ULTIMATE
UKULELE
TECHNIQUE & WARM-UP BOOK

FINGER WORKOUTS, GRADED PIECES & CHORD EXERCISES

FOR AUDIO AND VIDEOS FOR THIS BOOK VISIT:

https://brentrobitaille.com/product/ultimate-ukulele-technique-warmup-book

OR SCAN THE QR CODE:

BY BRENT ROBITAILLE

brentrobitaille.com

OTHER BOOKS BY BRENT ROBITAILLE

The Pop Rock Looper Pedal Book
The Blues Guitar Looper Pedal Book
The Jazz Guitar Looper Pedal Book
101 Blues Guitar Riffs & Solos in Open D Tuning
101 Blues Guitar Riffs & Solos in Open G Tuning
DADGAD Guitar Tuning - Celtic Flatpicking
Open D Guitar Tuning - Celtic Collection
Open G Guitar Tuning - Celtic Flatpicking
Classical Guitar Book in Open D Tuning
The Open D Christmas Songbook
Improve Your Guitar Chord Playing
Beginner Guitar Chord Book
The Slide Guitar Collection
Mandolin Blues Book
Celtic Collection for Mandolin
Celtic Mandola Book
Easy Classical Violin Tabs
Fiddle Tab - Celtic Collection
Holiday Collection for Fiddle Tab
Traditional Collection FiddleTab
Mastering Ukulele Fingerstyle
Celtic Collection for Ukulele
the Ukulele Christmas Songbook
Ukulele Blank Tab Collection and Reference Book
Cigar Box Guitar - Jazz & Blues Unlimited Book One & Two
Ultimate Collection – How to Play Cigar Box Guitar Vol. 1 & 2
Mandolin Blank Tab Collection & Reference Book
Cigar Box Guitar - Classical Collection
Cigar Box Guitar Blues Overload
101 Riffs for Cigar Box Guitar
Celtic Collection for Cigar Box Guitar
Cigar Box Guitar - The Technique Book
Holiday Collection for Cigar Box Guitar
Complete Cigar Box Guitar Chord Book

Audio - Video - Ebooks - Sheet Music Available at:

www.brentrobitaille.com

KALYMI MUSIC

PUBLISHED BY KALYMI MUSIC
©2025 Kalymi Music

Introduction

" Amateurs practice until they get it right. Professionals practice until they can't get it wrong."

—unknown

Have you ever noticed how good players make everything look effortless? They often seem to be thinking about something else entirely—smiling, relaxed, enjoying themselves. That's not just talent at work. It results from good "programming."

If you take away the emotional feeling part of playing a musical instrument, what remains is the purely physical task: the coordination of finger, hand, wrist, and arm movements. Before music can flow freely, these mechanical skills must become second nature. And that is the purpose of this ukulele book.

In The Ultimate Ukulele Technique and Warm-Up Book, we primarily focus on building the left-hand strength, dexterity, and precision (For deeper right-hand work, see Mastering Fingerstyle Ukulele.)

This book breaks down complex technical challenges into small, manageable tasks that, when practiced regularly, build toward mastery. Use one or several exercises as part of your daily warm-up routine. Since no tempos are indicated, start at a slow, comfortable pace. Once you've memorized the fingerings and can play cleanly, gradually work up to faster speeds.

Quick Tip

Write down your metronome tempos to track your progress.

The exercises are structured to help you develop skills progressively. First, you'll begin with one-finger workouts, then move to two-finger, three-finger, and four-finger challenges. You then move on to an extensive chord workout that includes essential chord progressions and blues and jazz. Finally, we will tackle eight graded pieces ranging from level one simple blues to level eight classical masterpieces.

Most exercises in this book are presented in tablature rather than standard notation. Why? Most ukulele players don't read music fluently, and those who do often struggle when reading higher up the neck. Tablature, along with clearly marked fingerings, offers a direct way for you to focus on building your technical skills.

Quick Tip

Rate each practice session from 1 to 10.
Ask yourself: What did I accomplish today?

Think of this book as a technical toolbox that you can return to again and again. Use it to warm up, strengthen your fingers, improve your chord-playing, develop fretboard knowledge, and open up a tension-free approach to ukulele playing.

Ready? Let's jump in!

CONTENTS – Ultimate Ukulele Technique & Warm-Up Book

CHAPTER SEVEN - EIGHT GRADED UKULELE PIECES

CHAPTER EIGHT – UKULELE RESOURCES

How to Read Ukulele Tablature

To read ukulele tablature, you need to know four things:

(1) **The 1st string on the ukulele (A) is the top line of the tablature.**

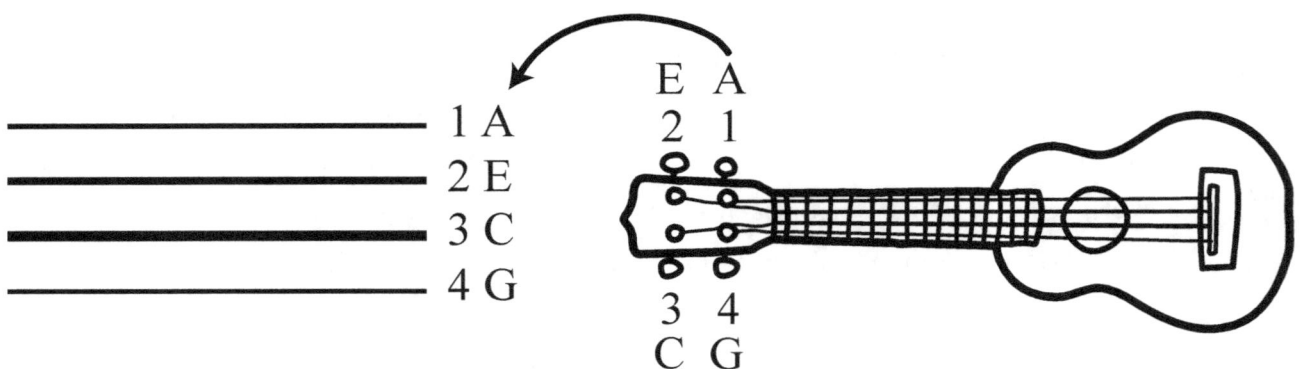

(2) **Play the string that the tab number is on.**

For example, the tab number is on the 2nd string (E), ➔
so pluck the 2nd string.

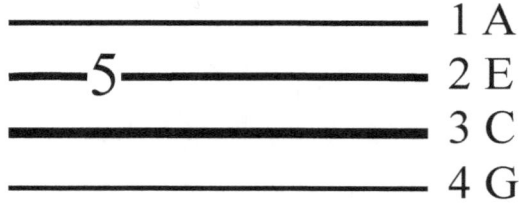

(3) **The number is the fret. If the number says 5, then put your finger on the 5th fret.**

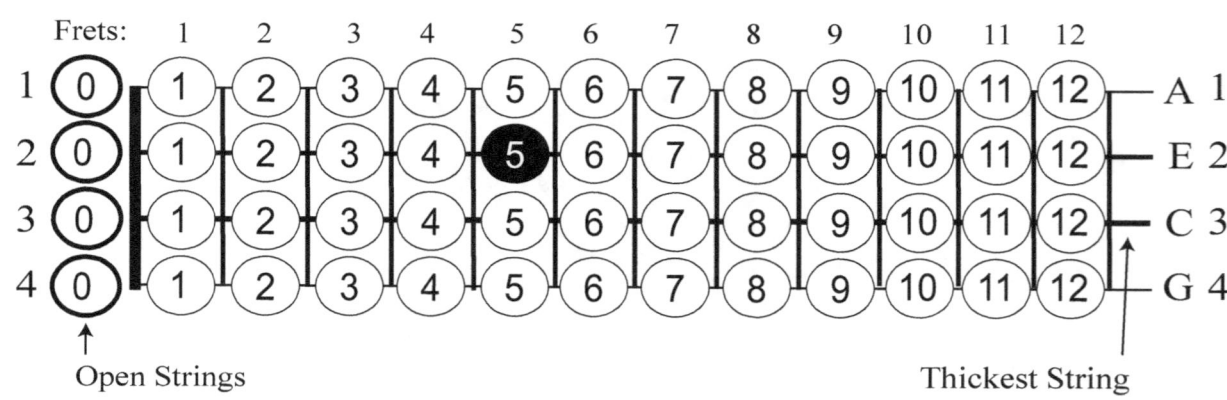

④ The last thing you need to know about reading ukulele tablature is **which finger to use**. Fingering can sometimes be confusing, as there's often more than one good choice for which finger to use. I will go into more detail in the following technique overview. Here are the finger numbers of the left playing hand (or right if you are left-handed):

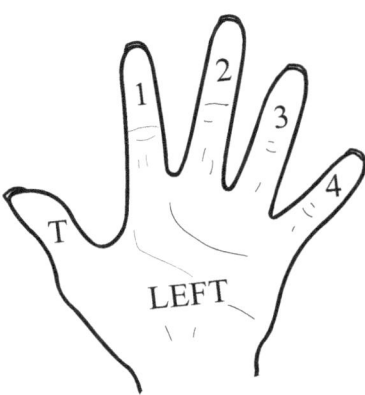

For a technique book to be complete, it is essential to have the fingers indicated in the tablature. Much effort has gone into providing what I think are the best fingerings for each exercise and piece, but remember, there is usually more than one option. Also, remember to ask yourself, "What note comes next"? Preparing for the following notes is often as important as the note you are playing. Here are some examples of finger markings:

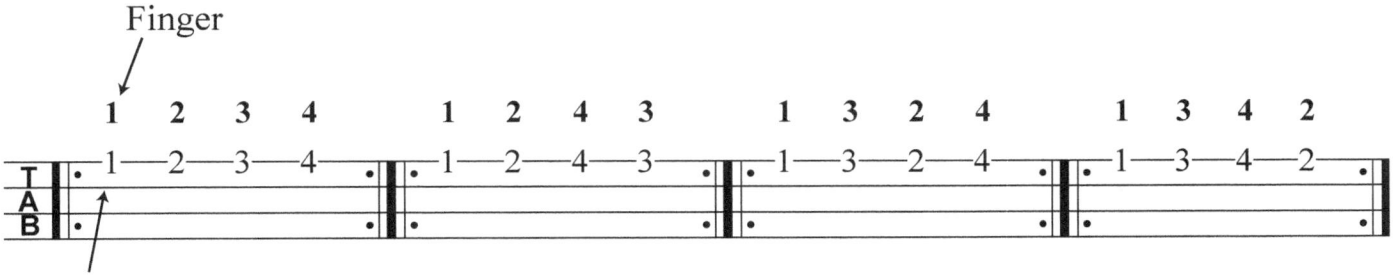

Here are some more examples of tablature:

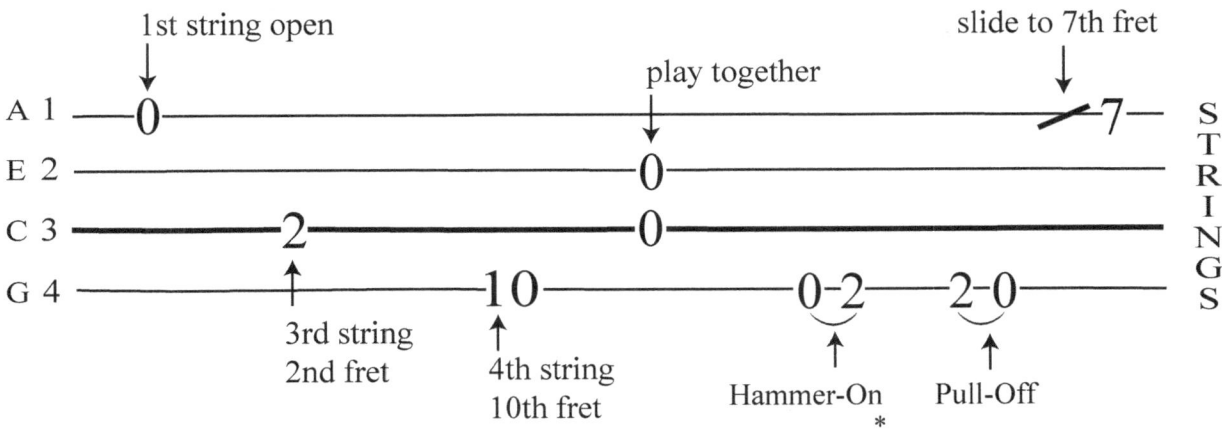

Throughout the book, you will learn about the other markings like hammer-ons, pull-offs and slides as shown above. There is much more to reading tablature, but these four points should get you going.

How to Read Ukulele Chords

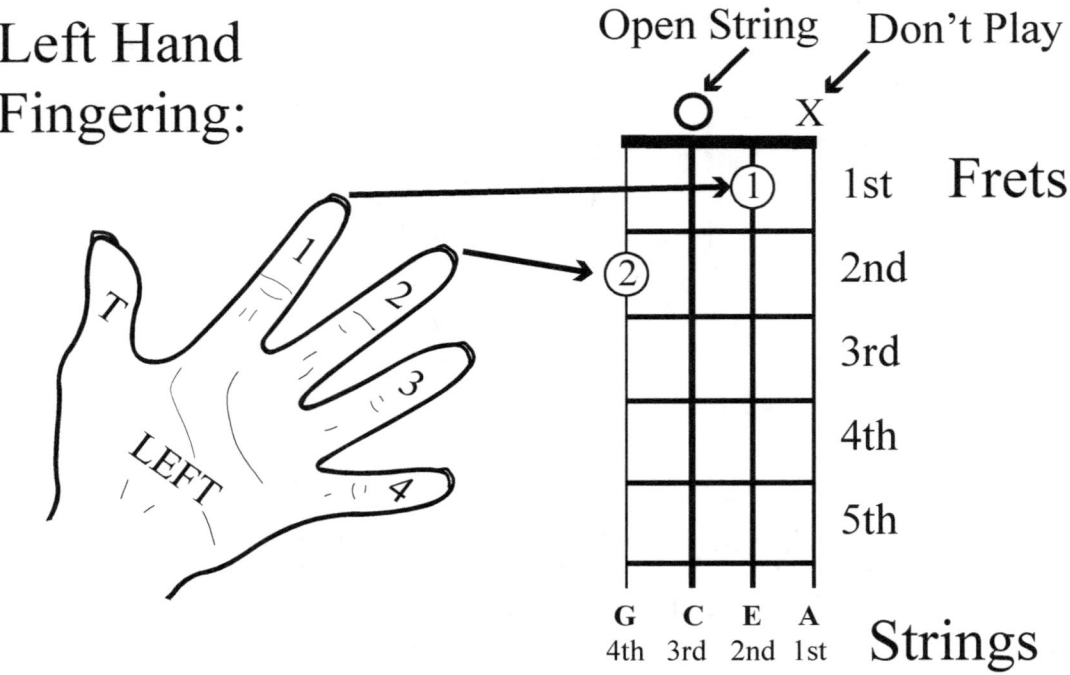

Barre Chords

Barre chords require covering several strings with one finger. In this example, place your 1st finger on strings 1 through 4 on the second fret – then add the 2nd and 3rd finger to form the G major chord.

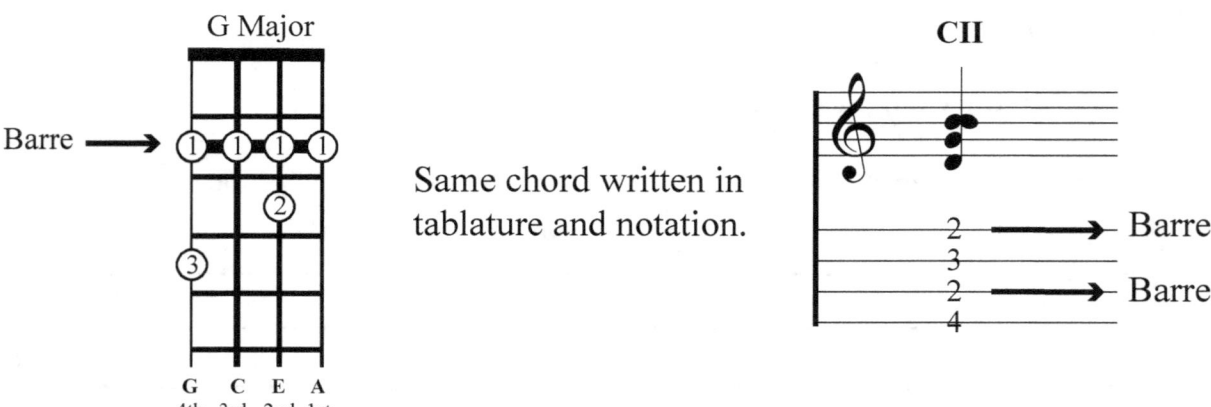

Same chord written in tablature and notation.

Barre chords are notated with a **C** and the Roman numeral for the fret. If you finger doesn't cover all the strings, a **¢** with a line though it is notated. For example, a full barre at the seventh fret is notated: **CVII** and a barre covering three or fewer strings on the seventh fret is notated **¢VII**. The line with a dash beside the **C** indicates how long to hold the barre down.

Mastering Ukulele Technique Overview

If you want to develop great technique on the ukulele, you need more than just hours of practice—you need smart, efficient practice. As a music teacher, I've seen many players hit a wall, frustrated that they don't know how to improve. Often, the real issue isn't time spent practicing but what they're practicing. Let's break it down and fine-tune your playing into four categories:

1. **Functional Tension and Finger Pressure**
2. **Placement and Posture**
3. **Fingering and Positioning**
4. **Mental Preparation**

Where do I begin?

Many players are motivated to play songs or riffs before first developing some basic technical abilities. However, without understanding basic ukulele techniques, you will likely get frustrated or worse, wasting hours developing bad habits.

It is true that nothing will replace many hours of practice, but we want to speed up the process and hopefully get you where you want to be sooner.

We could start with any of the four categories, but being aware of body tension is often overlooked as you adapt to holding onto a piece of wood with strings. The main point is to play with the least tension needed while remaining in control of your instrument.

1 - Functional Tension

Let's try an experiment. Play a note on your ukulele (any note) and analyze where the muscles are tense in your body (arm, shoulders, hand, neck, etc.). Identify which muscles are tense, then gently reduce the tension *except* in your hand and finger playing the note.

Next, put your attention on your fingers and thumb. Compare the pressure between your thumb and finger. Are they equal? Does your neck move when you play, and is your finger pushing down too hard?

The purpose of this experiment is not to reveal or undermine the physiology of hand mechanics but to bring awareness and put the tension where it belongs: between the thumb and finger. This type of tension is functional.

Of course, there is always tension in the wrist, arm, shoulder, and the rest of the body, but players often experience excess tension, preventing fluid movement of the hand and fingers. Poor habits can lead to strain-related issues like wrist pain, tendonitis, muscle fatigue and carpal tunnel syndrome, all of which are dysfunctional and you want to avoid.

To continue this experiment, pick up a pen or pencil with your left-hand thumb and use the same finger you used to play the note above. You will notice you need to push equally 50% with the thumb and 50% with the finger so the pencil doesn't drop.

An excellent exercise you can do anywhere is to hold the pencil as described above and alternate between your four fingers and thumb (you may have to move the thumb slightly so the pencil doesn't drop).

1st finger and thumb

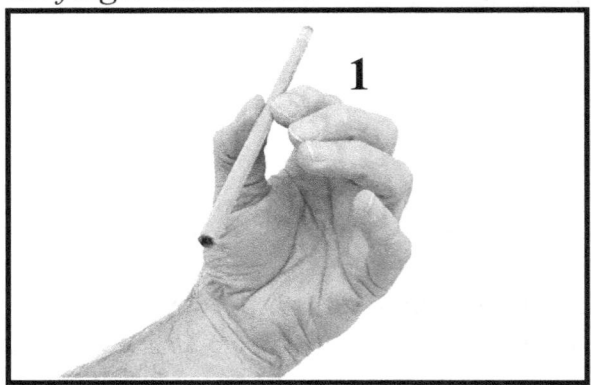

2nd finger and thumb

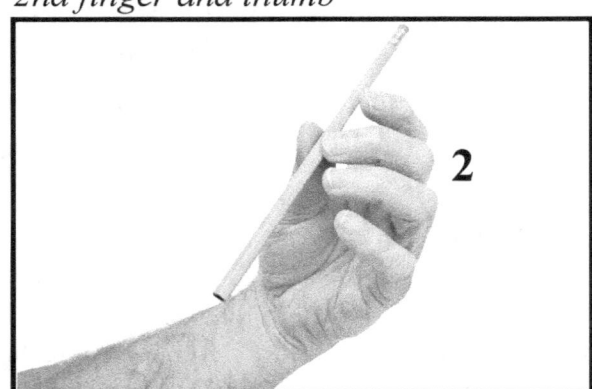

3rd finger and thumb

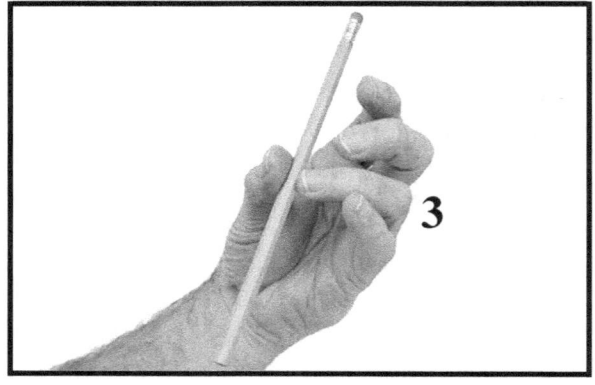

4th finger and thumb

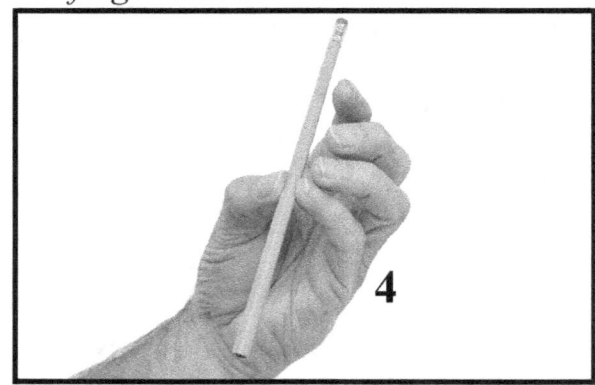

Finger Pressure

Another aspect of tension is how hard you push down on the strings or finger pressure. Let's try another experiment and play any note on your ukulele. Put the least amount of pressure as possible on the string without the note buzzing. Try to get a sense of how that feels on your finger.

Hopefully, you will notice that playing a note does not require nearly as much pressure as you think. You may have noticed that good players make everything seem effortless because they understand that excessive finger pressure slows you down and creates unnecessary tension in the hand.

We can take the idea of functional tension even further by including the spaces between the notes you play. Imagine if we were to analyze a series of notes in slow motion. One finger pushes down as another lifts, and maybe your hand moves to another position – A lot is going on! With all the complex finger, hand and arm movements (not to mention the required cognitive steps), there isn't time for you to process the complexity.

The only partial solution here is to be *aware* of the tension and play everything *very, very slowly*. Focus on one task at a time and ask yourself, what is good functional tension vs. dysfunctional tension?

Perhaps the best way to improve your technique is awareness. One thing that immensely helped me was breathing out and relaxing my shoulders before a challenging section. Doing this also relaxes my arm, hands and fingers. As it turns out, feeling relaxed improved my playing.

So, when practicing, take a sticky note, write down the word TENSION, and put it on your music stand where it's easily visible.

2 - Placement and Posture

Understanding tension is essential, but finger placement and posture are likely the number one issue most players notice from the start. Let's begin with finger placement, where the finger plays a note on the fretboard.

If you look at the frets on your ukulele, you likely notice the distances between the frets narrow as you move up the fretboard. The higher notes are closer together. Regardless of what fret or where you put a finger on the string, you are stopping the vibration of the note at the metal fret. That is, it doesn't matter where you put your finger down in the fret space because the note stops at the fret. See the illustration:

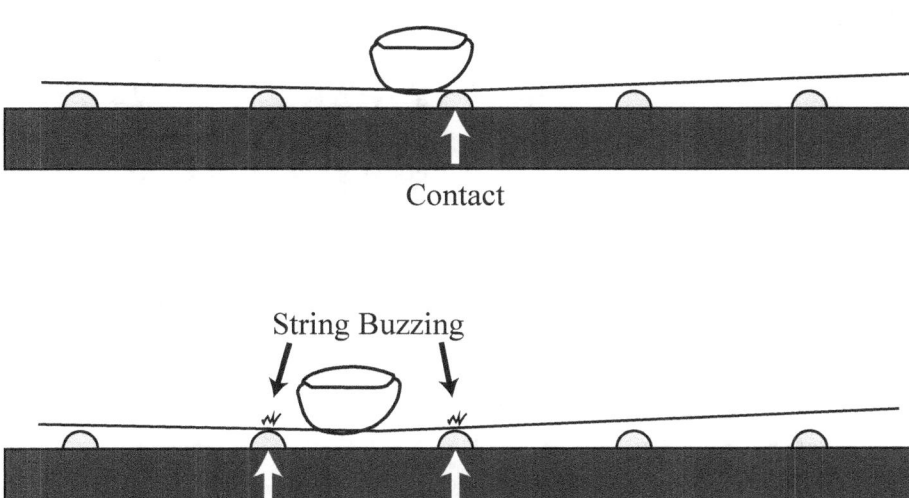

Contact

String Buzzing

If your notes are buzzing and sounding thin, it's not that you are pressing down too lightly; your finger is not placed correctly. The solution is often to move the finger closer to the fret; however, this is not always so simple. Primarily because our fingers are different sizes and shapes, and as it turns out, human evolution did not consider finger size when playing the ukulele!

So, we have to adapt the length of the fingers to the angle of the wrist and fretboard (And yes, the smallest digit, our fourth finger, is as essential as the other fingers). So, we adapt by the way we hold the ukulele. How do we do this?

First, there is no best way to hold a ukulele as each player's fingers, hand, and body size differ, and our music varies. All we can do is suggest what is ergonomically the most efficient way:

Posture: Sit or stand with a strap so the neck is tilted up to reduce wrist and hand tension.

Instrument Support: Hold the ukulele close to the body, use the forearm and strap to stabilize the ukulele to allow free movement.

Balance: As you play notes and chords, the neck will move as the pressure goes on and off the strings. Try maintaining balance between the forearm, strap, thumb and fingers so the neck stays relatively straight.

Chording: Keep the strumming arm and shoulder relaxed while the wrist is below the neck, and the fingers are curved. Keep a close eye on your wrist position so the notes ring clearly.

Good ergonomic habits help prevent strain-related issues like wrist pain, tendonitis, or muscle fatigue, making playing more enjoyable and sustainable. Once you are holding the ukulele in an ergonomic way, you can focus on other forms of efficiency referred to as *economy of motion*:

• Reducing excess finger, hand and arm motion to conserve energy and improve precision.
• Use the most efficient fingerings to minimize repositioning and avoid unnecessary stretching.

3 – Fingering and Positioning

Now that we have covered some ways our body has to adapt to this little four-string instrument, we can start thinking about fingering and positioning.

Finger Positions

Like most stringed instruments, the ukulele can be played in different positions. A position is when you place all four fingers on consecutive frets. For example, put your first finger on the first fret, your second finger on the second fret, your third on the third fret, and the fourth on the fourth fret. This is considered the first position:

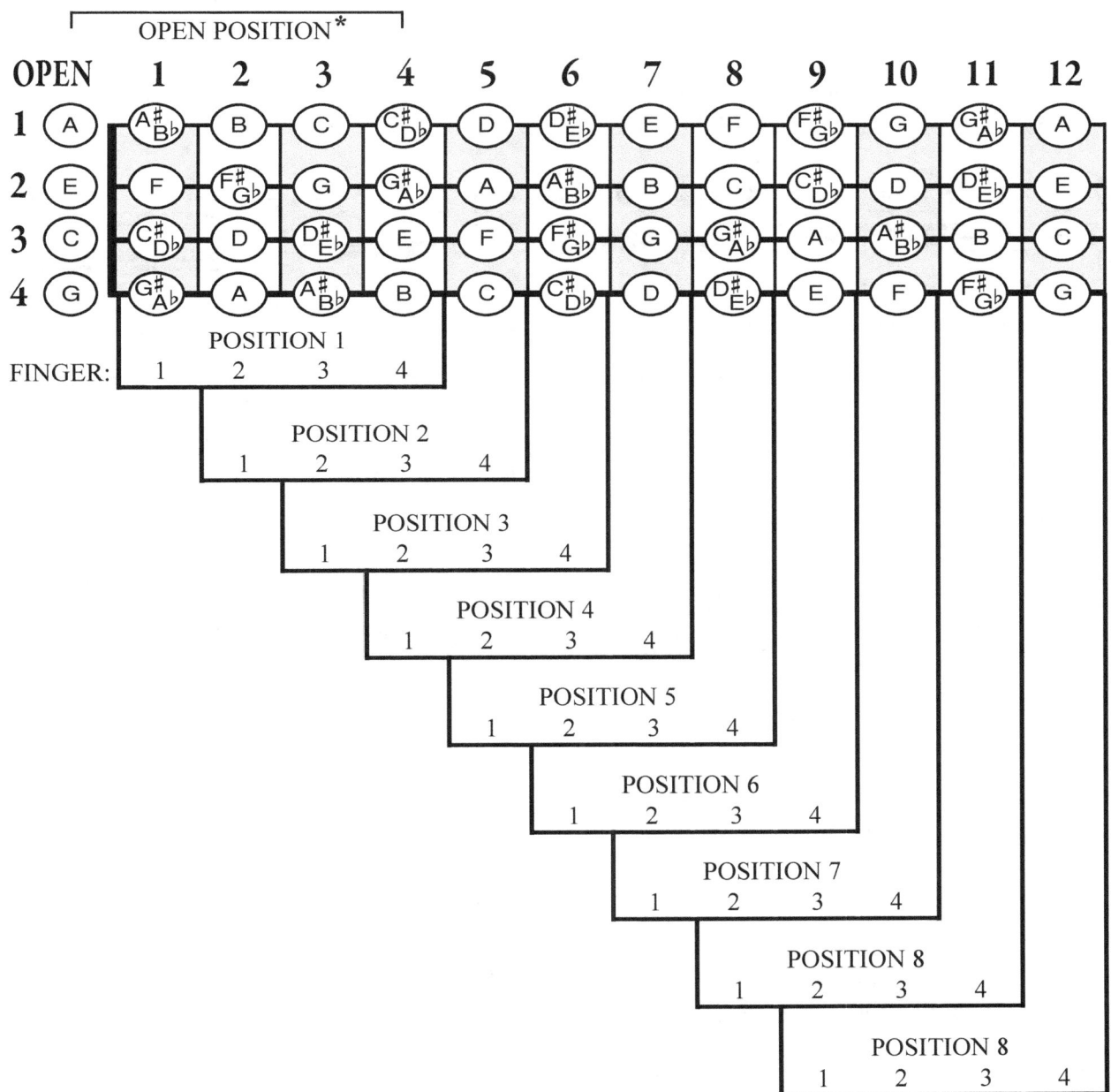

*
Open position and position one are the same, with the exception that open position includes the open strings.

14

To summarize, your first finger determines the position. Position playing is a nice, convenient way to place your hand, but as you know, this is not always the case. In fact, many exercises in the book attempt to develop this technique of playing in multiple positions.

Position playing should often be your first consideration to prevent your hand from moving excessively. However, music is random and extending fingers and quick hand movements are practically part of all the music you play.

Positioning and Preparation

Position playing is a good general approach to fingering any stringed instrument, but as mentioned, stretching and extending the fingers is necessary. The best advice is always to consider where you will end up. In other words, you have to prepare and always think ahead, or if you prefer, think backward from the last note to determine the best fingering.

For example, see how thinking backwards helps solve the most challenging fingering situations, as in the excerpt below of the opening notes of Flight of the Bumblebee:

So, we play right to left instead of playing from left to right. After reversing the notes, one logical fingering appeared. The hand symbol above the note indicates when to change positions:

And here is the original with the position changes and the correct fingering:

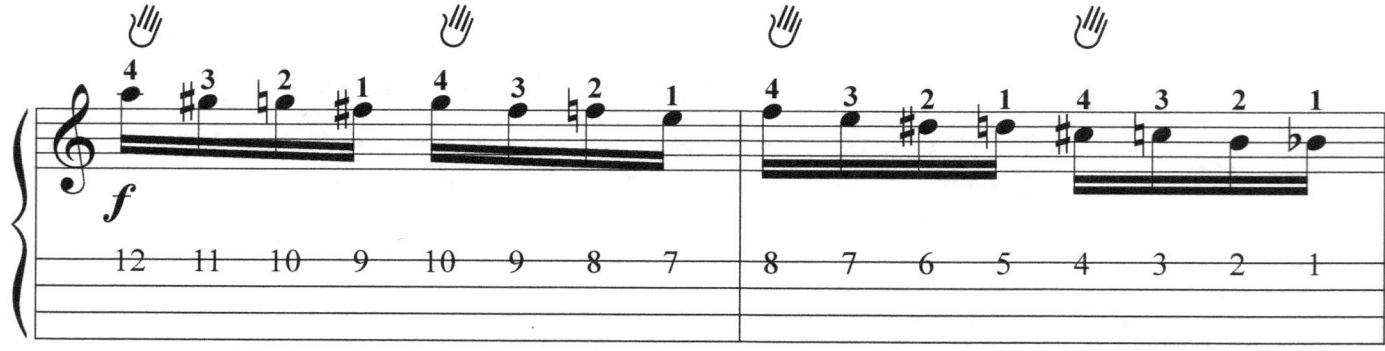

While many players may not be interested in or feel inclined to tackle pieces like Flight of the Bumblebee, the goal is to develop technique. You don't need to learn the entire piece; just focus on a few measures and turn them into small exercises.

4 - Mental Preparation

Last but not least is mental preparation, not in the psychological sense but in terms of memory and the learning process. Here are five tips:

1) ***Stick to a good fingering***. It might seem obvious, but most players rush through this step and instead use whatever finger is most convenient. While convenient fingering is often correct, take a few extra seconds to try alternate fingerings and work backwards if you are stumped.

2) ***Write down a fingering*** if none are indicated. The process of writing will help solidify your memory. I also found that focusing on which finger to play in fast passages helps. Instead of thinking about a lot of notes, I think of only a few and which finger I need.

3) ***Begin beyond slow***. There are so many moving parts when learning an instrument, and regardless of your level, give yourself a break and actually slow down. Also, reduce multitasking and focus on what you are trying to improve upon. For example, tap out the rhythm if this is an issue or write down any tricky fingerings.

4) ***Study away for your instrument***. Once you have a fingering that works and are playing at a comfortable speed, another step to prepare mentally is to study your music before and after you practice. A study by Lotze et al. (2003) showed that when musicians visualize playing, their brains activate the same regions as if they were physically playing.

5) ***Practice without looking*** at your hands. Of course, this will produce some unwanted sounds initially, but you develop a more accurate sense of touch and the ability to anticipate notes. Eventually, the more familiar you are with your music, the less you will rely on looking.

These are just a few suggestions to help with the mental preparation required to develop a strong and secure music repertoire.

Alright, we are almost ready to get to work, but there's one more thing to discuss: Practice Schedules.

"Practice is the best of all instructors." — Publilius Syrus

Ukulele Practice Tips and Schedules

Here are a few tips to help you get the most out of your ukulele practice. By setting clear goals, tracking your progress, and keeping your sessions interesting, you'll build habits that lead to real improvement over time.

Getting Started: How to Approach Your Practice

One way to improve your technique is to identify the area that needs the most attention. This book is organized into four main sections:

- **Finger Exercises** (Chapters 1–4)
- **Chord Practice** (Chapters 5–6)
- **Graded Pieces** (Chapter 7)
- **Ukulele Resources** (Chapter 8)

The most straightforward approach would be:

- Start with the 1-finger exercises and work your way to the 4-finger exercises.
- If you want to focus more on chord playing, you can jump ahead to Chapters 5 and 6.
- Work through the graded pieces in Chapter 7 once you feel comfortable with the finger exercises.
- Refer to the resource section scales, arpeggios, chords and fingerboard charts as necessary.

If you prefer not to work through the book in the order provided, then skim through it to get acquainted with the material and work on specific techniques as they arise.

Keep Motivated

There is no doubt that maintaining a consistent practice routine is the most challenging part of learning something new or improving your existing skills. Regardless, students who stick to a regular practice routine will see faster improvement than those who practice only occasionally. Here are a few suggestions to keep you motivated and help you progress faster:

1. Set SMART Goals

Adapting the SMART goal framework to your practice (first introduced by George T. Doran in 1981) will help you stay motivated to practice by keeping track of your goals.

So, when you practice, set **S**pecific, **M**easurable, **A**chievable, **R**elevant, and **T**ime-bound goals to keep focused. For example:

- _Specific_: "I will practice the 1-finger exercise at 80 BPM (on my metronome) for one week."
- _Measurable_: "I will start at 40 BPM and gradually increase to 80 BPM."
- _Achievable_: "I understand the exercise and will increase the speed by 5 BPM daily."
- _Relevant_: "This will develop finger control and coordination to improve my technique."
- _Time-bound:_ "One week is possible to reach this goal."

2. Track Your Progression on a Calendar or App

For a more traditional method, make a weekly practice schedule and mark down when and what you practice (if you prefer, use a time management app to monitor your progress).

Here is a basic practice schedule* that you can adapt and personalize according to your goals. You can do as little as 5 minutes daily with the main idea to be consistent.

I'd also suggest you rate your daily or weekly progress on a 1 to 10 scale. So, if you got through all your daily exercises and feel you progressed, then give yourself an 8 or more.

TIME	PRACTICE	MON	TUES	WED	THUR	FRI	SAT	SUN	Rate 0-10
5 – 10 minutes	1, 2, 3 or 4-finger exercises								
5 – 10 minutes	Chord Practice								
10 – 20 minutes	Graded Pieces								
5 – 10 minutes	Music theory, rhythm, reading, ear training.								
Weekly	Planning: new repertoire, composition, improv, etc.								
Extra									

*I've included a blank schedule at the back of the book you can copy.

Maintaining a consistent daily practice schedule is challenging and impossible for most people, but keep positive by acknowledging your progress. Also, keep it interesting, change your routine, and recognize that your journey will have ups and downs.

Quick Tip

One of the best ways to track your progress is to record yourself playing and compare.

Quick Tip

Find other musicians or a teacher and work towards a performance. The performance can be anything (it could be you and your cat), but setting a specific date is a great motivator.

Alright, enough's enough! Let's get going with the one-finger exercises.

CHAPTER ONE - 1 FINGER EXERCISES

In our first set of exercises, we will use only one finger at a time. While it may seem simple, the real goal is to learn to move your arm and elbow smoothly. Think of your elbow as a pivot point that guides your hand along the neck. As you move higher up the neck, your elbow shifts slightly away from your body, helping your wrist stay relaxed and balanced to avoid unnecessary tension in your hand and wrist.

Go through each exercise using all four fingers, one at a time. For example, start with your first finger, then play with the second finger, and so on. The fingering is shown over the tablature line. Always strive for a clear tone on each note, and keep your finger close to the fret to avoid buzzing or muted notes.

Chromatic Scales

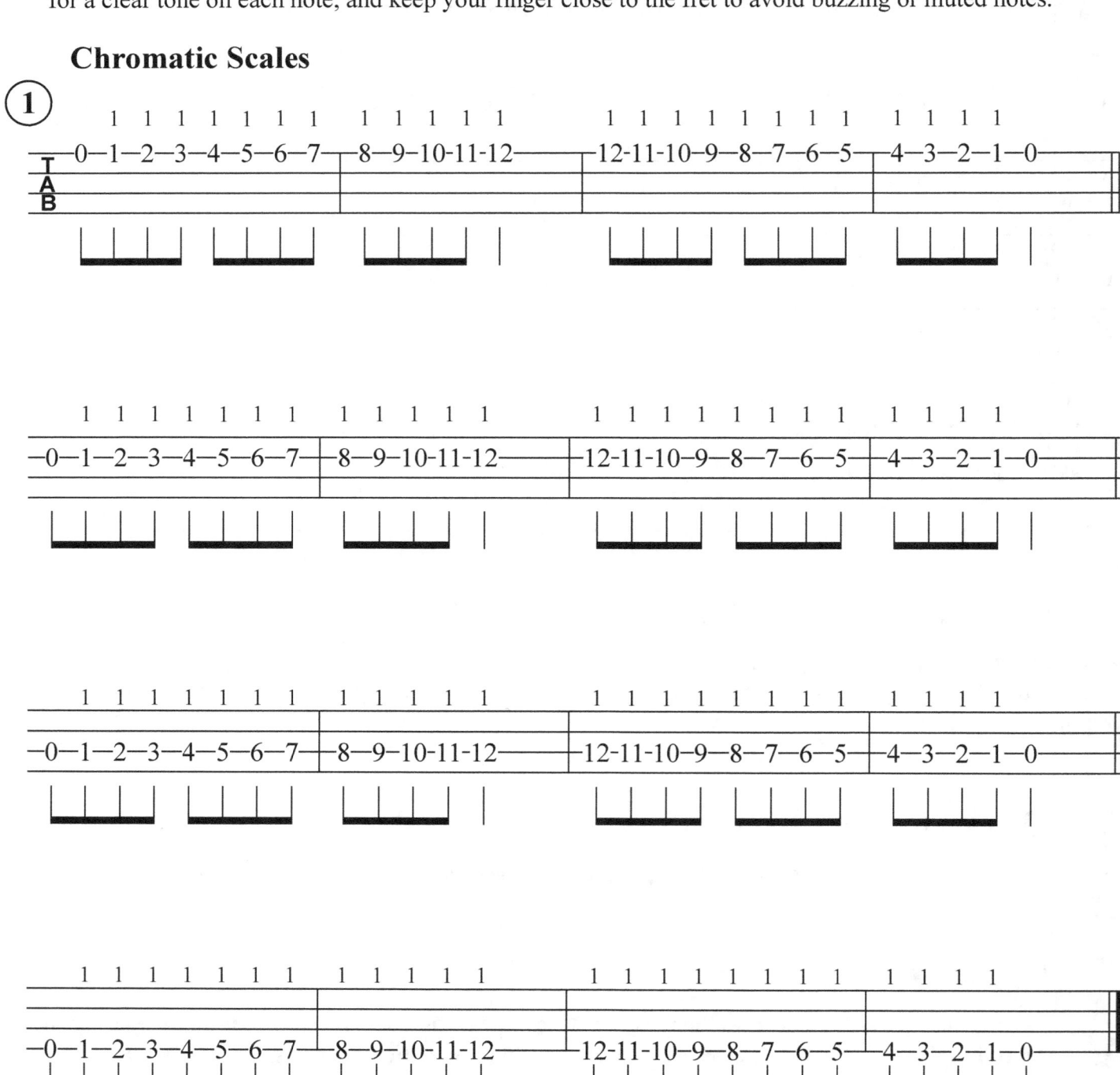

Major Scales

In exercise 2, we will play the major scale on each string using one finger at a time. The following exercise shows the first finger above the tablature line but go through each exercise using all four fingers.

A Major Scale

②

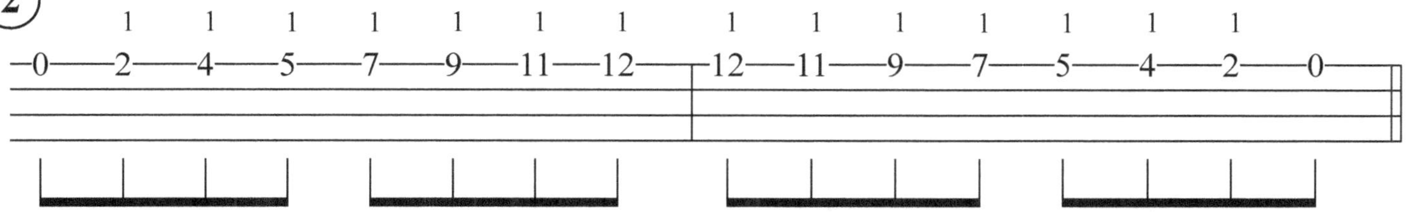

| 1 | 1 | 1 | 1 | 1 | 1 | 1 | 1 | 1 | 1 | 1 | 1 | 1 | 1 |

```
—0——2——4——5——7——9——11——12——┼12——11——9——7——5——4——2——0——
```

E Major Scale

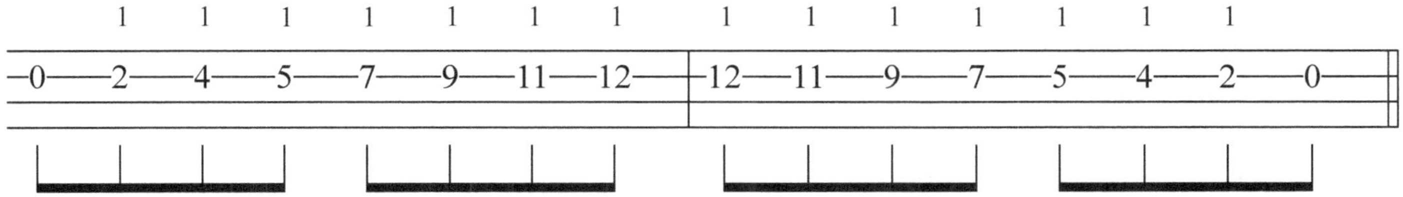

| 1 | 1 | 1 | 1 | 1 | 1 | 1 | 1 | 1 | 1 | 1 | 1 | 1 | 1 |

```
—0——2——4——5——7——9——11——12——┼12——11——9——7——5——4——2——0——
```

C Major Scale

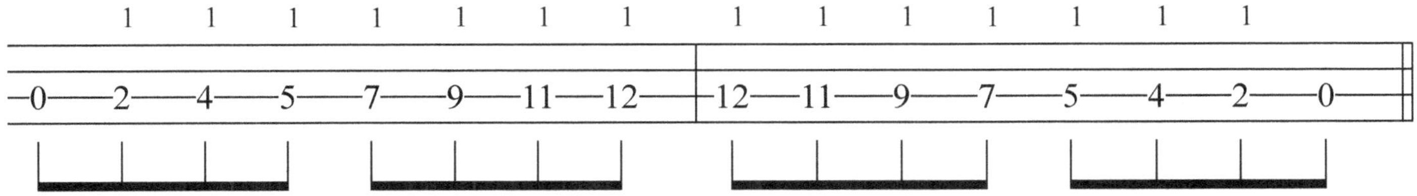

| 1 | 1 | 1 | 1 | 1 | 1 | 1 | 1 | 1 | 1 | 1 | 1 | 1 | 1 |

```
—0——2——4——5——7——9——11——12——┼12——11——9——7——5——4——2——0——
```

G Major Scale

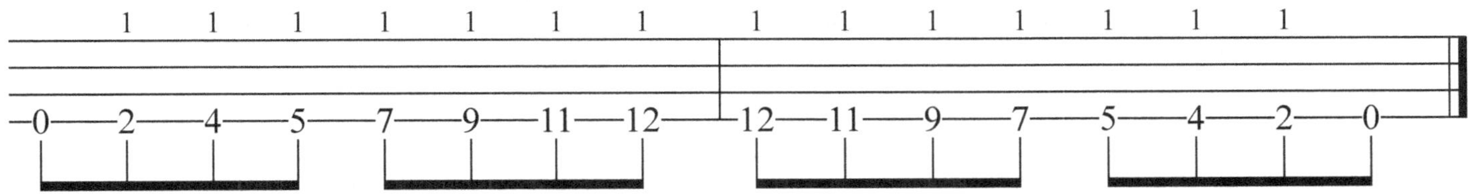

| 1 | 1 | 1 | 1 | 1 | 1 | 1 | 1 | 1 | 1 | 1 | 1 | 1 | 1 |

```
—0——2——4——5——7——9——11——12——┼12——11——9——7——5——4——2——0——
```

Arpeggios

When you play the notes of a chord separately, it is called an arpeggio. In exercise 3, we will arpeggiate the notes of the major and minor chords. Again, practice with all four fingers and listen carefully for a clear tone on each note.

Major Arpeggio Pattern

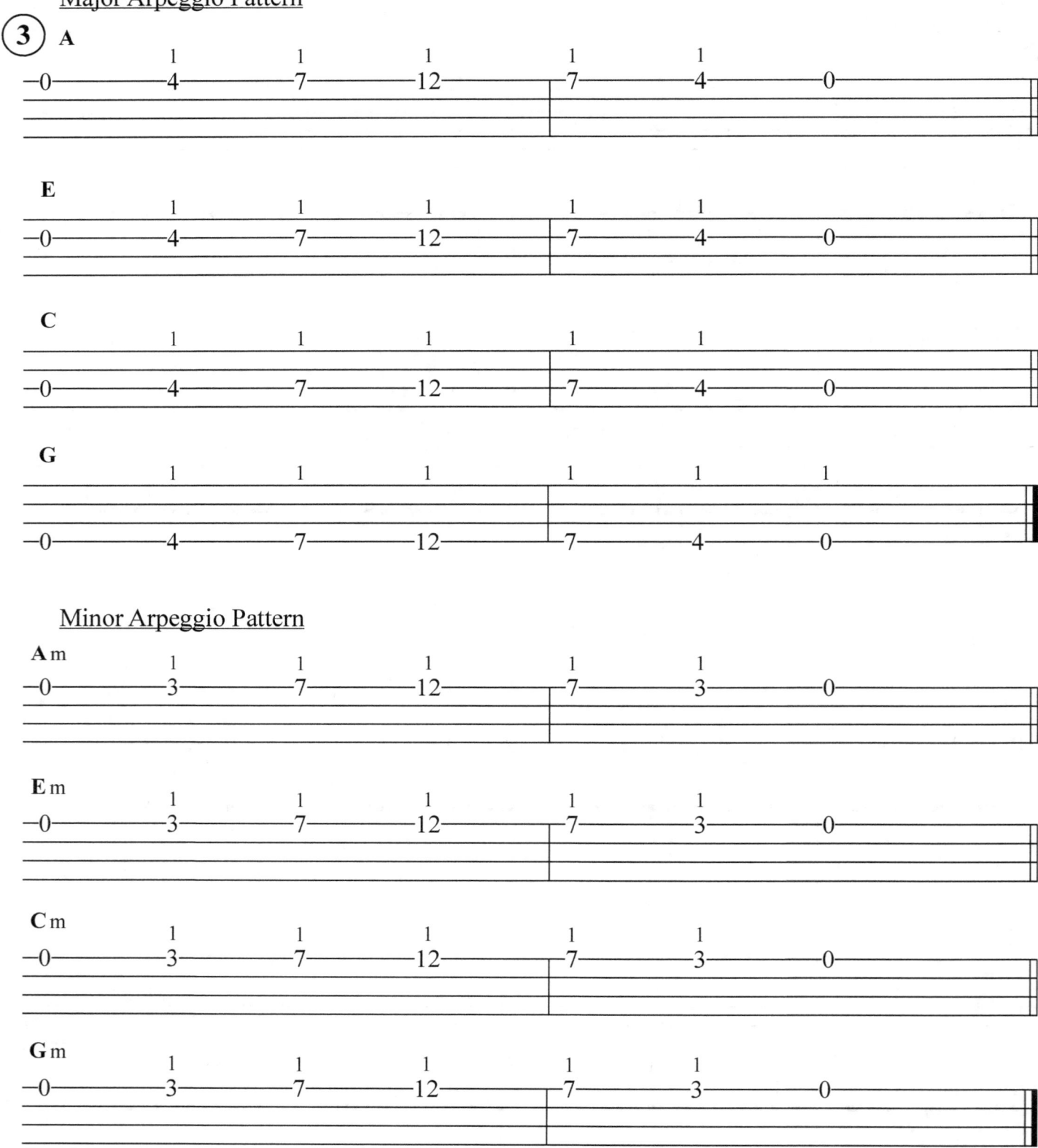

Minor Arpeggio Pattern

Big Leaps

In the next set of exercises, we use the notes of the major and minor scales but use leaps between the notes. Pay special attention to how your elbow and shoulder pivot as you move up and down the neck. You are looking for a smooth, seamless movement between the notes. Use a metronome and start slowly!

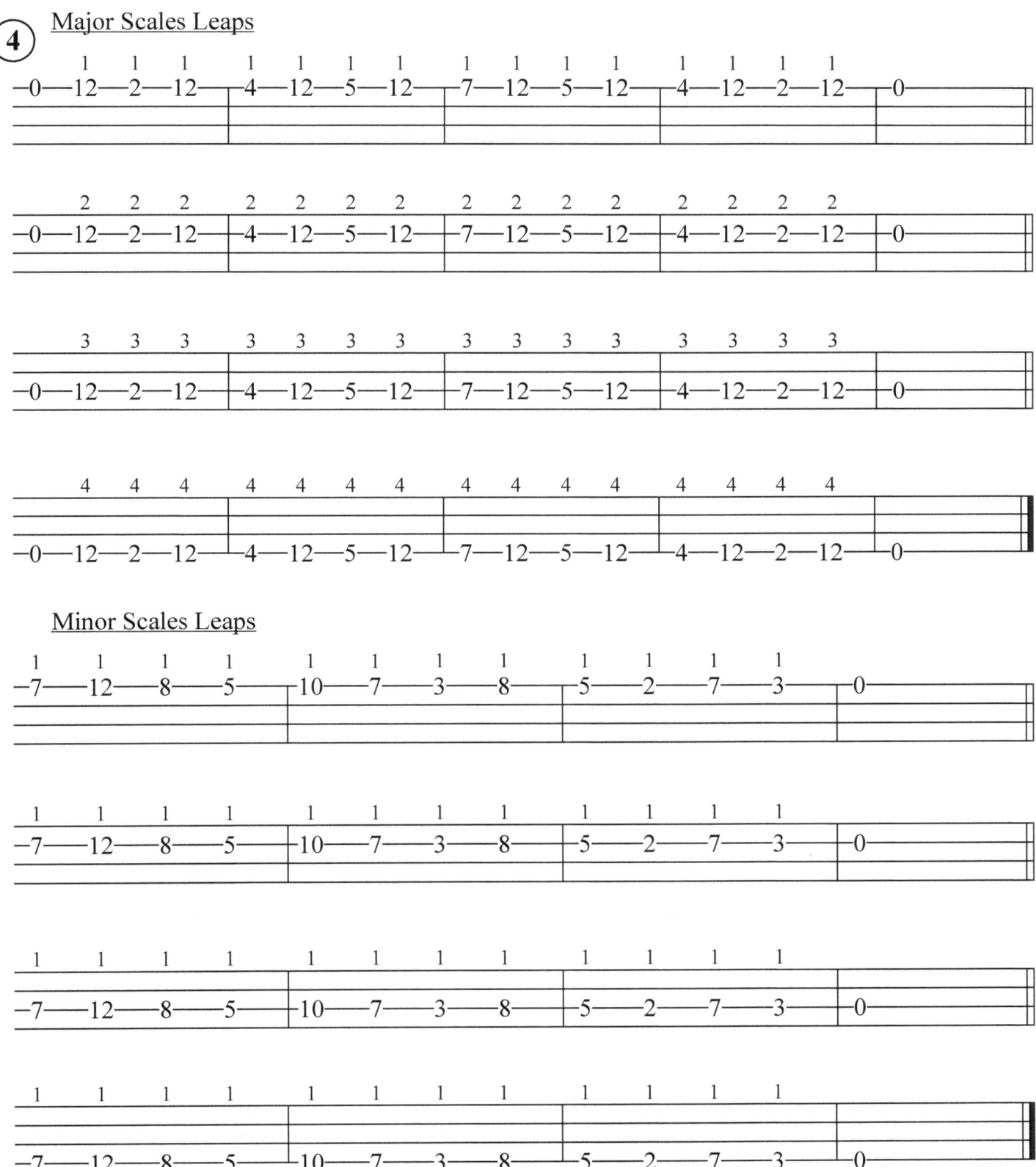

(4) <u>Major Scales Leaps</u>

<u>Minor Scales Leaps</u>

String-Skipping

Exercise 5 is excellent for developing your note accuracy, though a challenge using only one finger at a time. Keep your wrist loose and try not to tense up. The string-skipping exercises outline a major and dominant 7th chord (arpeggio). Refer to the chord diagrams to help memorize the arpeggio/chord shape.

Use 1st finger only, then repeat with 2nd, 3rd and 4th.

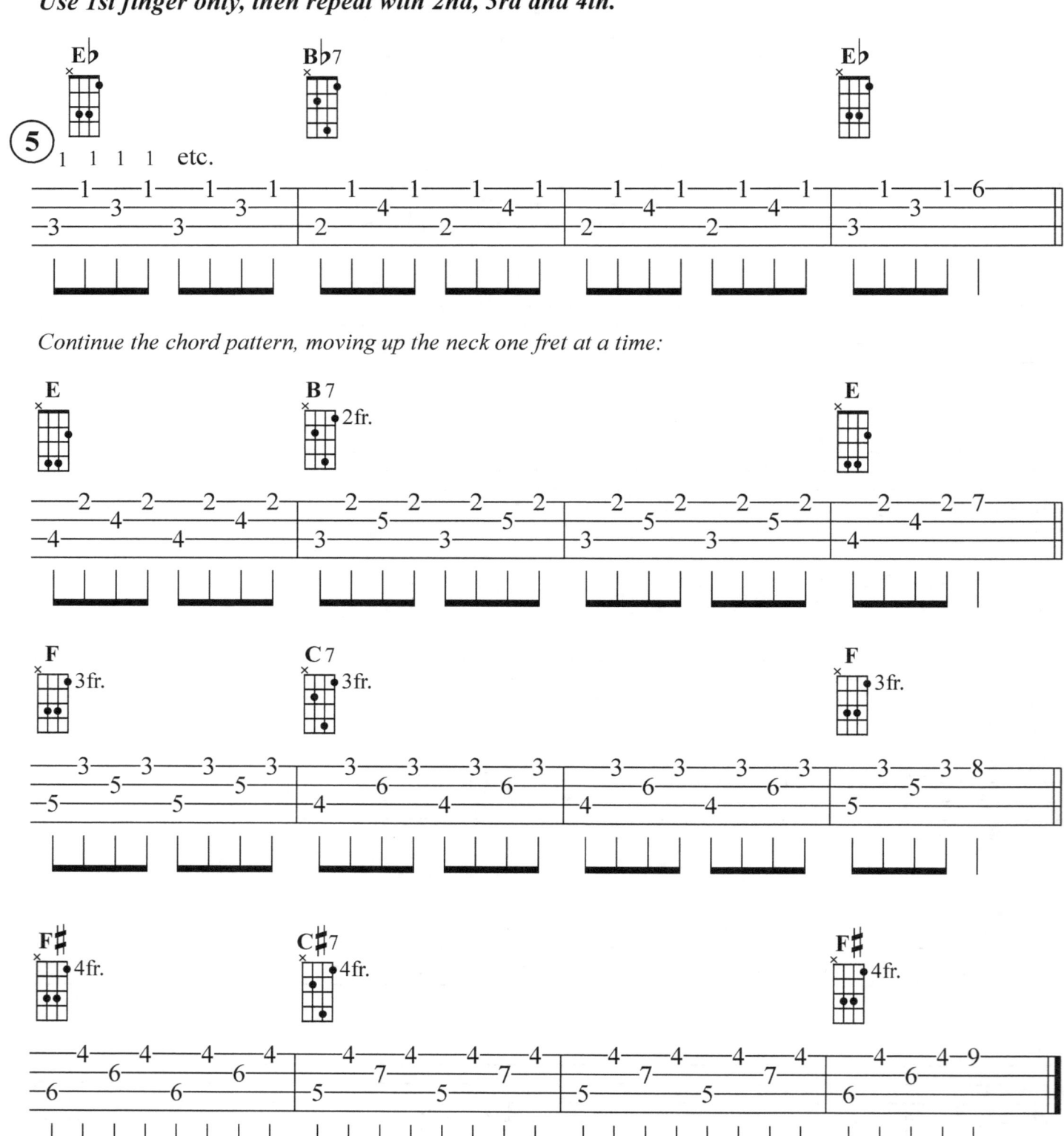

Continue the chord pattern, moving up the neck one fret at a time:

Hammer-On Exercises

A hammer-on is when you pluck a note and slap the finger down *without plucking it again*. The hammer-on is notated with a curved line (slur) over top of the tab number. A hammer-on requires you to attack the string with enough strength to hear the second note loudly. Listen for a consistent volume between the plucked and unplucked notes. If you can't hear the second note, strike the string harder until you produce two notes with equal volume and tone.

Use 1st finger only, then repeat with 2nd, 3rd and 4th.

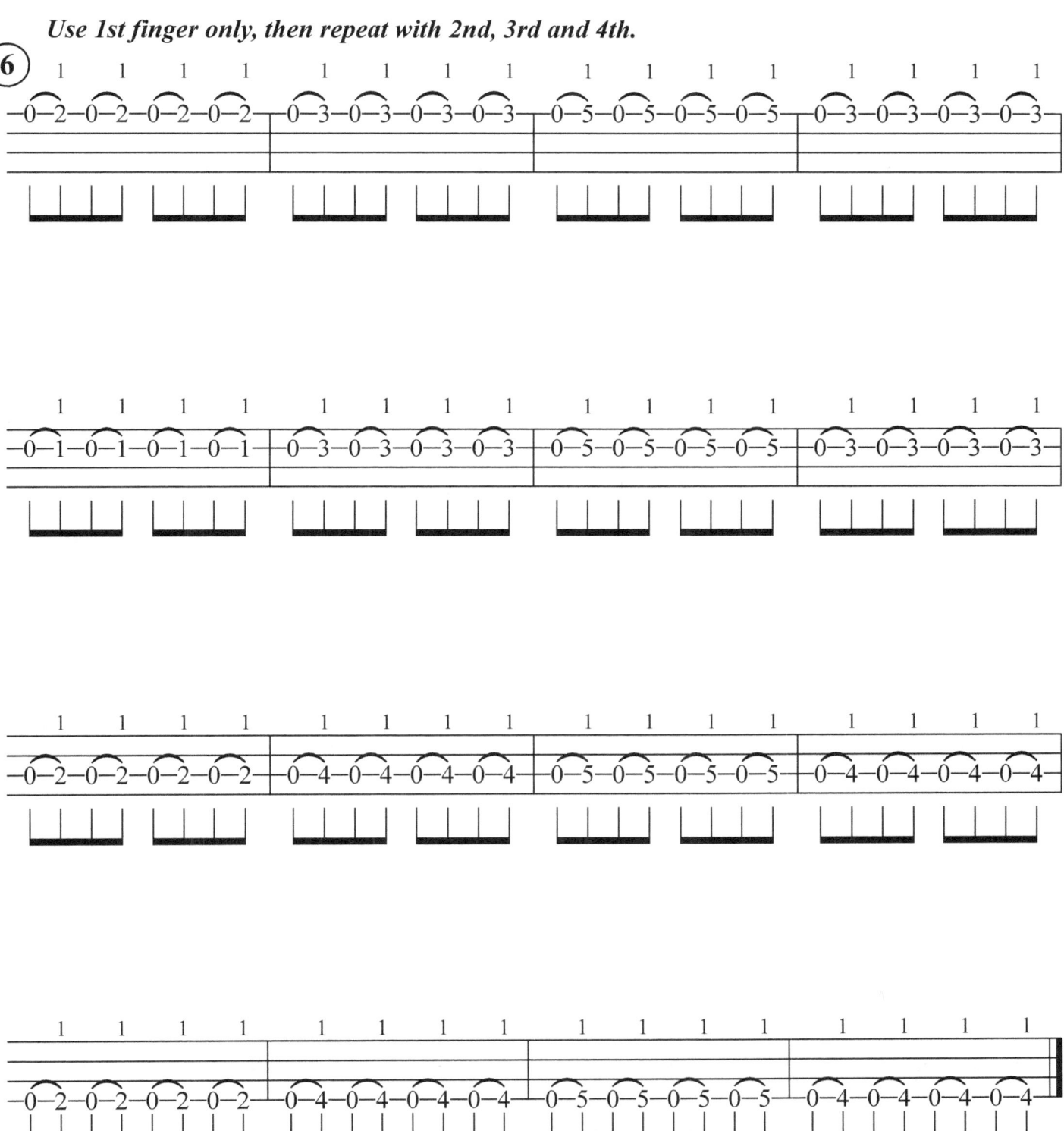

Pull-Off Exercises

A pull-off is when you pluck a note and then pull off the finger *without plucking the string again* (the reverse of a hammer-on). To do a pull-off, you must grip the string and slightly pull down on it hard enough to make the string vibrate again. Listen for an equal volume on both notes and an even eighth-note rhythm.

Use 1st finger only, then repeat with 2nd, 3rd and 4th.

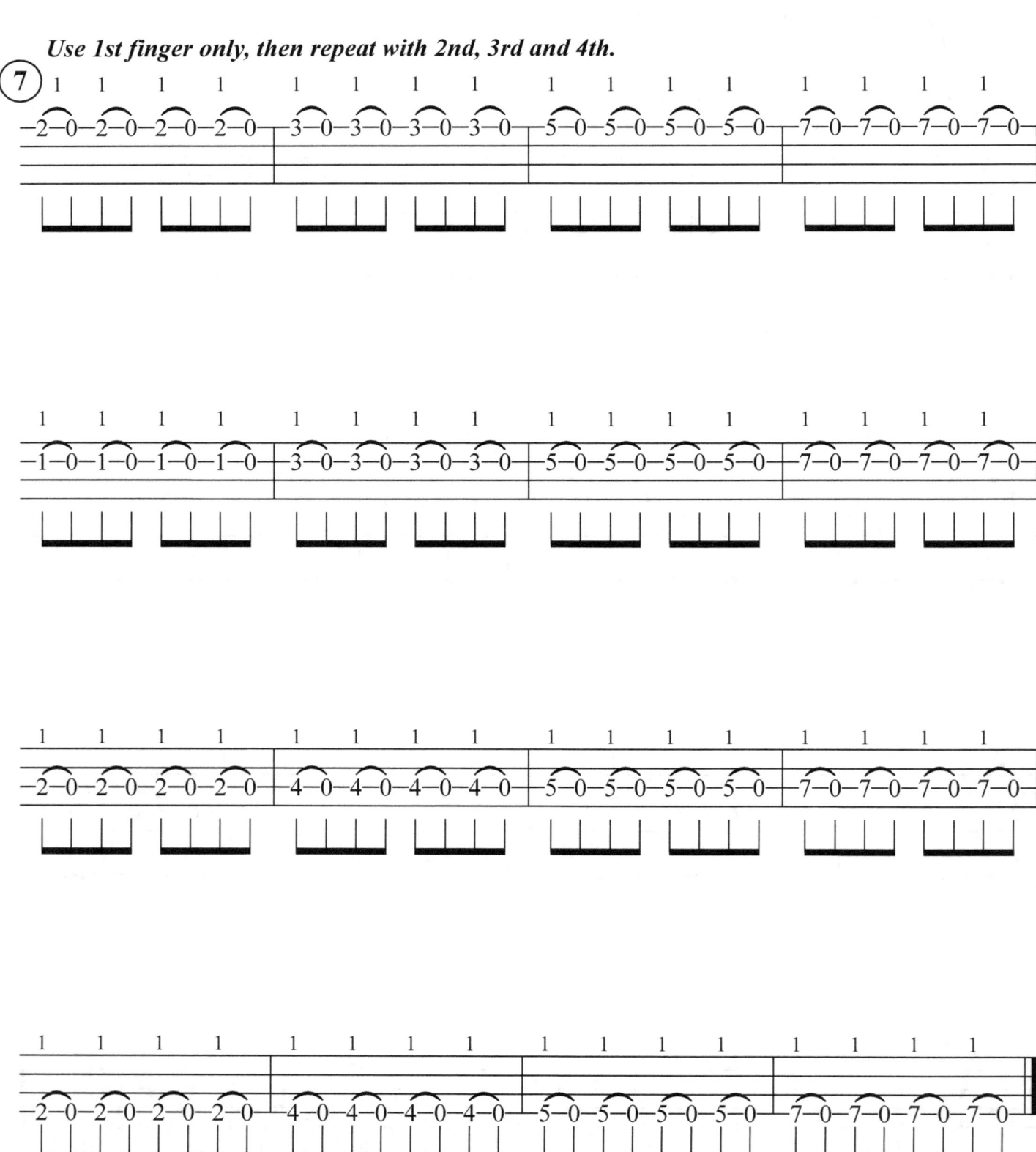

Trill Exercises

A trill is a musical ornament where you quickly alternate between two notes (usually a combination of hammer-ons and pull-offs). The trill is notated with a "tr" symbol above the note. Trill exercises are considered one of the best for building endurance and finger strength. Work through all four fingers and keep an even rhythm, volume and clear tone.

Ex. 1

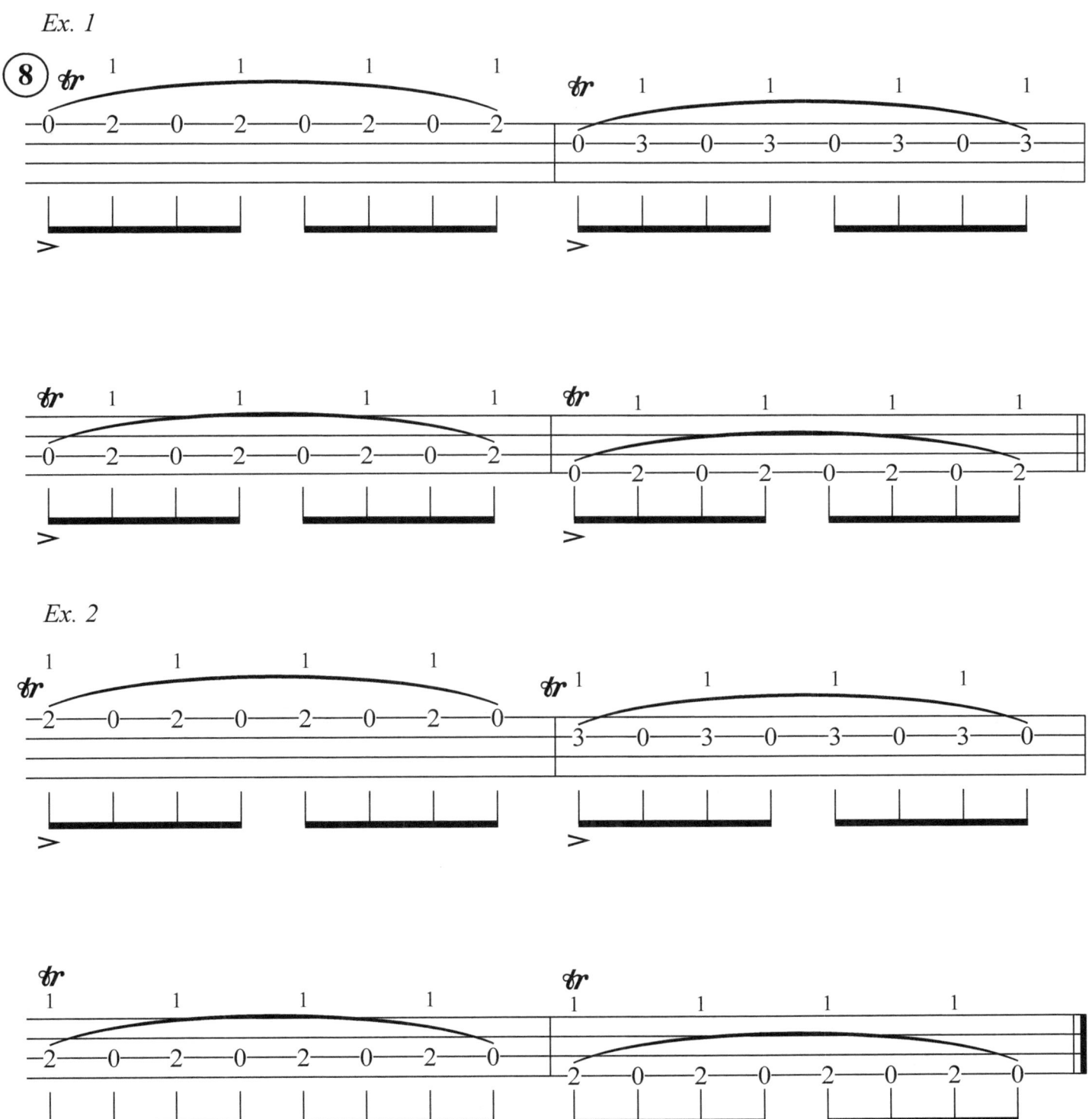

Ex. 2

Sliding Exercises

A slide is notated with a diagonal line and a curved slur connecting two notes(/). Keep downward pressure on the string as you slide up or down to the following note. The exercise below uses the notes from the Bb pentatonic scale. Play with all four fingers, one finger at a time and strive for an even volume between notes.

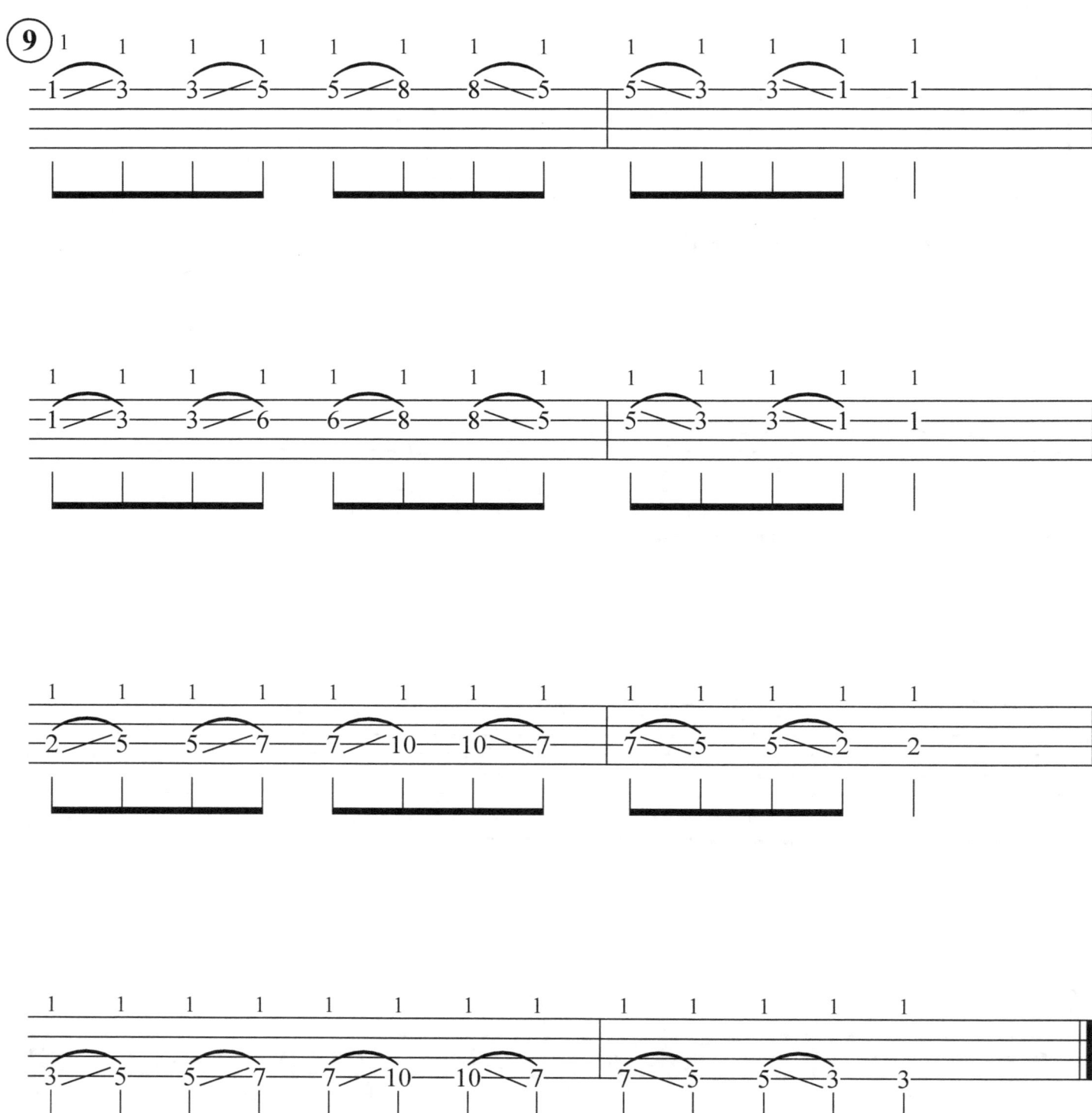

Barre Exercises

In our final one-finger exercise, we will work on making finger barres. A barre is where you hold down a finger on two or more strings. A full barre is notated with a C, which is related to the Spanish word cejilla, which means capo. A ½ before the C means a partial barre.

Keep the barre finger close to the fret and maintain even pressure on the strings. Barres can be played with any finger, so practice the exercise with all four fingers.

*Tip - Always scan ahead in the music to see if a chord can be formed with a barre. If you see the same number or note close together; this might indicate a barre.

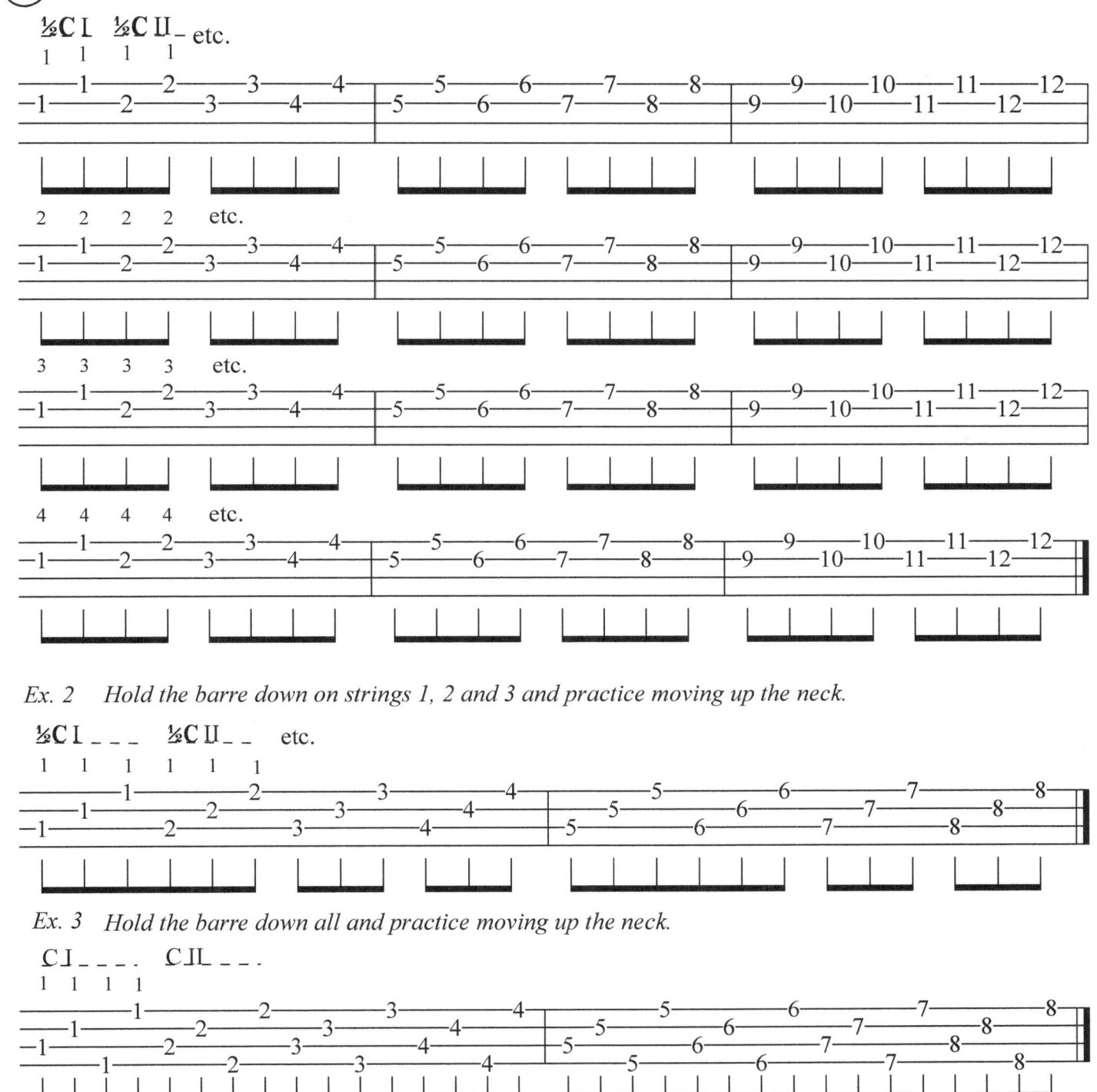

Ex. 2   Hold the barre down on strings 1, 2 and 3 and practice moving up the neck.

Ex. 3   Hold the barre down all and practice moving up the neck.

CHAPTER TWO - 2 FINGER EXERCISES

In our next set of ten exercises, we will use two fingers at a time. In exercise 1, two-finger combinations, there are twelve possible movements with two fingers. Follow the fingering carefully and always strive for a clear tone without fret rattling. Move the two-finger combinations to practice in different positions and fret distances.

Though these exercises are geared to the left-hand workout, you should also monitor your right-hand fingering once the left-hand fingering is secure. Most exercises in the book work best with alternating fingers or down/up if you use a pick. Here are some fingerings you can work through if you are fingerpicking the exercises:

i-m m-i i-r m-r.

Two-Finger Combinations

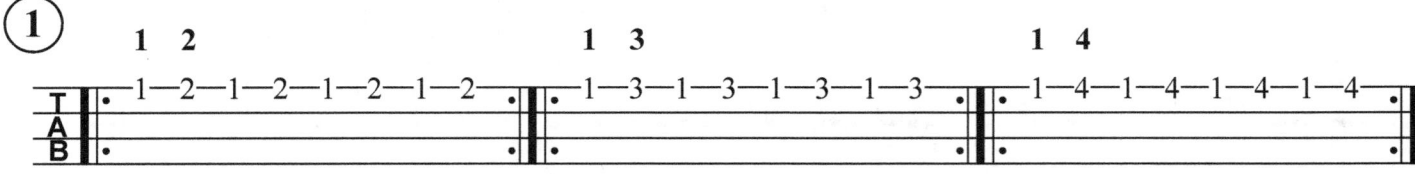

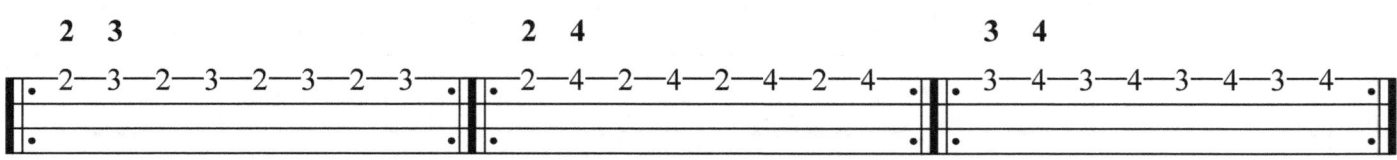

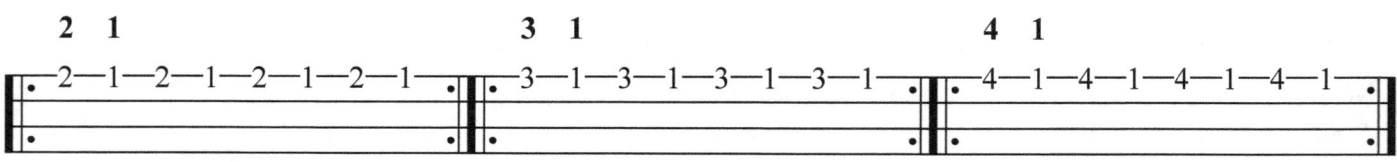

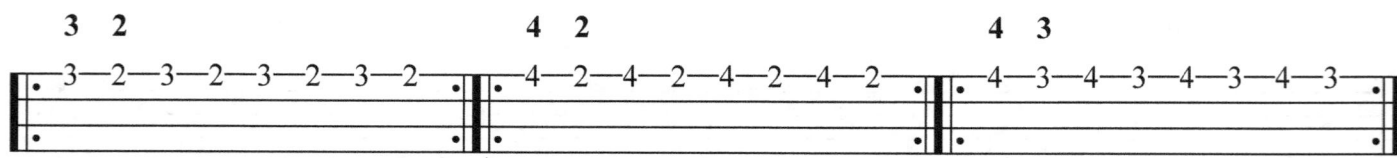

Two-Finger Hammer-On and Pull-Off Exercises

This might seem redundant, but repeat exercise 1 using hammer-ons and pull-offs. Remember, the curved slur line indicates a hammer-on or pull-off. The hammer-on always goes from a lower to a higher number, and the pull-off goes from a higher to a lower number. Use a metronome to keep an even rhythm and work towards an equal volume on both notes.

Hammer-On Exercises

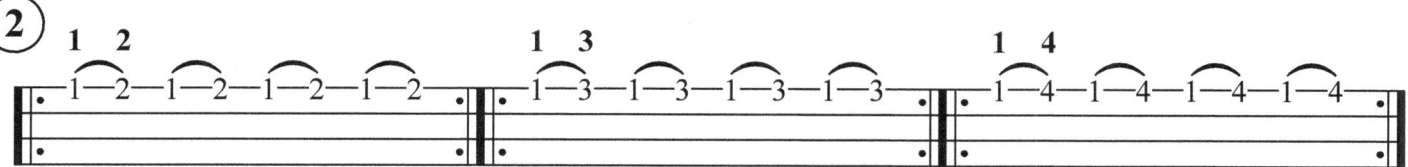

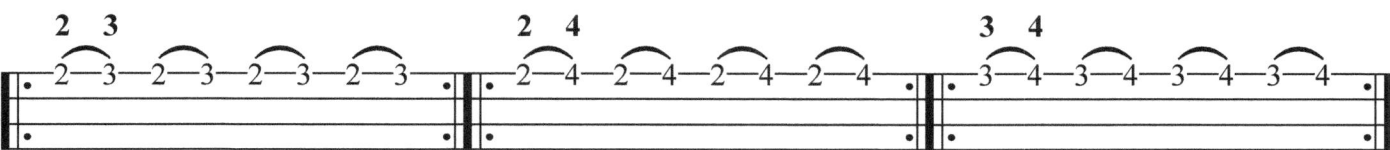

Pull-Off Exercises

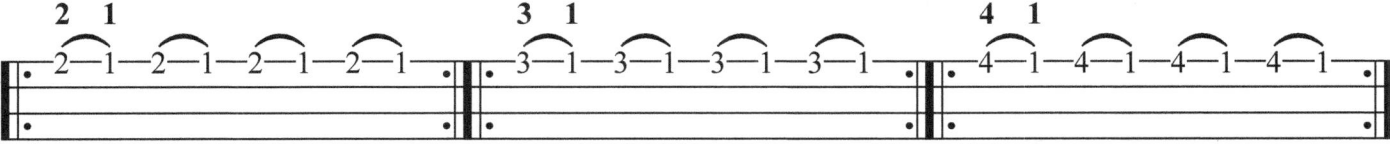

Box Exercises

Imagine outlining a small box with your fingers as you work through exercise 3. These exercises, like most, can be moved around the neck. For added practice, try applying hammer-ons and pull-offs.

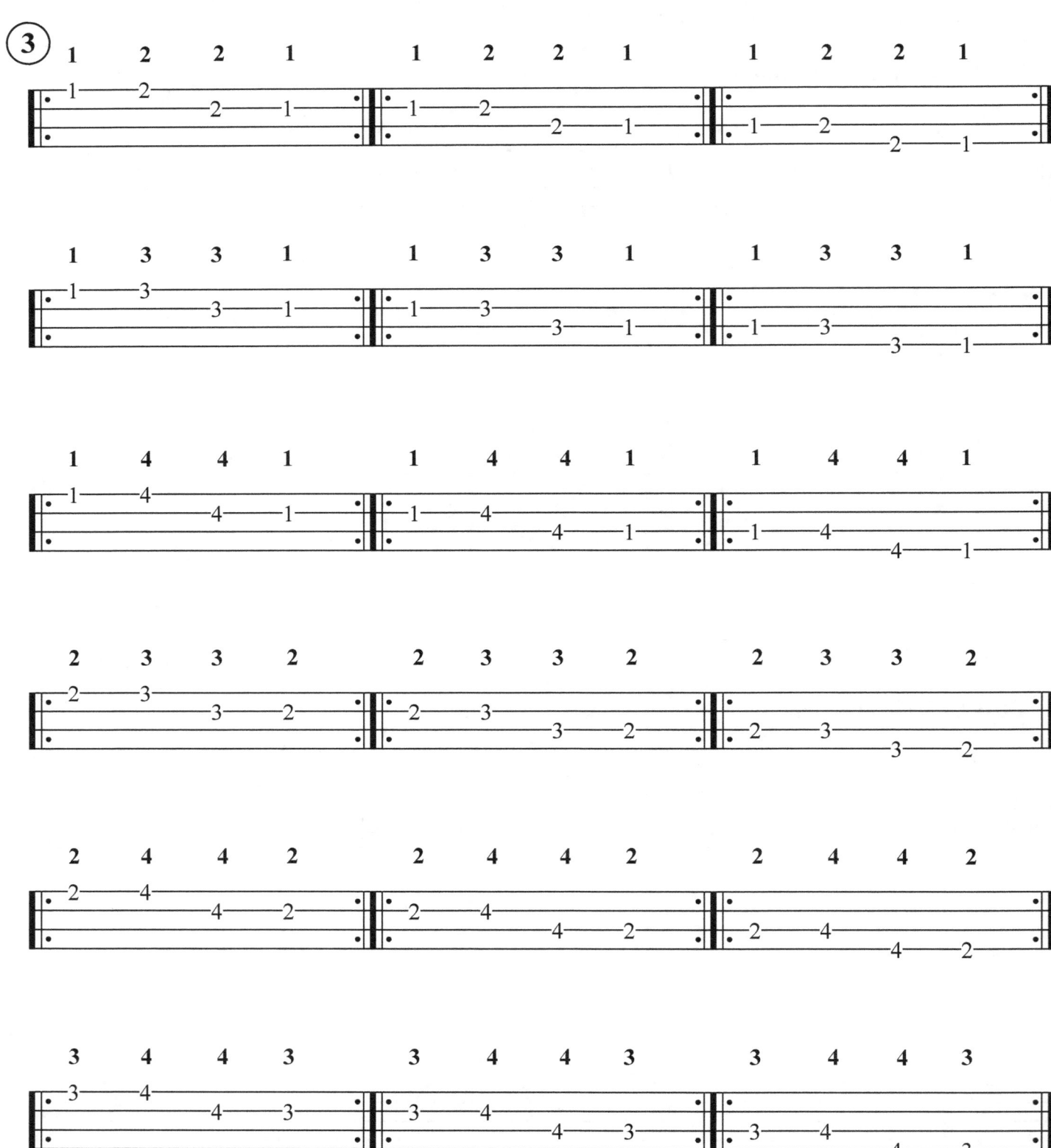

Pivot Exercises

Here are some challenging exercises requiring focus and coordination. In exercise 4, you have to hold one finger down while pivoting the other finger between strings. Carefully follow the fingering and observe the text above each exercise.

(4)

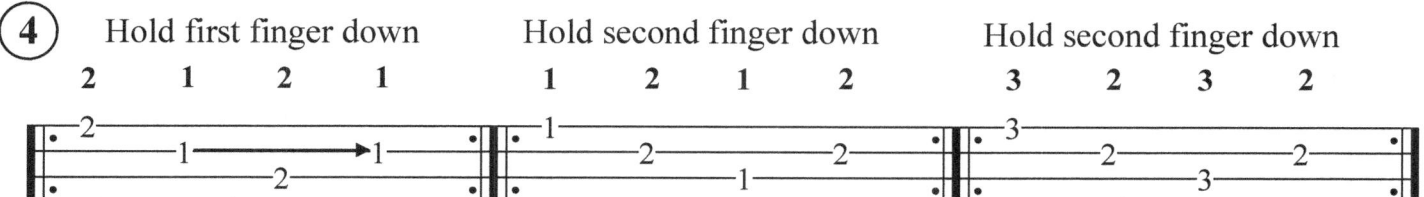

Barre Chord Exercises Using Two-Fingers

We will apply some more barre chord exercises to familiar ukulele chord shapes. Notice the barre markings in Roman numerals that indicate which fret to barre. Listen for a clear tone on each string and avoid any string buzzing by keeping your finger close to the fret and even pressure on the strings.

Ex. 1

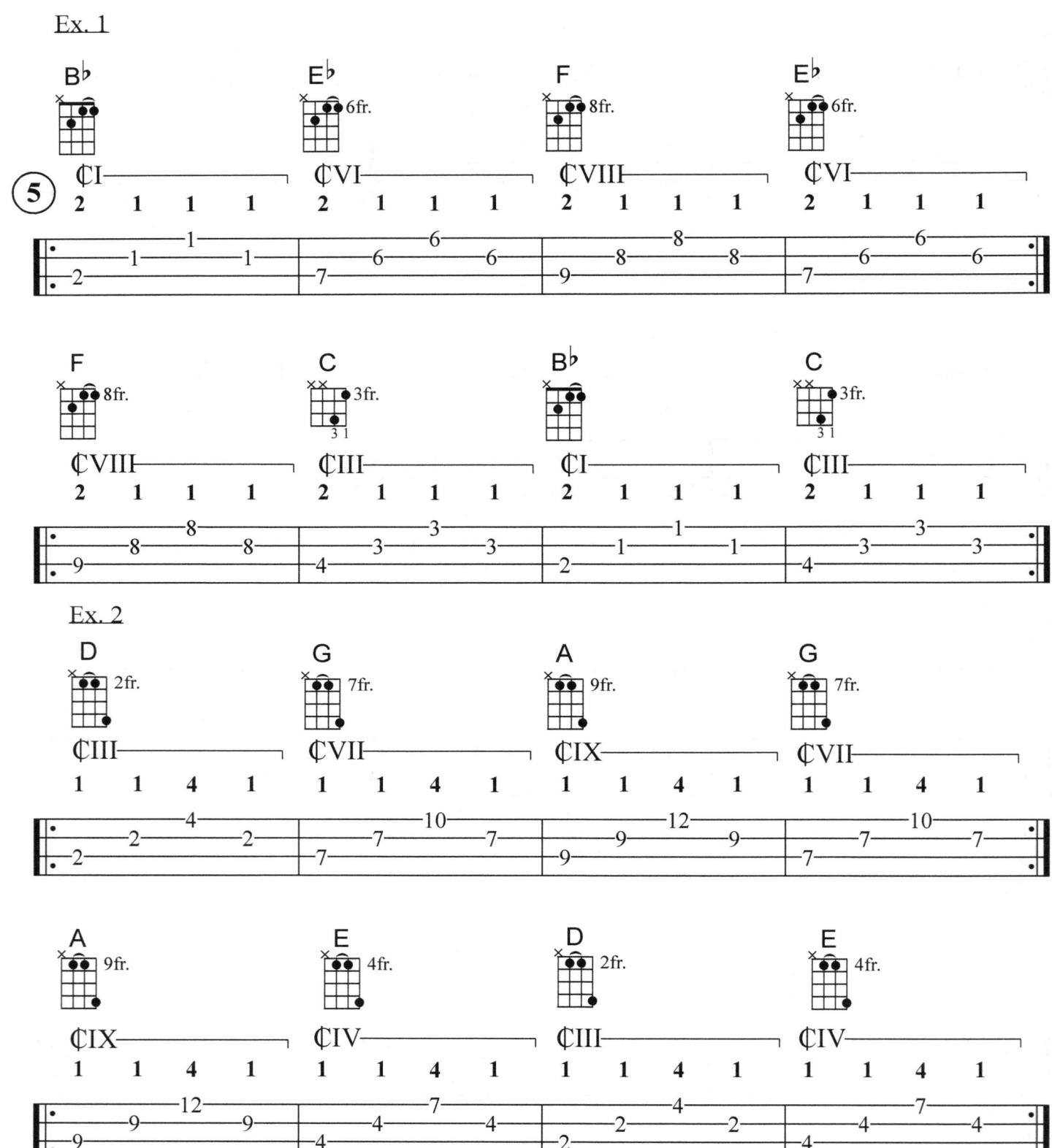

Ex. 2

Finger-Swap Exercises

Here's an excellent exercise to help with position changes on your ukulele. In this group of exercises, use two different fingers on the same fret. In other words, swap one finger with another on the same note.

<u>Ex. 1</u>

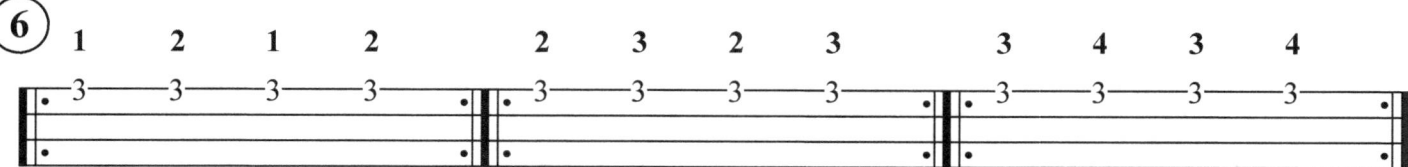

| 1 | 2 | 1 | 2 | | 2 | 3 | 2 | 3 | | 3 | 4 | 3 | 4 |

```
⑥ ┌──3───3───3───3──┐┌──3───3───3───3──┐┌──3───3───3───3──┐
  │                 ││                 ││                 │
  └─────────────────┘└─────────────────┘└─────────────────┘
```

| 1 | 3 | 1 | 3 | | 1 | 4 | 1 | 4 | | 2 | 4 | 2 | 4 |

```
┌──3───3───3───3──┐┌──3───3───3───3──┐┌──3───3───3───3──┐
│                 ││                 ││                 │
└─────────────────┘└─────────────────┘└─────────────────┘
```

<u>Ex. 2</u>

We continue the same exercises but up the neck on a smaller fret width. For more practice, repeat the finger-swapping exercises on different frets and strings.

| 1 | 2 | 1 | 2 | | 2 | 3 | 2 | 3 | | 3 | 4 | 3 | 4 |

```
┌──8───8───8───8──┐┌──8───8───8───8──┐┌──8───8───8───8──┐
│                 ││                 ││                 │
└─────────────────┘└─────────────────┘└─────────────────┘
```

| 1 | 3 | 1 | 3 | | 1 | 4 | 1 | 4 | | 2 | 4 | 2 | 4 |

```
┌──8───8───8───8──┐┌──8───8───8───8──┐┌──8───8───8───8──┐
│                 ││                 ││                 │
└─────────────────┘└─────────────────┘└─────────────────┘
```

Sliding Exercises

We continue with another set of sliding exercises using two fingers. Pay attention to the fingers marked above the tablature, and keep even pressure on the string as you slide. In Ex. 2 below, there are larger leaps between the notes. Slide up and then strike the note again.

Ex. 1

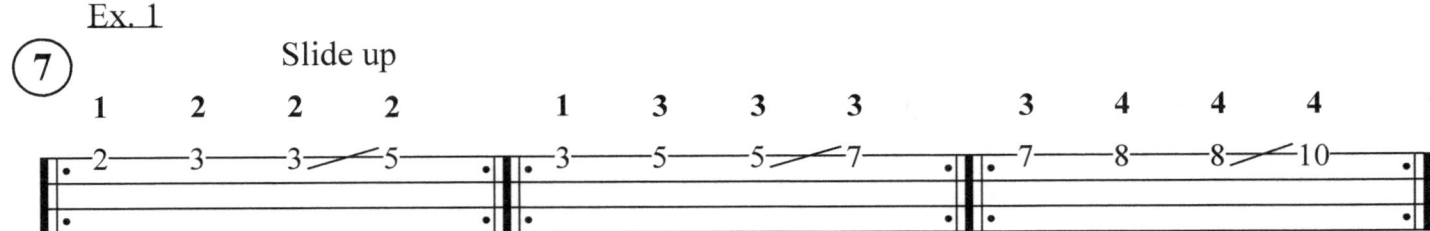

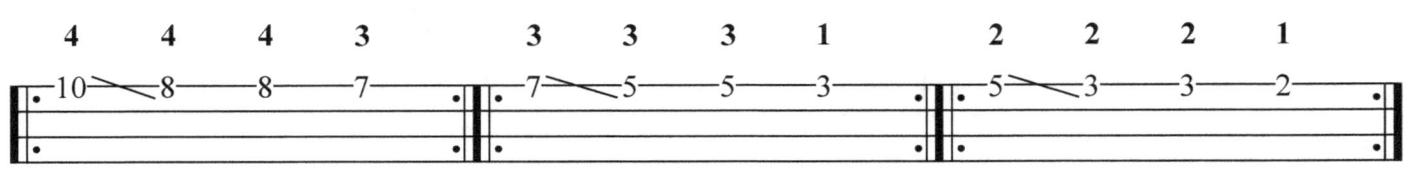

Ex. 2

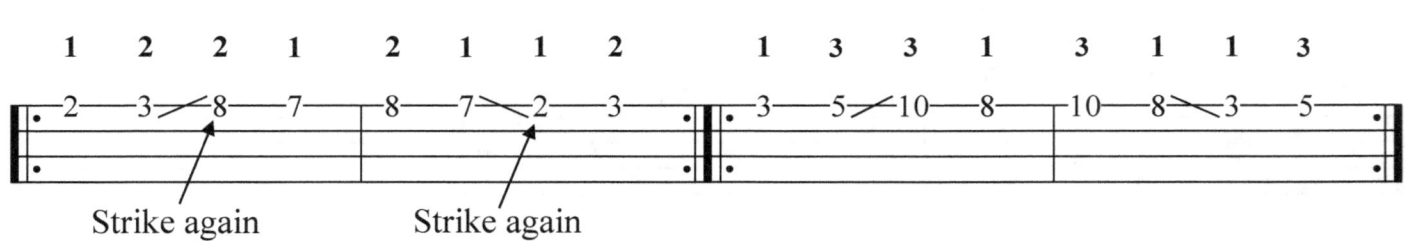

Adding the slur line over the number means to play legato. In other words, don't strike the string again.

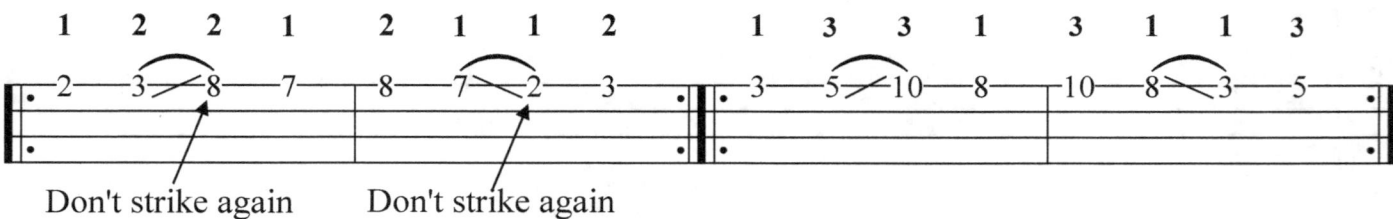

Two-Finger Trill Exercises

 The two-finger trill exercises are similar to what you did in chapter one. Pluck the string once, hammer on, and pull off without plucking the string again. Move the trills to different frets and strings for extra practice.

 Notice the slur line over the top of the notes indicates that you should play the notes legato, meaning connect the notes closely together. Strive for an even eighth-note rhythm.

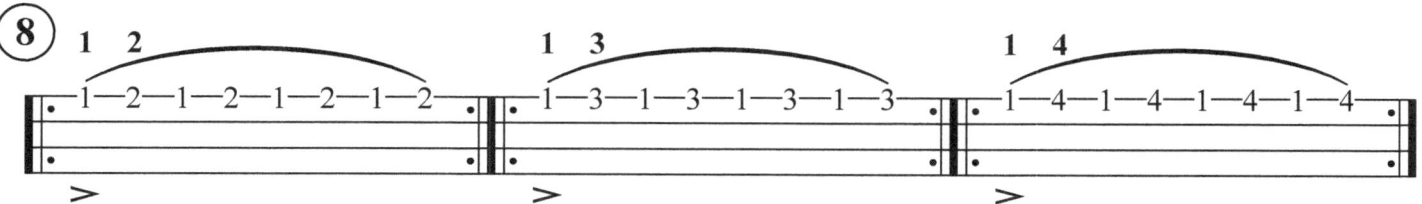

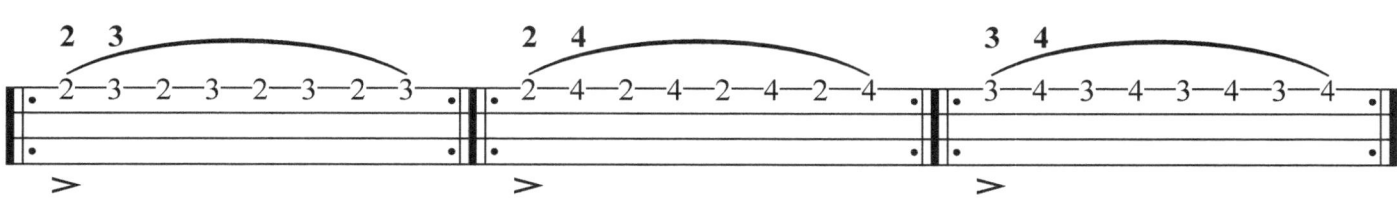

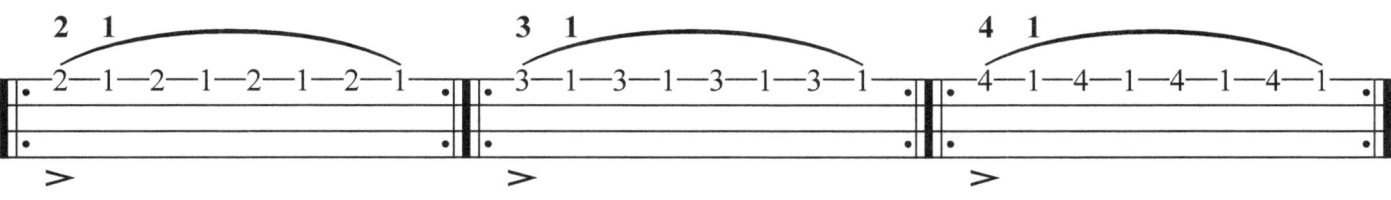

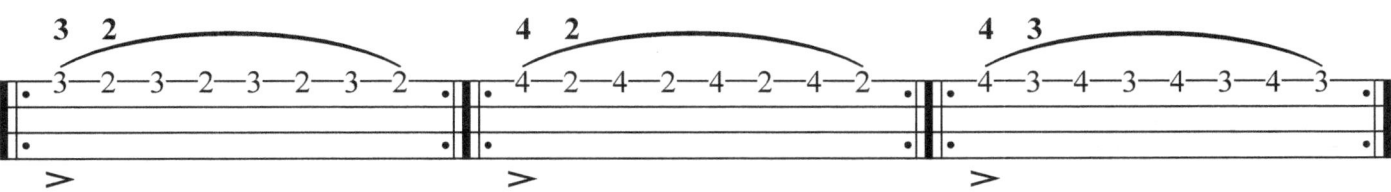

Two-Finger Arpeggios

Let's return to our arpeggio patterns with two fingers and dominant and minor 7th arpeggios. Observe the fingering and listen for a good tone by aiming close to the fret.

Dominant 7th Arpeggio Pattern

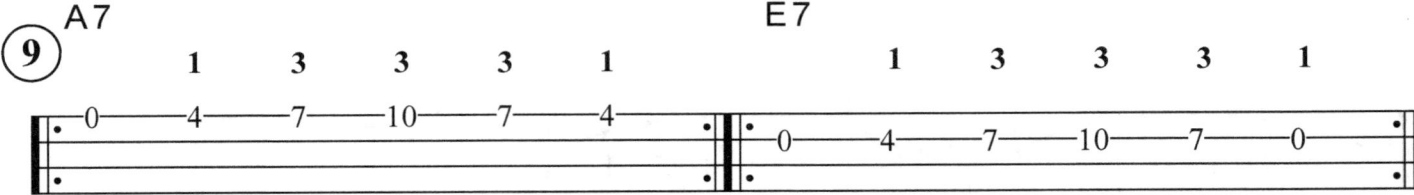

Same A7 and E7 arpeggio and fingering, but using two strings.

Minor 7th Arpeggio Pattern

Same Am7 and Em7 arpeggio and fingering on two strings.

Guide Finger Exercises

A guide finger is when your left-hand finger remains in contact with a string while shifting between notes and chords. In other words, when you keep the finger on the string as you "guide" your finger up and down the neck.

In Ex. 2, we will use intervals of thirds to connect the two notes together. Hold the fingers down on both notes as you shift around the neck. For added practice, slide between the notes.

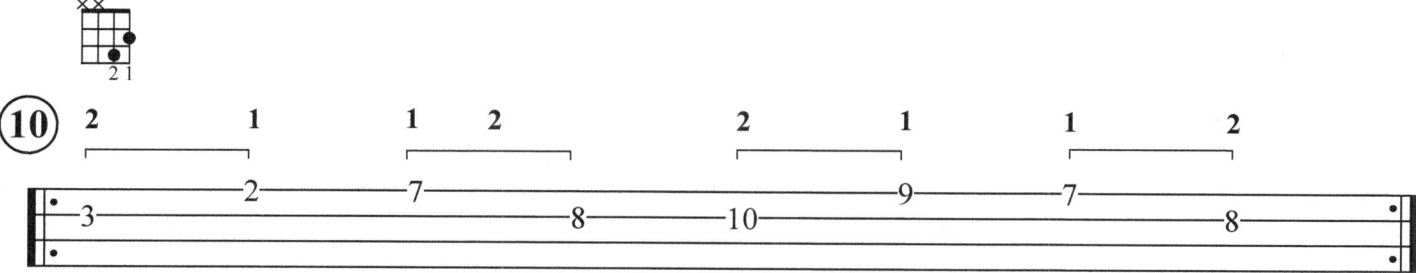

Keep fingers on the strings.

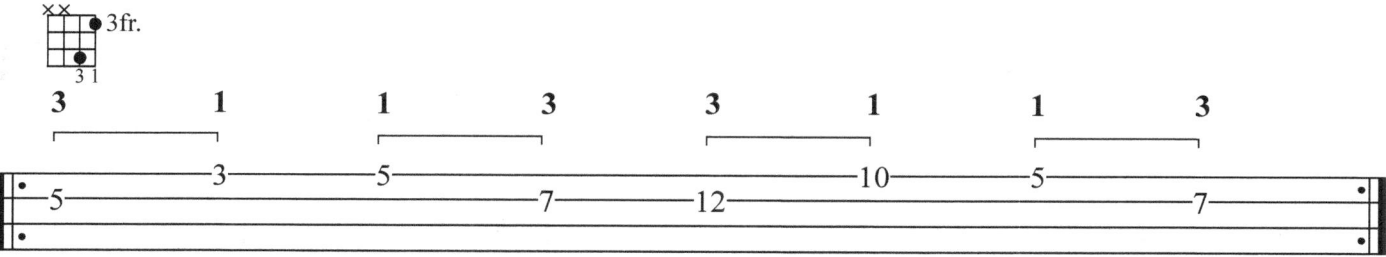

Ex. 2 The next exercise uses a combination of barres and two finger shapes.

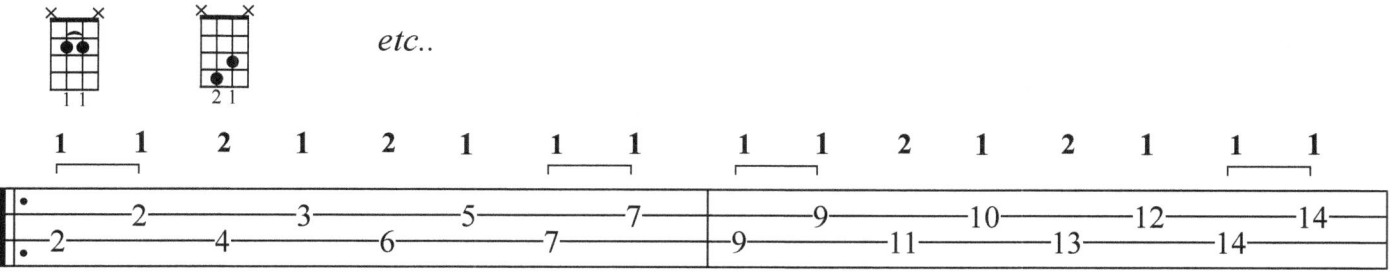

CHAPTER THREE - 3 FINGER EXERCISES

We started with one and two and now move on to the three-finger exercises. With three fingers, there are now 24 possible combinations. And you guessed it, we will go through all the combinations. As always, follow the fingerings above the tablature and keep an ear to produce a clear, full sound on each note.

The exercise below shows the fingers on the first string but move to other strings and positions for a complete workout. Dust off your metronome and start slow.

Three-Finger Combinations

1

1 2 3 1 2 3	1 2 4 1 2 4	1 3 2 1 3 2	1 3 4 1 3 4
1—2—3—1—2—3	1—2—4—1—2—4	1—3—2—1—3—2	1—3—4—1—3—4

1 4 2 1 4 2	1 4 3 1 4 3	2 1 3 2 1 3	2 1 4 2 1 4
1—4—2—1—4—2	1—4—3—1—4—3	2—1—3—2—1—3	2—1—4—2—1—4

2 3 1 2 3 1	2 3 4 2 3 4	2 4 1 2 4 1	2 4 3 2 4 3
2—3—1—2—3—1	2—3—4—2—3—4	2—4—1—2—4—1	2—4—3—2—4—3

3 1 2 3 1 2	3 1 4 3 1 4	3 2 1 3 2 1	3 2 4 3 2 4
3—1—2—3—1—2	3—1—4—3—1—4	3—2—1—3—2—1	3—2—4—3—2—4

3 4 1 3 4 1	3 4 2 3 4 2	4 1 2 4 1 2	4 1 3 4 1 3
3—4—1—3—4—1	3—4—2—3—4—2	4—1—2—4—1—2	4—1—3—4—1—3

4 2 1 4 2 1	4 2 3 4 2 3	4 3 1 4 3 1	4 3 2 4 3 2
4—2—1—4—2—1	4—2—3—4—2—3	4—3—1—4—3—1	4—3—2—4—3—2

Three-Finger Hammer-Ons & Pull-Offs

Now, apply hammer-ons and pull-offs using the same three-finger combinations. For added practice, try speed bursts (slow-fast) once you are comfortable with each fingering.

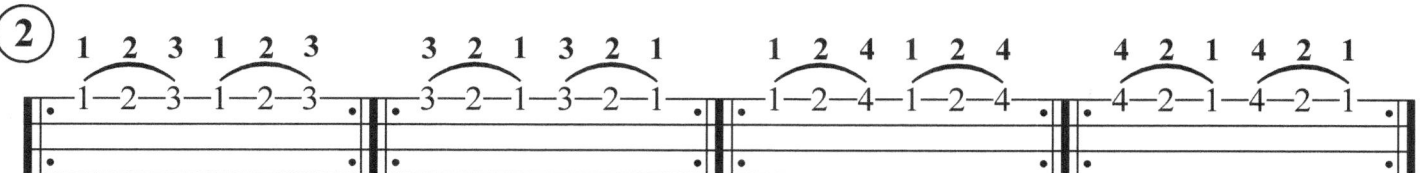

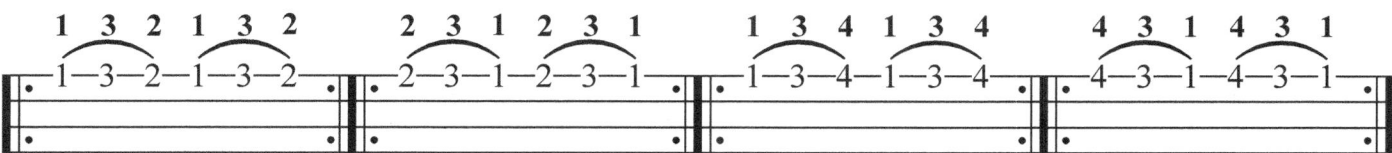

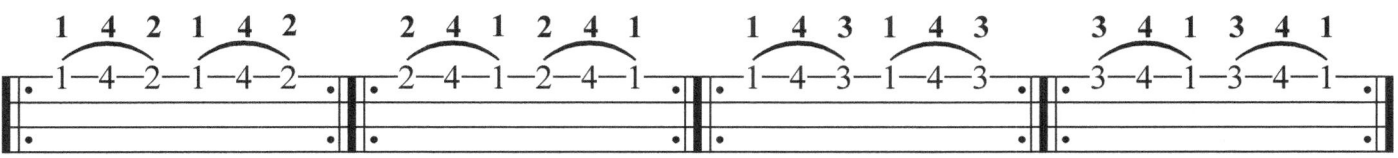

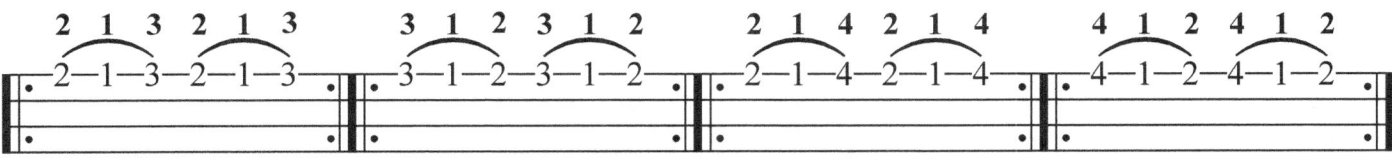

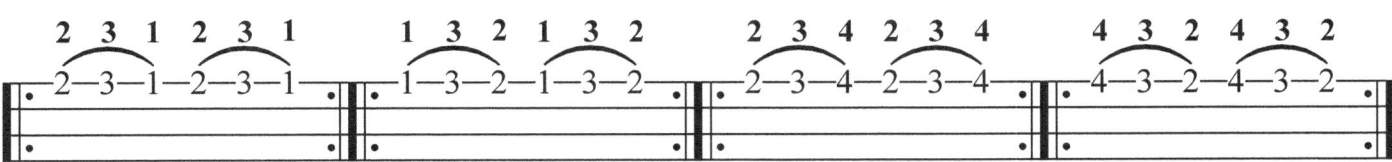

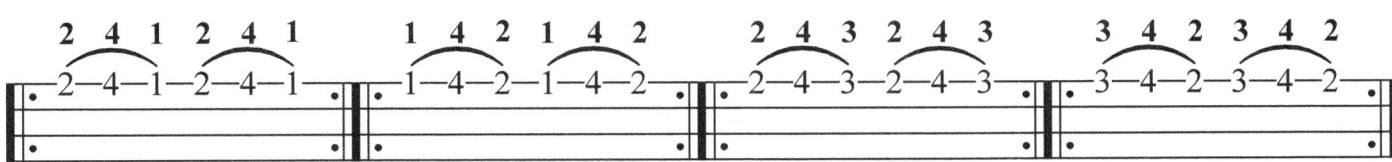

40

Triangle Exercises

In exercise 3, we are going to practice switching chords. All the chords have a triangle shape and should be easy to remember. Here are a few chord-switching tips to keep in mind:

1) Try to land all the fingers in a chord together. Instead of playing a chord one finger at a time, try to drop all three fingers together.
2) Form the chord and hover the fingers overtop the chord, then quickly drop all fingers together.

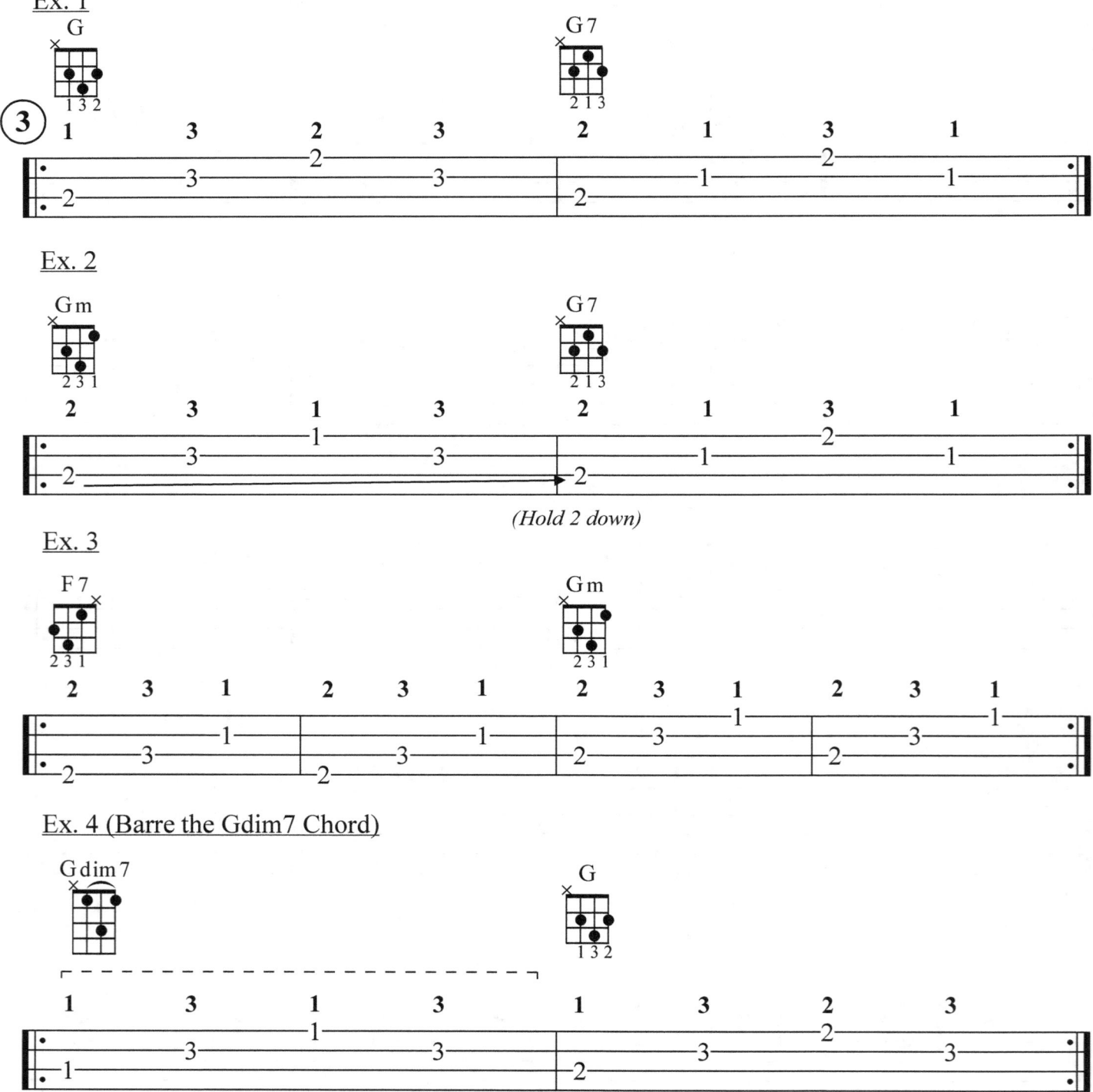

Criss Cross Exercises

The next set of exercises requires you to pivot (hold down a finger) as you move your wrist to form the chords. After you have memorized an exercise, try to do the chord shapes around the neck. Increase the speed as you become more proficient.

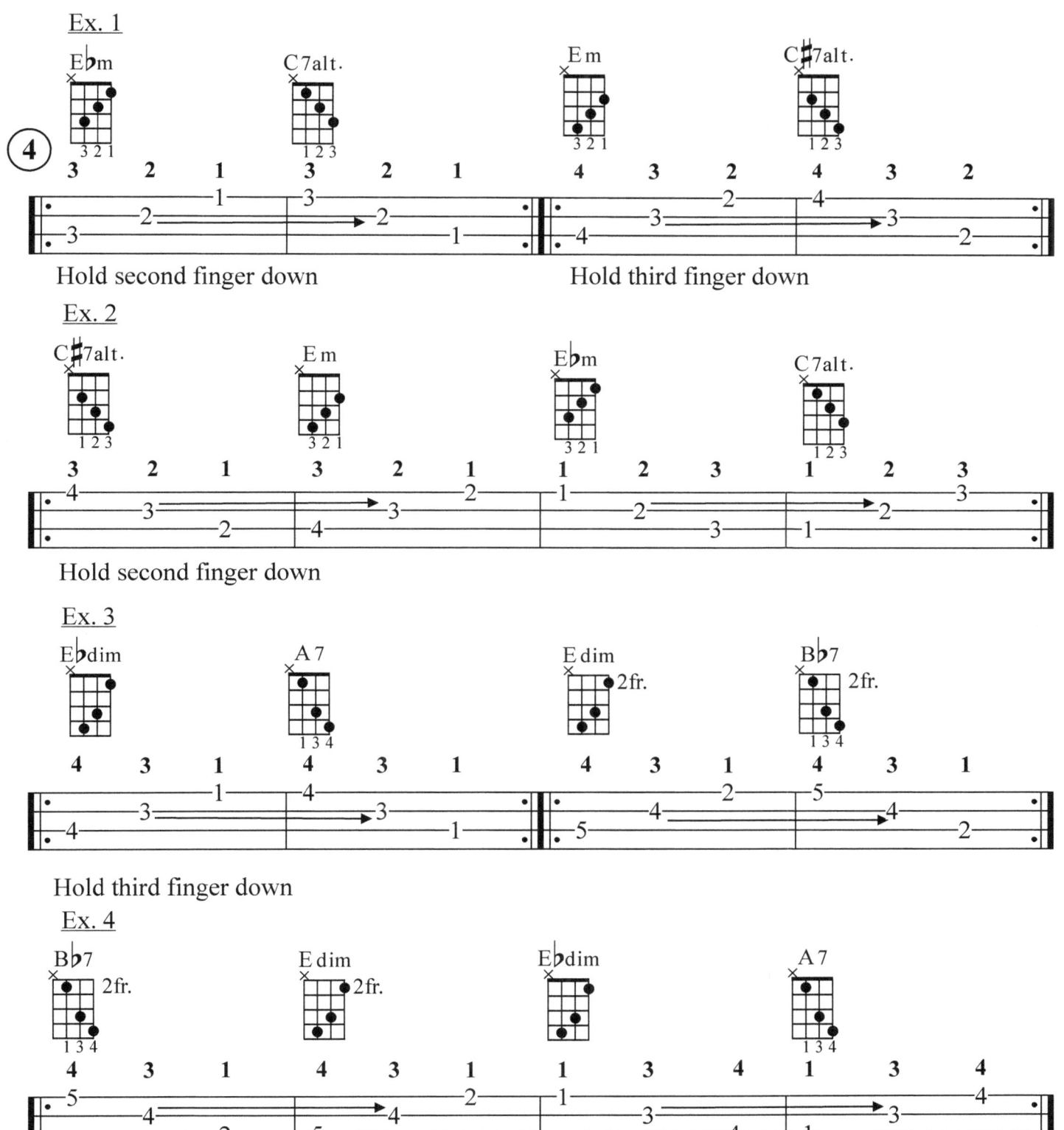

Ex. 1

Hold second finger down   Hold third finger down

Ex. 2

Hold second finger down

Ex. 3

Hold third finger down

Ex. 4

Scales in Thirds and Sixths

As we did in an earlier exercise, we will play melodic intervals in 3rds and 6ths. Develop the technique of keeping one finger down, which acts as a guide as you move up and down the scale. Try memorizing the finger patterns, as thirds and sixths are frequently used in all styles of music.

C Major Scale in Thirds

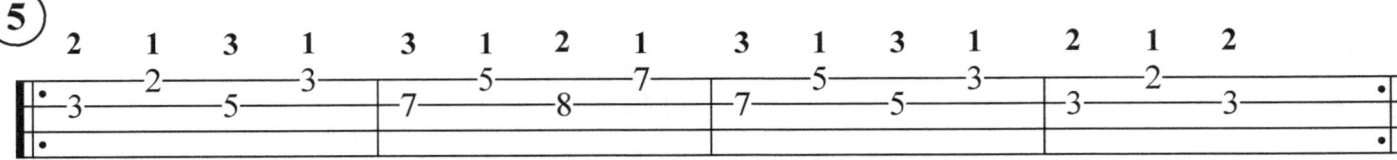

Keep 1st finger onstring - use as a guide

C Major Scale in Thirds

Keep 2nd finger onstring - use as a guide

G Minor Scale in Thirds

Keep 1st finger onstring - use as a guide

F Major Scale in Sixths

Keep 2nd finger on 3rd string - use as a guide

Bb Major Scale in Sixths

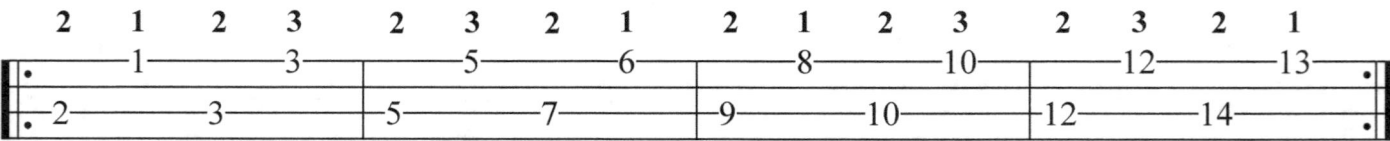

Keep 2nd finger on 3rd string - use as a guide

Pentatonic Scales and Patterns

In our next exercise, we will explore the pentatonic major scale. The pentatonic major is a five-note scale frequently used in improvising. We start with the basic one-octave scale and then apply variations. This scale is moveable, as shown in the Db pentatonic major scale below.

C Pentatonic Major   Variation 1

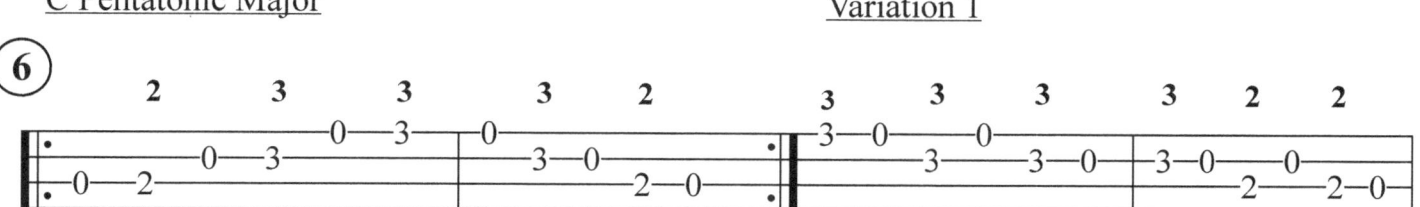

Variation 2   Variation 3

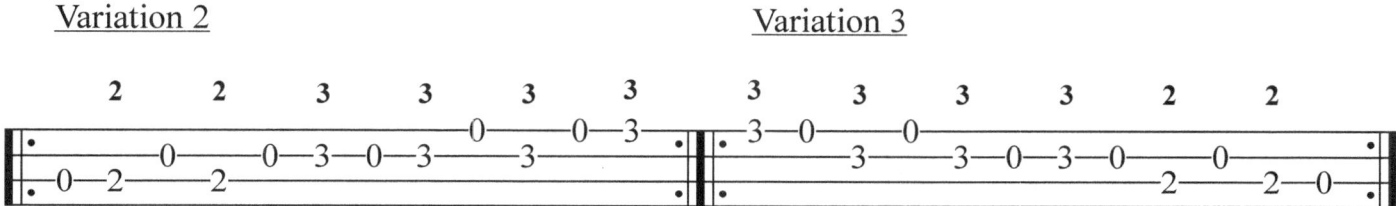

D♭ Pentatonic Major   Variation 1

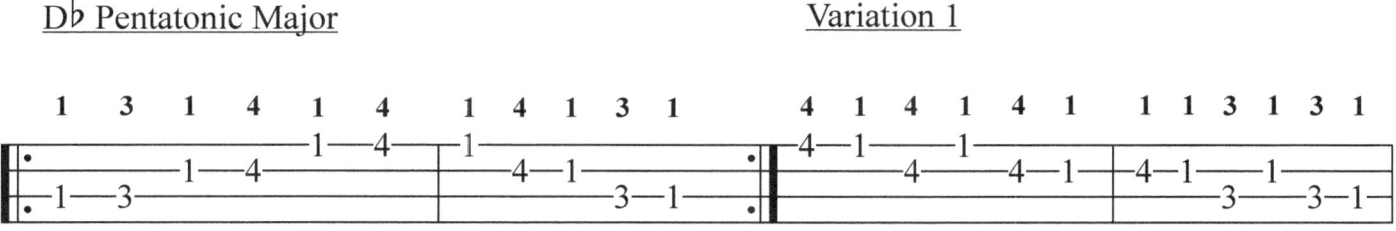

Variation 2   Variation 3

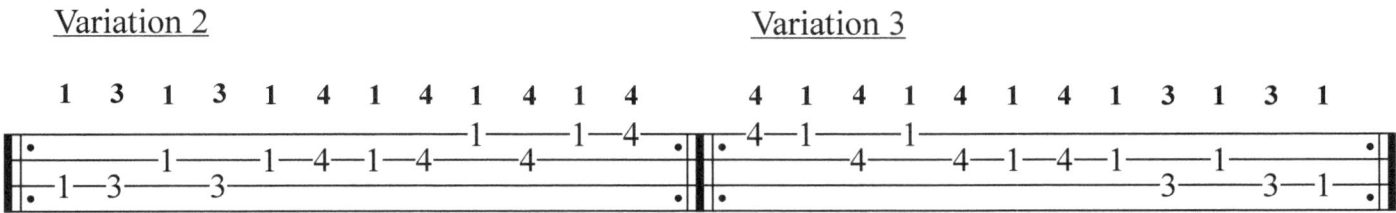

Legato Slurs with Three Fingers

A legato slur is when you strike the string once and then play consecutive notes using hammer-ons and pull-offs. Legato slurring is a common technique but presents a few challenges. The first is to keep an equal volume on all the notes played. You can do this by striking the first note with enough attack that the other notes don't fade away.

Similarly, hammer on and pull off with enough force to articulate the notes clearly. You may also need to use a barre when switching strings.

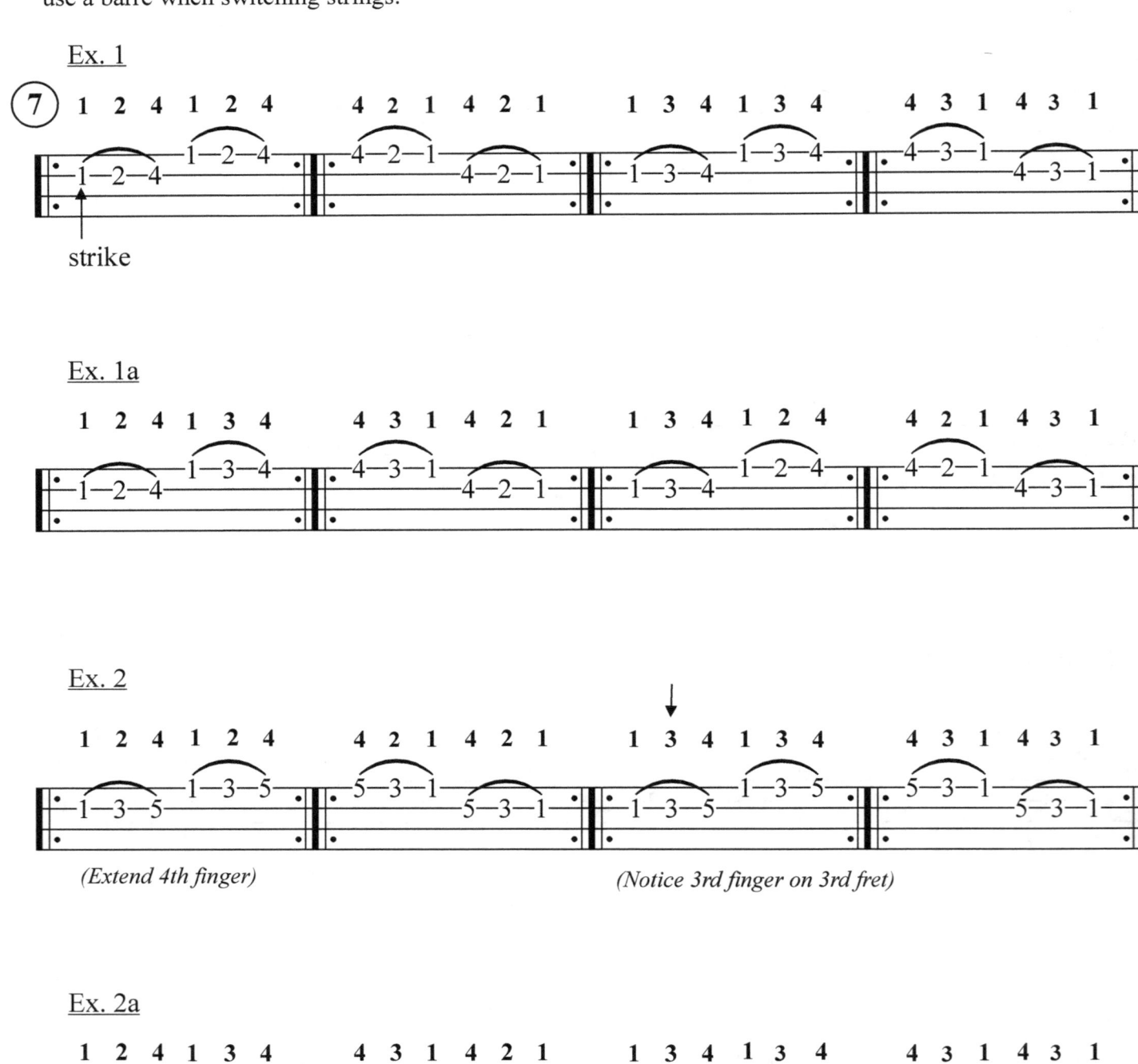

Ex. 1

strike

Ex. 1a

Ex. 2

(Extend 4th finger)   (Notice 3rd finger on 3rd fret)

Ex. 2a

The Turn - Ornamentation with Three Fingers

Turns were common in earlier types of classical music but continue to be heard in all styles of music. The turn is similar to a legato slur but adds an extra note or two and is notated: ∾. Turns require a combi- nation of hammer-ons and pull-offs as they circle a target note. Like the previous exercise, use equal velocity on the first and subsequent notes to maintain an equal volume.

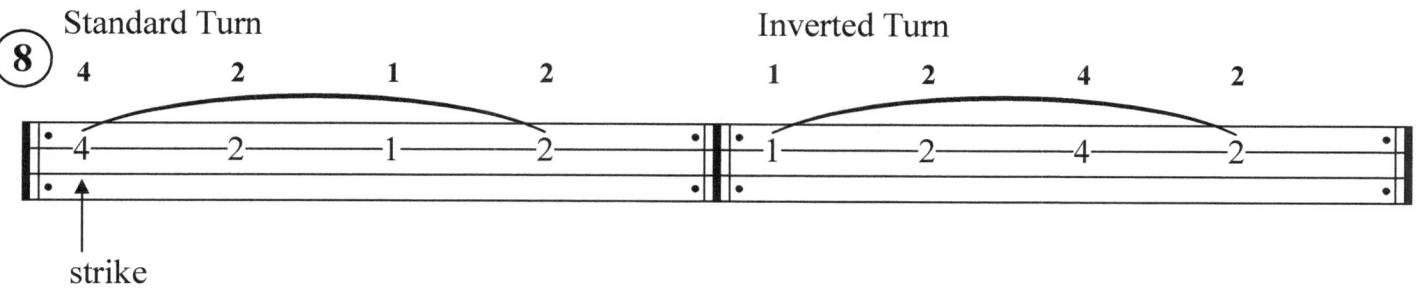

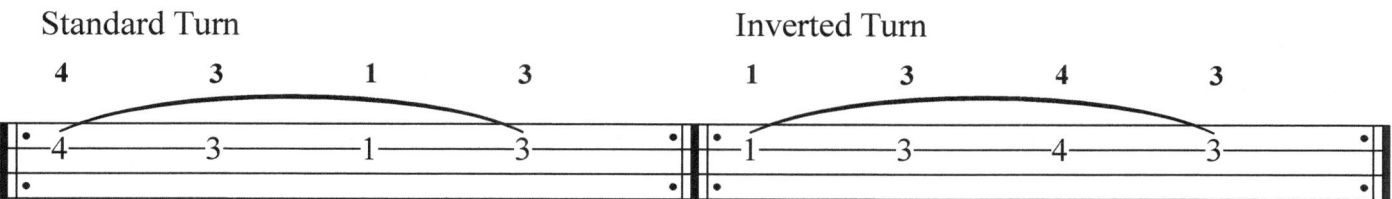

Variation 1

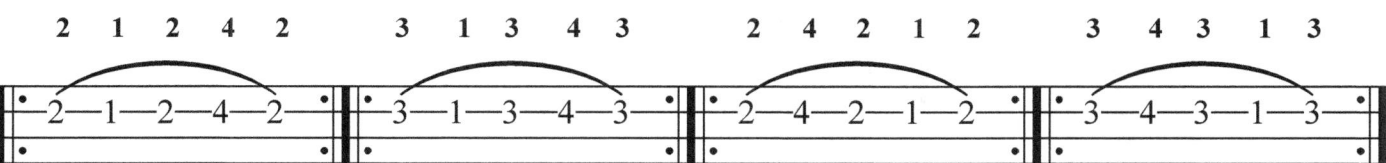

Playing a Scale with Turns

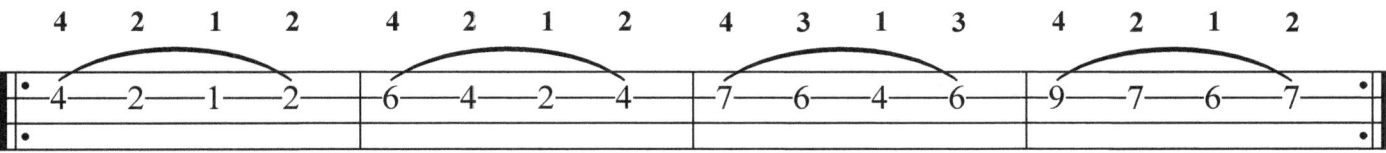

Three-Finger Stretch (Extensions)

Now it's time to stretch those fingers with the extension exercises. Pay close attention to the tablature number and match the corresponding finger (see arrows). Try to reach close to the fret and produce a nice, clear tone. I suggest you move these exercises up the neck to negotiate the different fret distances.

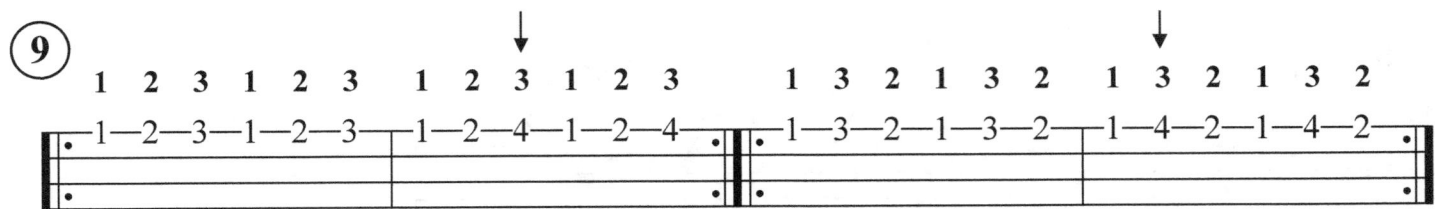

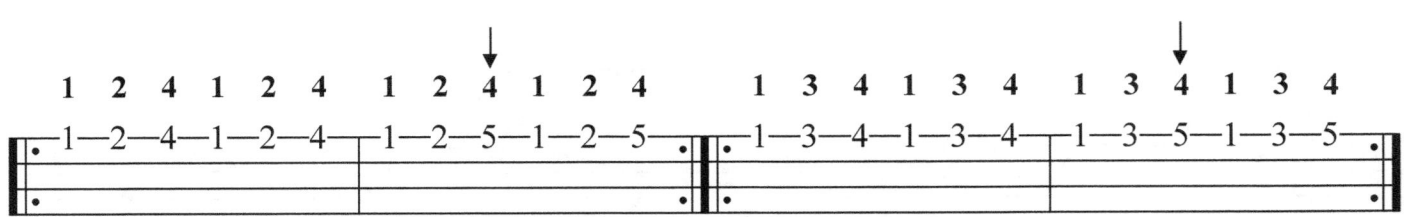

Ex. 2

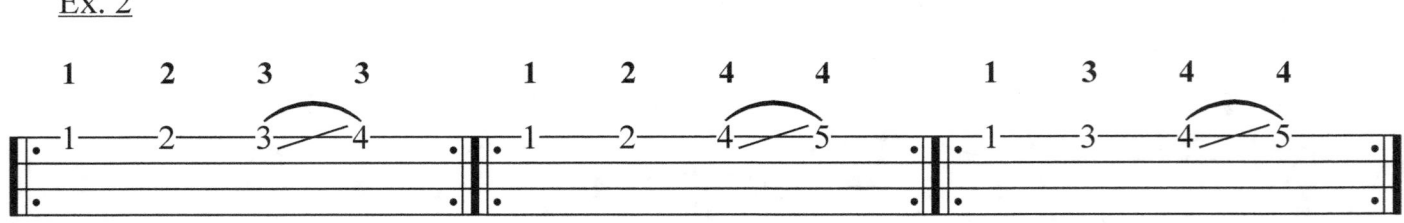

Ex. 3

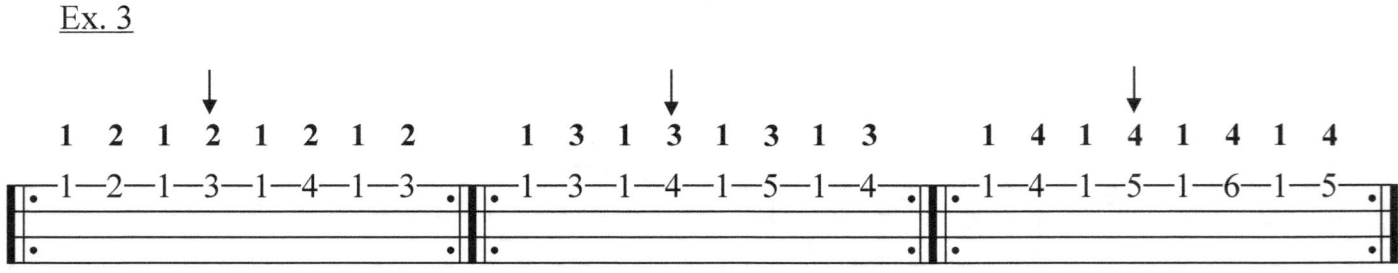

Exercise Ten – Introduction to Rhythm Exercises

In the final exercise of this section, we will apply a variety of rhythms and accents on the C major scale. Before we play the exercises, let's review how to read and play rhythm and give a few technique tips.

How to Read Rhythms

Most students learning to read music struggle with reading rhythms, so if that is you, you are not alone. The problem with our notation system is that it is visually inaccurate. Maybe we should think about rhythm as how long a note rings and represent it with a line equal to the length of the note.

So, a long note could be shown with a long line and a short note with a short line. The chart below makes better sense visually but is not feasible when written down:

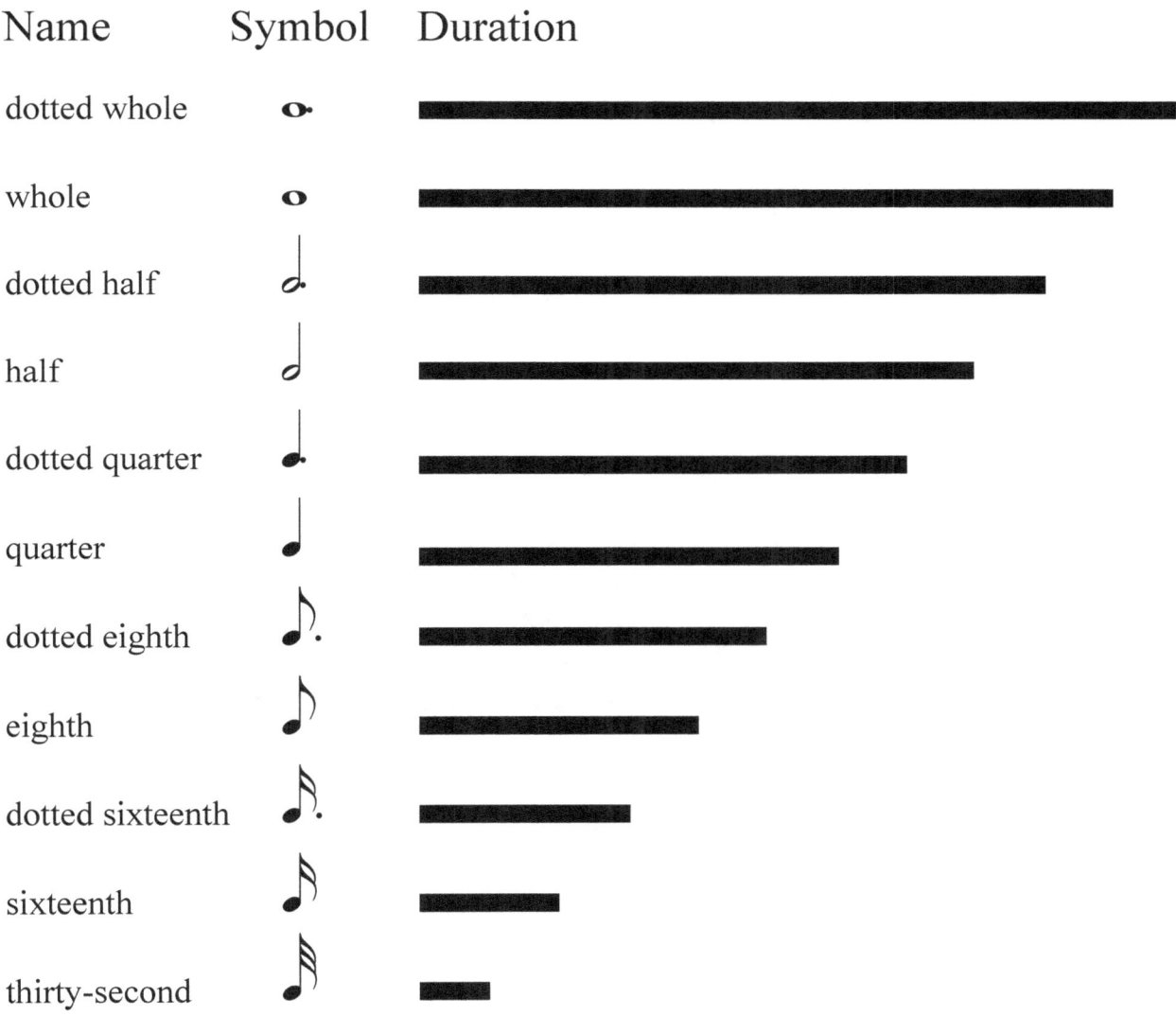

Time Signatures and Subdivisions of the Beat

When you listen to music, you probably have noticed recurring rhythm beats. These beats are organized into groupings and notated with time signatures. The most common time signature is 4/4.

Rhythm is all about structured time, but I'll use another visual example of an apple basket to explain rhythm and subdivisions of the beat. I can place four apples in the basket below, and each apple equals one beat. In music, we call these apples quarter notes, which are notated below:

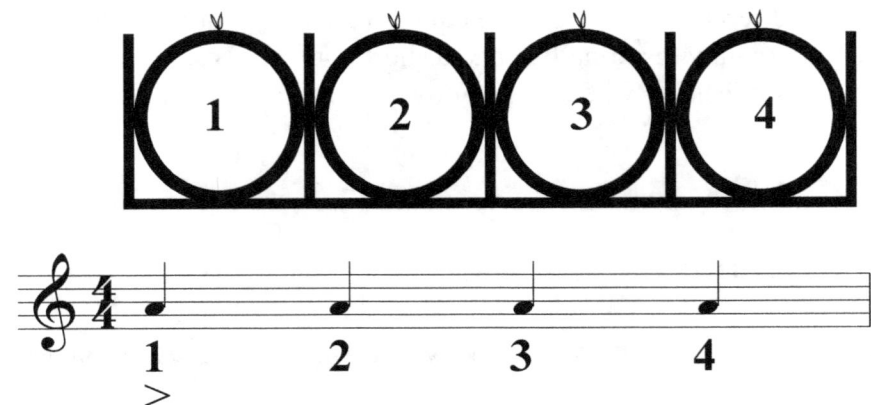

The example above is in 4/4 time, which has a stronger accent on the first beat. Clap your hands and count evenly (1, 2, 3, 4), putting an accent (>) on the 1.

So, we have 4 quarter notes (apples) in a bar, but let's divide each apple in half. Now we have eight pieces of apple or what we call eighth notes.

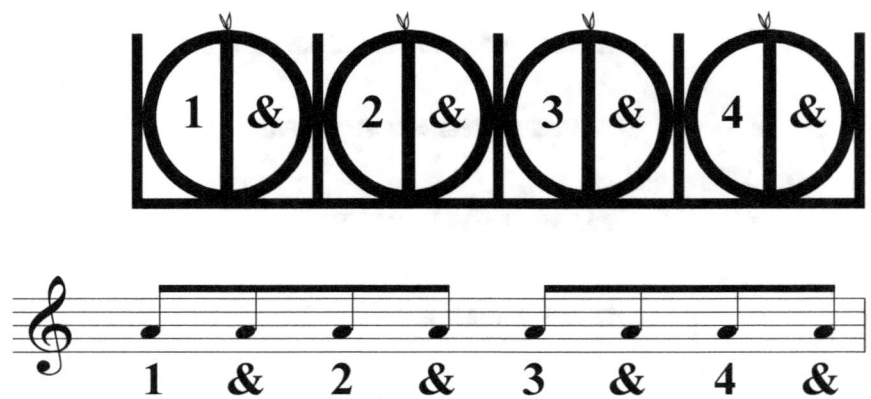

It is standard practice to count our eighth notes using a speech rhythm (a word, number or syllable pattern that mimics a musical rhythm) using the number and &. So, you count this 1 & 2 & 3 & 4 & to help keep your place in the measure of 4/4 time.

We are not done yet! We will cut each piece of apple in half again, so now we have four notes or pieces of apple in each beat. We call these shorter subdivisions of the beat sixteenth notes, and we count them: 1e&a 2e&a 3e&a 4e&a:

1 e & a 2 e & a 3 e & a 4 e & a

Playing the Rhythms

Ok, let's learn some of the rhythms in exercise 10, but first, let's do a little exercise.

Run your right-hand* finger evenly across the line below from left to right. Put your finger on the page at the start of the line (where the circle is) and evenly move your finger in the direction of the arrow. Remember to keep a steady pace as you move your finger along:

Now, let's add our speech rhythms to help keep our place in the bar. Repeat moving your finger along the line, **but this time count:**

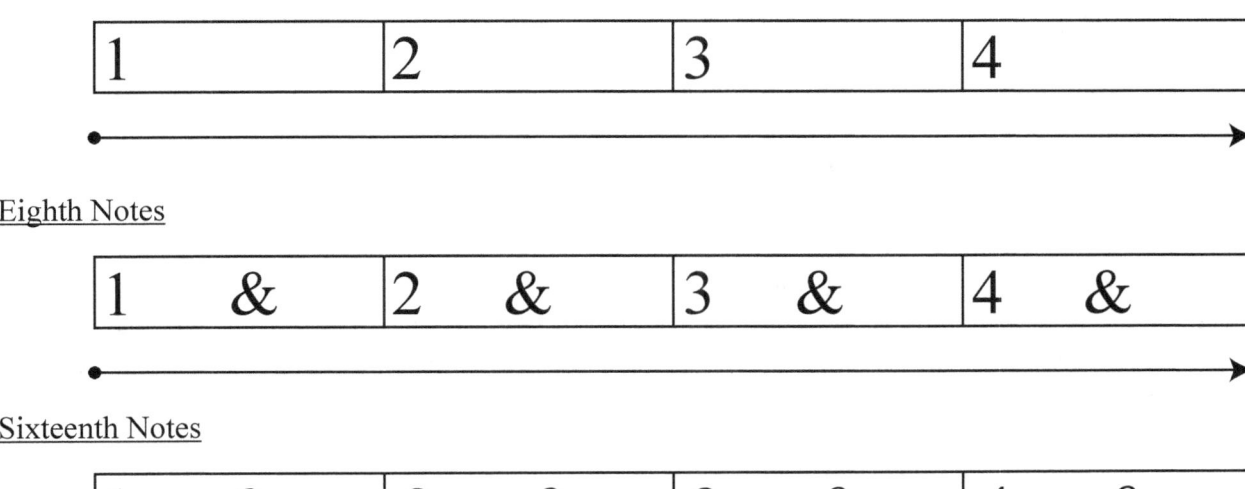

That was easy, right? Now, we can learn six rhythms that correspond to exercise 10. Here, we will only show one beat (or apple) below, but remember, each beat can be repeated up to four times in a bar (or basket) in 4/4 time.

Now, we will run our right-hand finger along the line, but this time, **tap your left-hand finger where the arrows are**. That is, use both hands – the right to smoothly move across the page while the left-hand finger taps the rhythm where the arrows are.

1	e	&	a	
↓	↑	↓	↑	♪♪♪♪
↓		↓	↑	
↓	↑	↓		
↓	↑		↑	
↓			↑	
↓	↑			

Before the next exercise, repeat the tapping exercise above, but **switch hands.** Use your left hand to run along the line while the right-hand taps the rhythm. Repeat these exercises until you are comfortable.

A Few More Rhythms

Until now, we have been using the 4/4 time signature, but the following exercise is in 3/4. So, only count to three. The 3/4 time signature is commonly used in waltzes.

1	2	3
↓	↓	↓

Returning to our first exercises above, we could think of dividing the apple into three parts. Here, we would have 3 apple pieces in each beat. When we divide in 3, we call this a triplet. Triplets are used in all time signatures, but we will go back and apply them to our 4/4 time signature. Now, we will use the speech rhythm 1-&-a, 2&-a, etc.:

1	&	a	
↓	↑	↓	♪♪♪

Ok, our last rhythm! You might recognize the following rhythm from Ravel's "Bolero." Here, we are in the 4/4 time signature with an eighth note and a triplet and will use slightly different counting. Let's divide the beat into two:

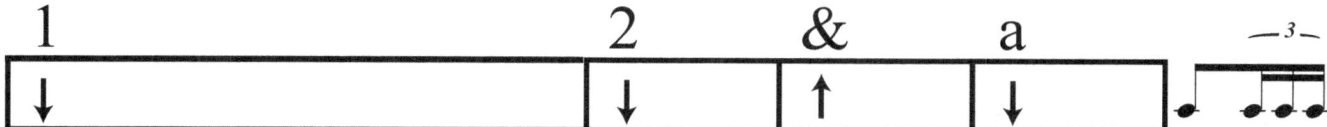

Fingering and Other Practice Tips

Like many exercises in this book, you can use multiple fingerings or picking patterns to develop your right-hand technique. As a reminder, here are the finger names:

t = thumb, i = index, m = middle, and r = ring

Now, here are 6 two-finger patterns and 4 three-finger patterns you can apply to exercise ten:

- Two-finger patterns: ***im, mi, ir, ri, mr, and rm.***
- When there are three notes in a group, try these fingerings: ***i-m-a, a-m-i, m-i-a, and m-a-i.***

If you use a pick, the most crucial technique to develop is alternate picking. That is, down-up. There are exceptions but for the most part, stick with down-up picking. The down pick is usually on the first beat, and the upstroke follows.

Other Practice Tips

• Practice with a metronome to help keep a steady beat. Think of the metronome as another musician rather than an unrelenting machine you work against. Relax and play with the metronome, not against it.

• Apply different scales and riffs with the rhythms in exercise 10. For example, you could play your minor, blues or pentatonic scales. Whatever you practice, try to apply a variety of different rhythms to help develop your right and left-hand coordination.

• Play the scales forward and backward and in random order. Just because you are playing a scale doesn't mean you have to go in a linear order. Shake it up and make up your own scale variations.

Alright, I hope you have a better understanding of rhythm. Let's go to exercise ten!

"It does not matter how slowly you go as long as you do not stop."

— Confucius (551–479 BCE)

Rhythm Exercises

Play through exercise ten with the accents and rhythm indicated in the notation line. For more information, see the introduction to rhythm exercises on the previous page.

Ex. 1 - Accents

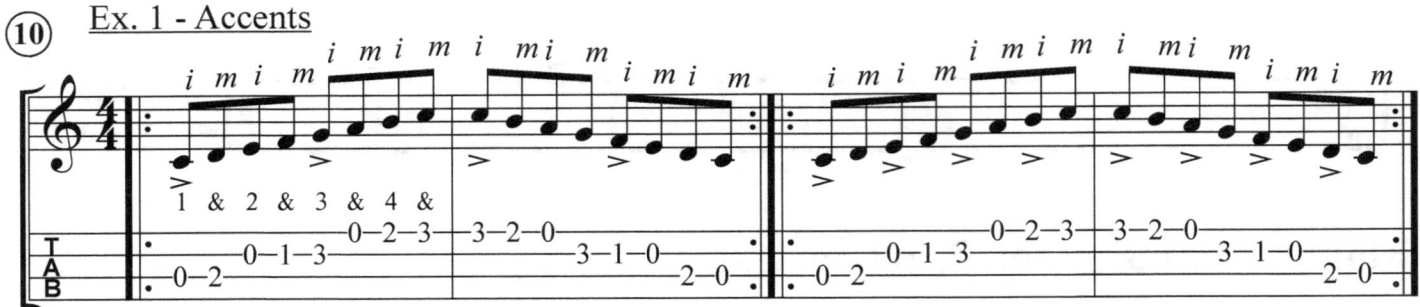

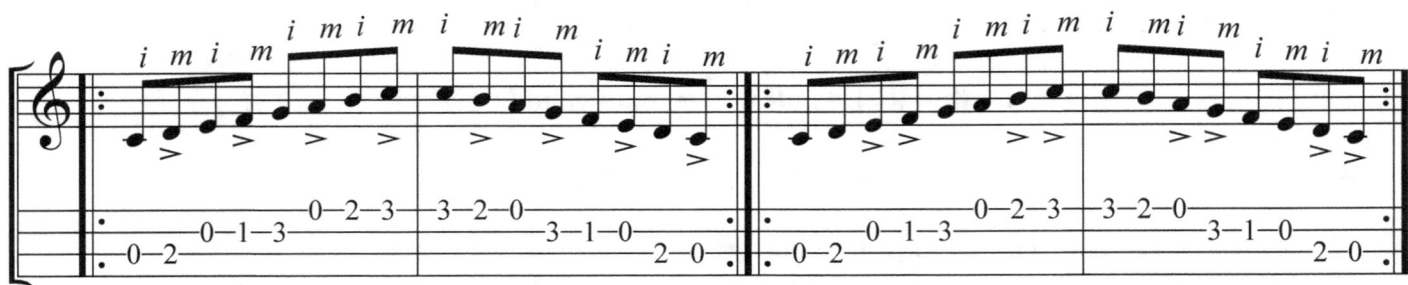

Ex. 2 - Rhythm Groupings

Rhythm 1

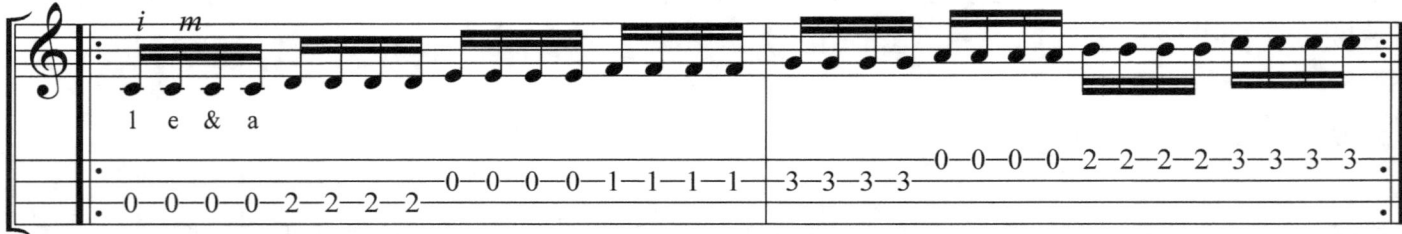

Rhythm 2

Rhythm 3

Rhythm 4

Rhythm 5

Rhythm 6

Rhythm 7

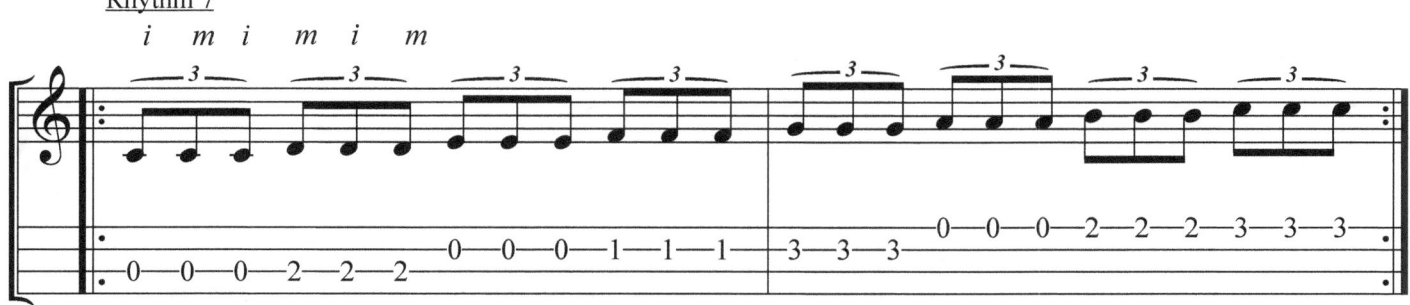

Rhythm 8

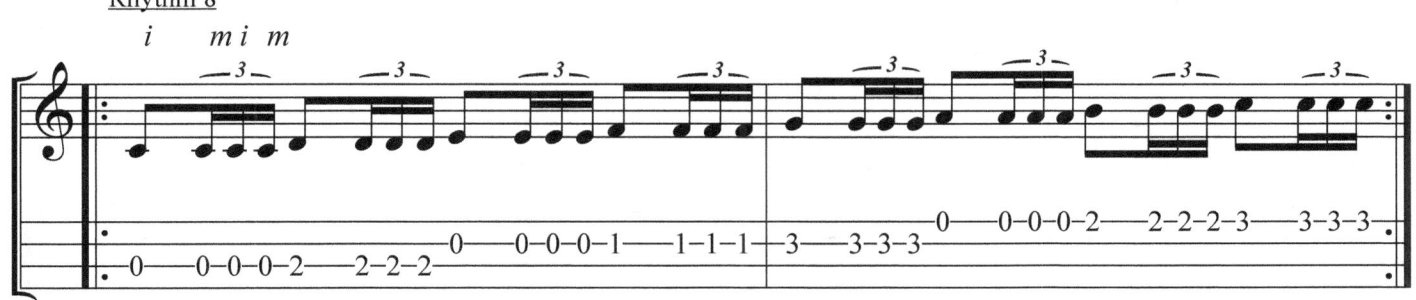

CHAPTER FOUR - 4 FINGER EXERCISES

Alright, our last set of exercises uses all four fingers. You may think these exercises look more like math problems than music, but remember, these exercises teach you how to move your fingers, not your soul.

With four numbers, there are 24 possible combinations (4 x 3 x 2 x 1 = 24). Once you've played through all 24 combinations, your fingers will have moved in every possible pattern. Start slow and even, but eventually work towards speed bursts for each pattern. For example, you could play each pattern slowly and then fast. For a complete workout, play the patterns on all strings or move a pattern up the neck one fret at a time.

Four Finger Combinations

①
| 1 2 3 4 | 1 2 4 3 | 1 3 2 4 | 1 3 4 2 |

TAB: —1—2—3—4— | —1—2—4—3— | —1—3—2—4— | —1—3—4—2—

| 1 4 2 3 | 1 4 3 2 | 2 1 3 4 | 2 1 4 3 |

—1—4—2—3— | —1—4—3—2— | —2—1—3—4— | —2—1—4—3—

| 2 3 1 4 | 2 3 4 1 | 2 4 1 3 | 2 4 3 1 |

—2—3—1—4— | —2—3—4—1— | —2—4—1—3— | —2—4—3—1—

| 3 1 2 4 | 3 1 4 2 | 3 2 1 4 | 3 2 4 1 |

—3—1—2—4— | —3—1—4—2— | —3—2—1—4— | —3—2—4—1—

| 3 4 1 2 | 3 4 2 1 | 4 1 2 3 | 4 1 3 2 |

—3—4—1—2— | —3—4—2—1— | —4—1—2—3— | —4—1—3—2—

| 4 2 1 3 | 4 2 3 1 | 4 3 1 2 | 4 3 2 1 |

—4—2—1—3— | —4—2—3—1— | —4—3—1—2— | —4—3—2—1—

Four Finger Hammer-Ons & Pull-Offs

Now, let's apply hammer-ons and pull-offs using the same four-finger combinations. Though challenging, keep an even volume and rhythm on each note. Maintaining consistent volume will require you to hammer on and pull off the finger with enough force that the string attack allows the string to ring.

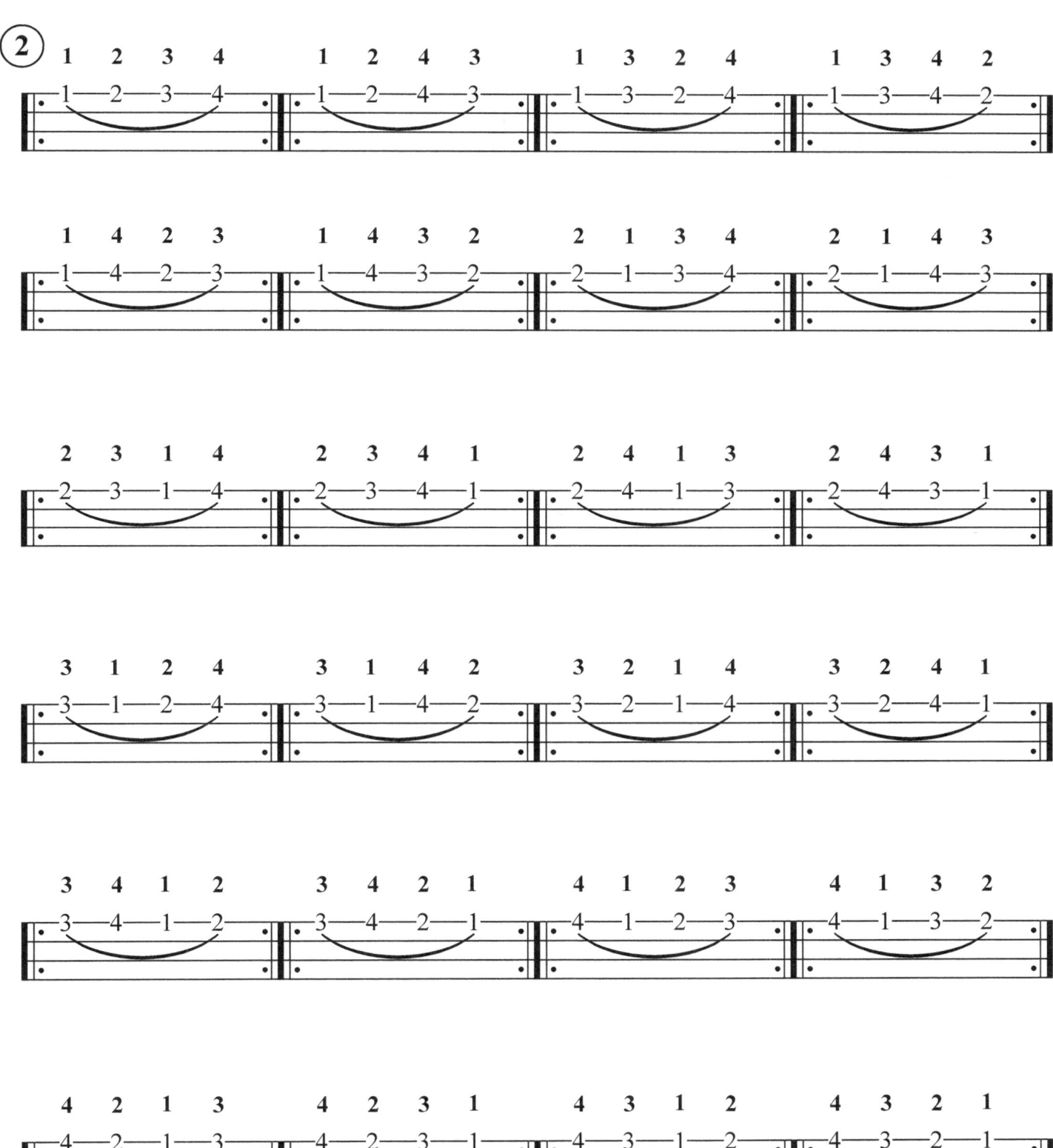

Finger Challenge #1 - Download Ladder

The following exercise is one of the most challenging in the book. It sounds like a pose you'd do at yoga, but the downward ladder will stretch your fingers to the limit. Holding the fingers in the chord shape above the tab is essential to get the most from this exercise. This exercise involves holding the chord while stretching one finger at a time down the neck, as indicated by the arrow.

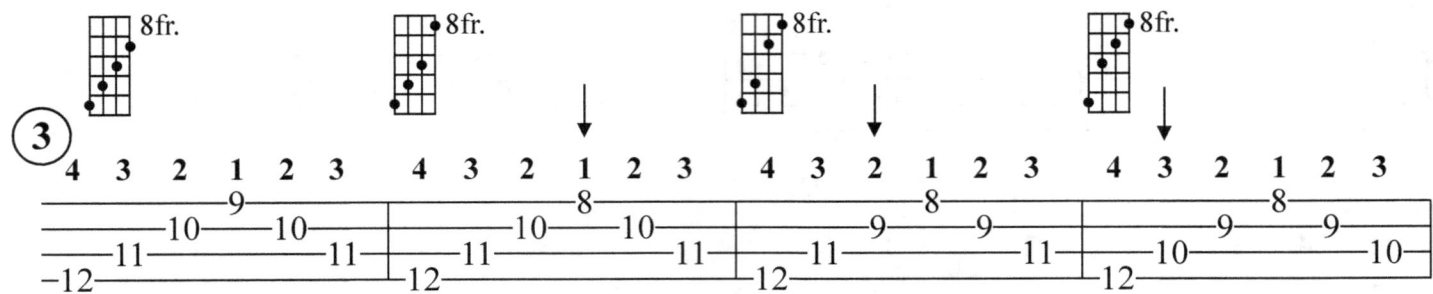

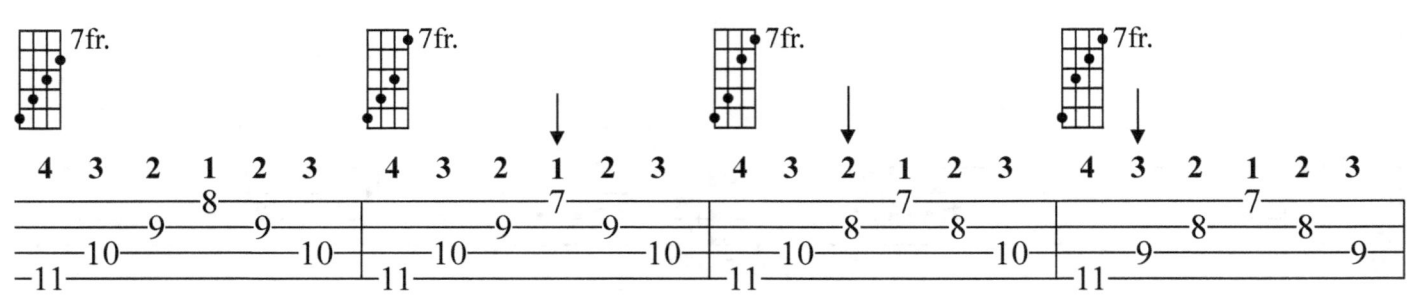

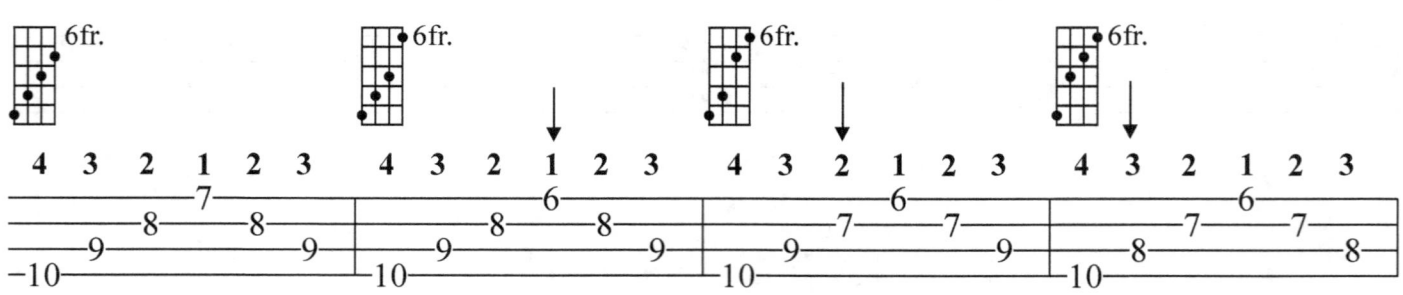

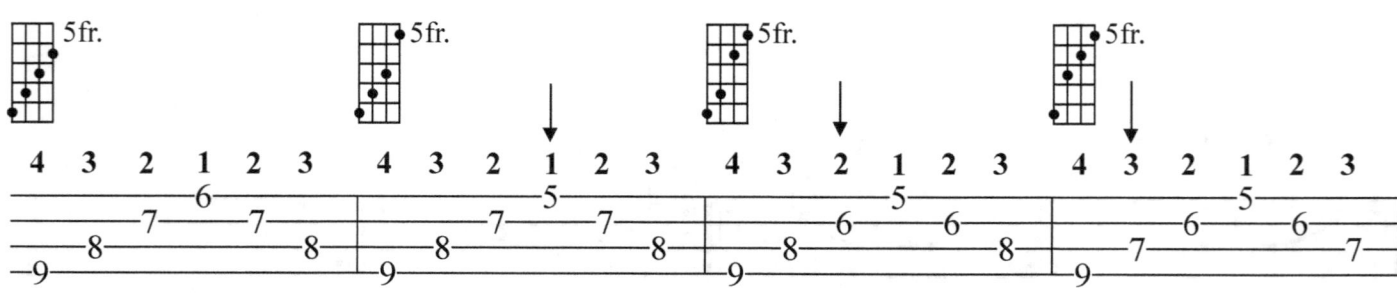

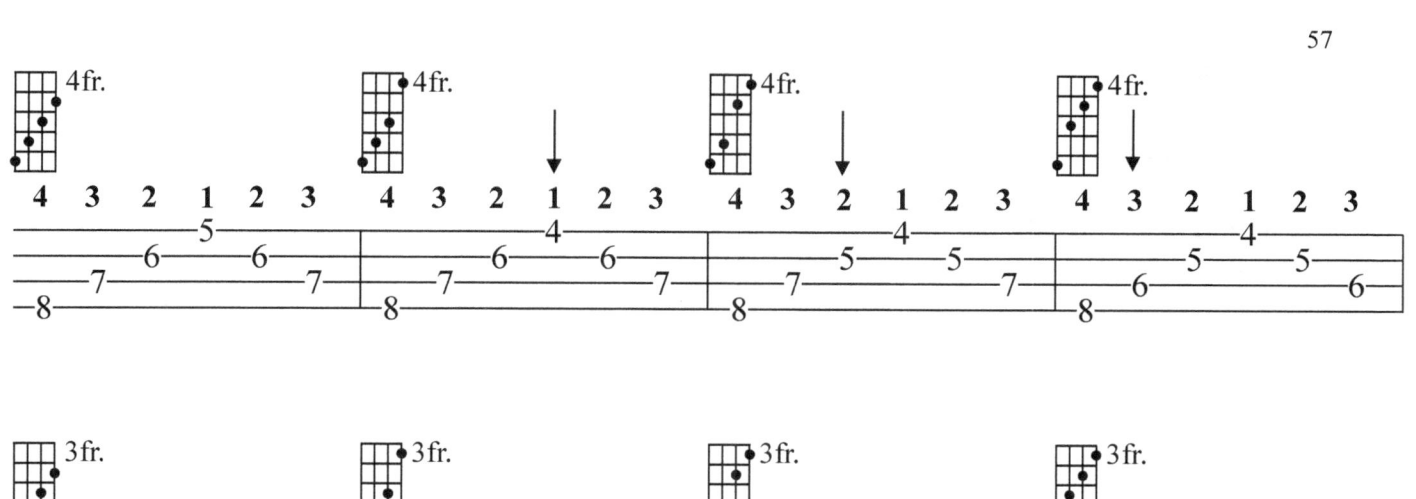

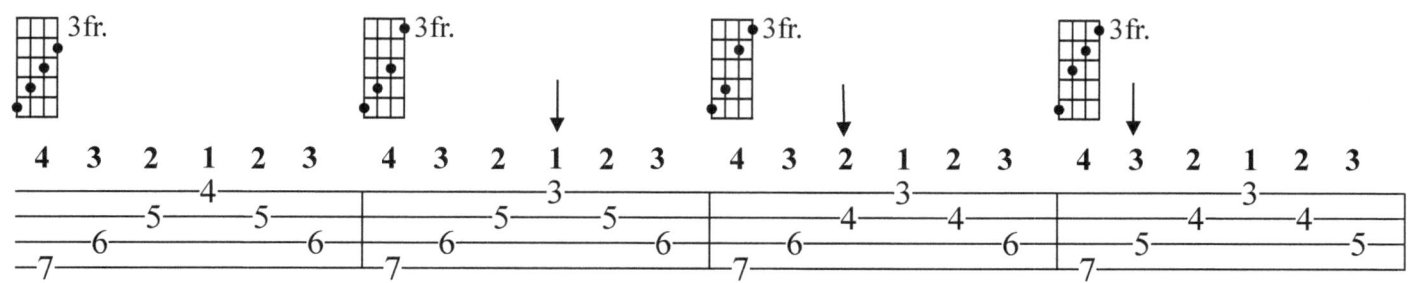

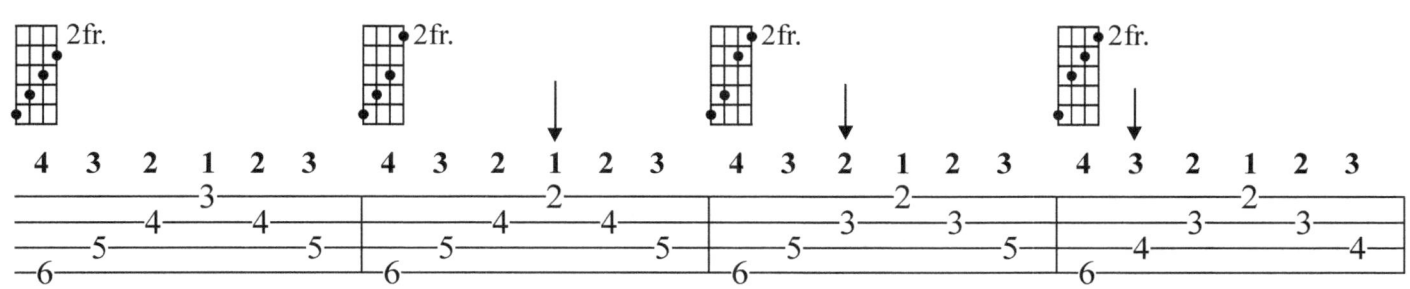

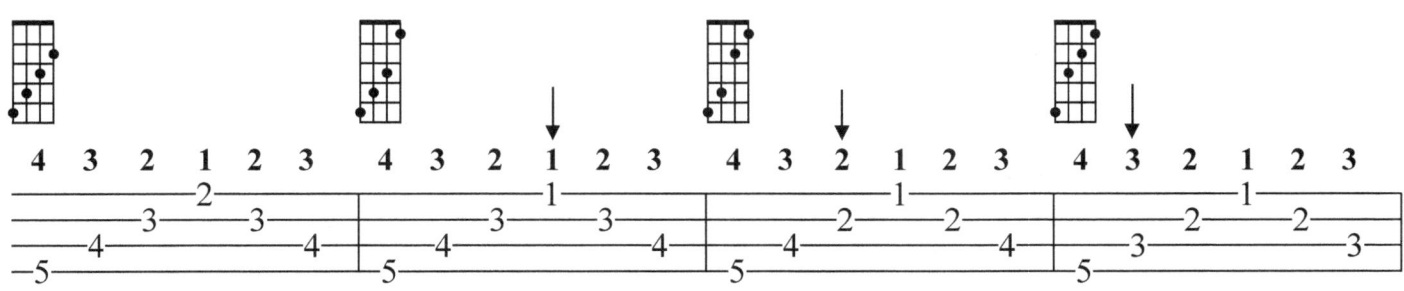

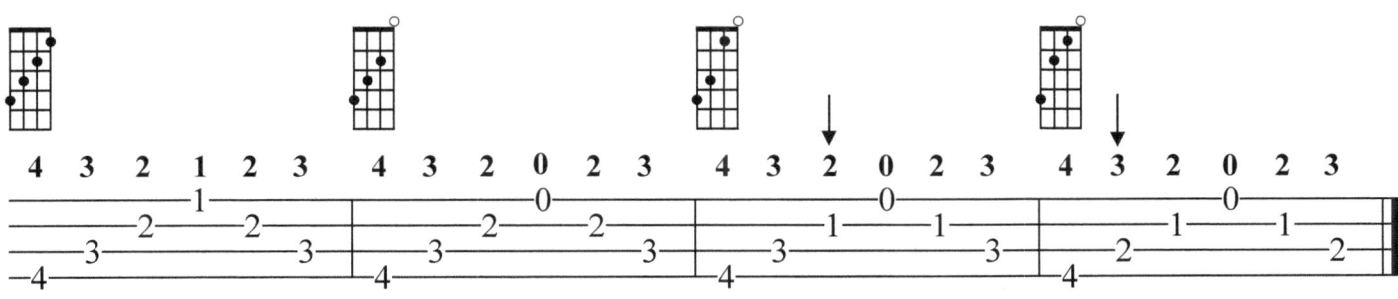

Finger Challenge #2 - Upward Ladder

Now, we will do the reverse finger movement from the previous exercise. On the upward ladder, as indicated in the chord diagram, we hold the fingers down and gradually move one finger at a time. Listen for a clear tone and adjust the angle of your ukulele as needed to prevent wrist discomfort. This exercise is suitable for fingers or a pick.

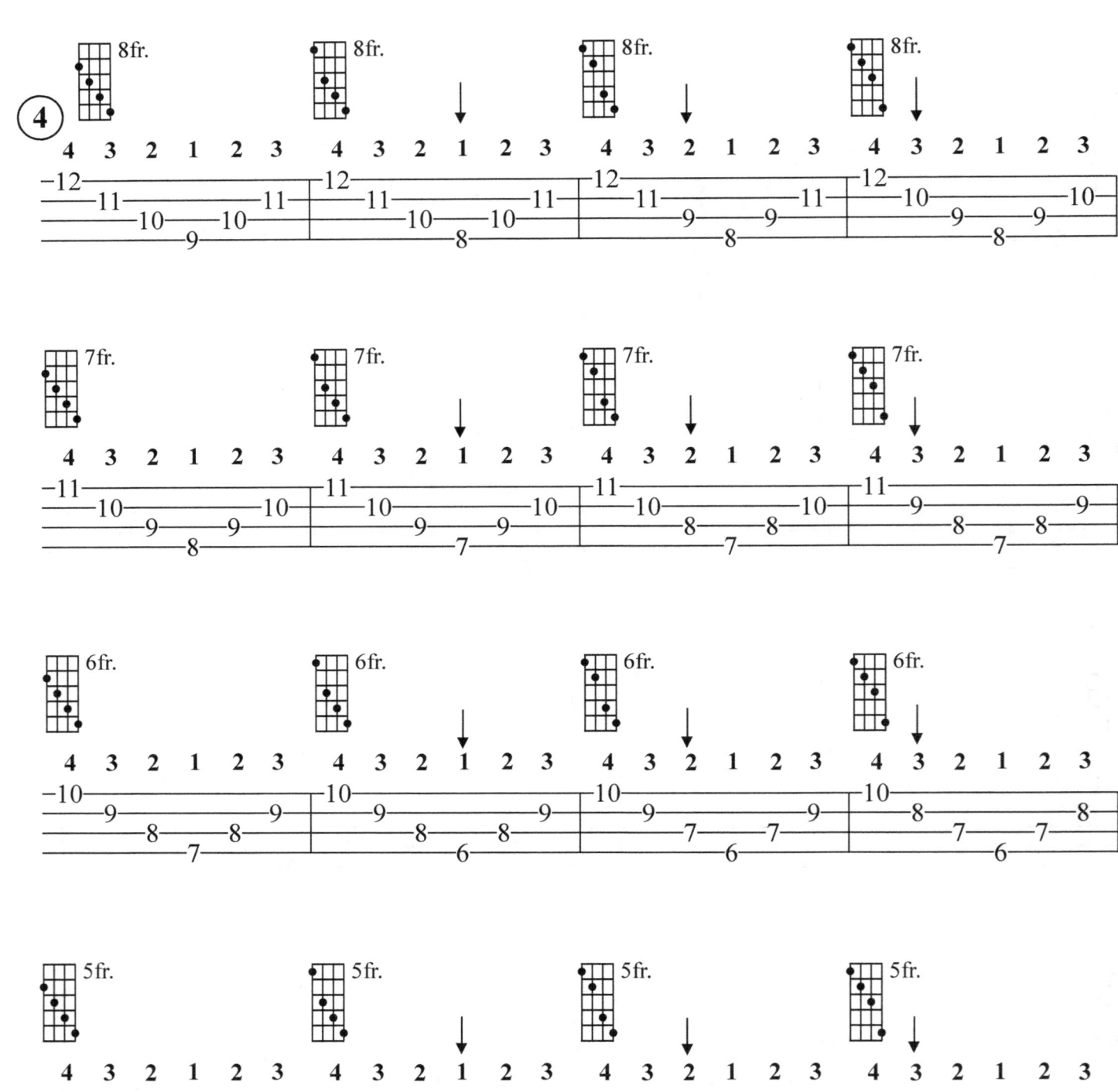

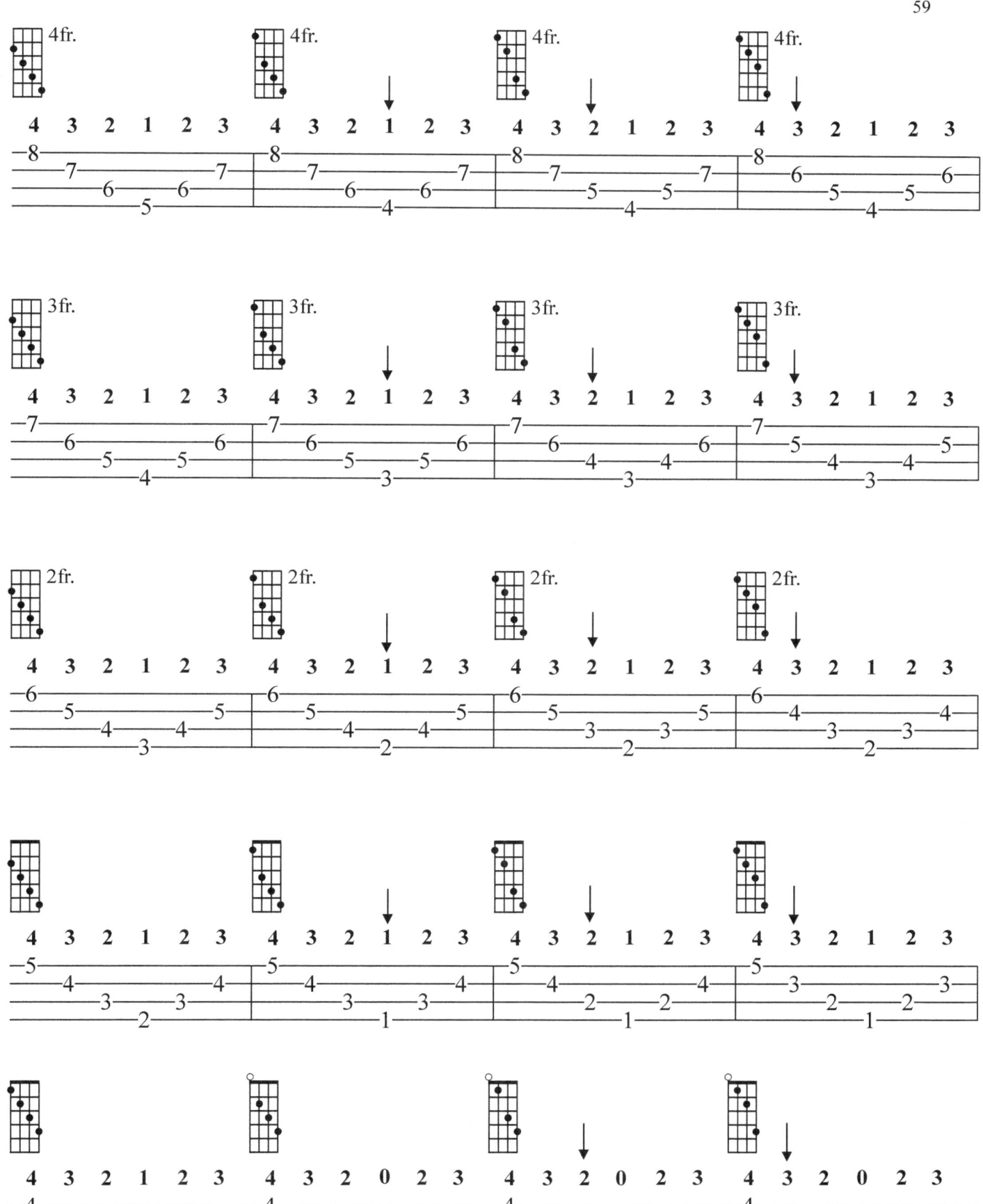

59

String Skipping Exercise

In Exercise Five, we'll apply the major scale pattern while incorporating string skipping as we move up the neck. This exercise is especially effective on standard "high G" ukulele tuning but also works well with Low G, baritone, soprano, or tenor tunings. Use whichever fingering or picking style feels most comfortable.

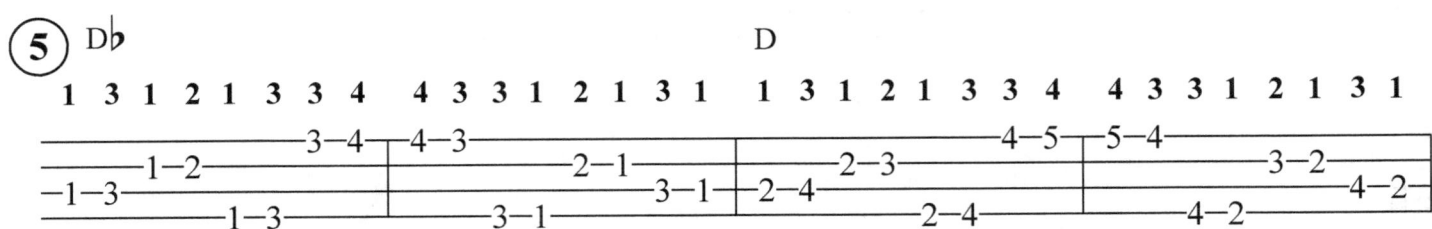

5   Db   D

```
1  3  1  2  1  3  3  4    4  3  3  1  2  1  3  1    1  3  1  2  1  3  3  4    4  3  3  1  2  1  3  1
----------------3-4--4-3-----------------------------------------------4-5--5-4------------------
----------1-2-----------------2-1-----------------------2-3------------------------3-2-----------
--1-3-----------------------------3-1--2-4------------------2-4------------------------4-2-------
----------1-3-----------3-1-----------------------2-4--------------------4-2---------------------
```

Eb   E

```
1  3  1  2  1  3  3  4    4  3  3  1  2  1  3  1    1  3  1  2  1  3  3  4    4  3  3  1  2  1  3  1
----------------5-6--6-5-----------------------------------------------6-7--7-6------------------
----------3-4-----------------4-3-----------------------4-5------------------------5-4-----------
--3-5-----------------------------5-3--4-6------------------4-6------------------------6-4-------
----------3-5-----------5-3-----------------------4-6--------------------6-4---------------------
```

F   F#

```
1  3  1  2  1  3  3  4    4  3  3  1  2  1  3  1    1  3  1  2  1  3  3  4    4  3  3  1  2  1  3  1
----------------7-8--8-7-----------------------------------------------8-9--9-8------------------
----------5-6-----------------6-5-----------------------6-7------------------------7-6-----------
--5-7-----------------------------7-5--6-8------------------6-8------------------------8-6-------
----------5-7-----------7-5-----------------------6-8--------------------8-6---------------------
```

G   Ab

```
1  3  1  2  1  3  3  4    4  3  3  1  2  1  3  1    1  3  1  2  1  3  3  4    4  3  3  1  2  1  3  1
----------------9-10--10-9---------------------------------------------10-11--11-10--------------
----------7-8-----------------8-7-----------------------8-9------------------------9-8-----------
--7-9-----------------------------9-7--8-10----------------8-10------------------------10-8------
----------7-9-----------9-7-----------------------8-10------------------10-8---------------------
```

A   Bb

```
1  3  1  2  1  3  3  4    4  3  3  1  2  1  3  1    1  3  1  2  1  3  3  4    4  3  3  1  2  1  3  1
----------------11-12--12-11-------------------------------------------12-13--13-12--------------
----------9-10----------------10-9--------------------10-11------------------------11-10---------
--9-11----------------------------11-9--10-12--------------10-12-----------------------12-10-----
----------9-11----------11-9----------------------10-12-----------------12-10--------------------
```

Modal Scale Climber

Now, we will play seven different types of scales called Modes. Modes are scale patterns derived from the major scale, each starting on a different degree and creating a unique sound or mood. To play the modes, all we have to do is shift the major scale up the neck one note at a time.

Each measure outlines a different fingering pattern and diagram corresponding to one of the seven modes. For added variety, apply the rhythms from Chapter Three, exercise 10 and work on memorizing fingering patterns shown above the tab.

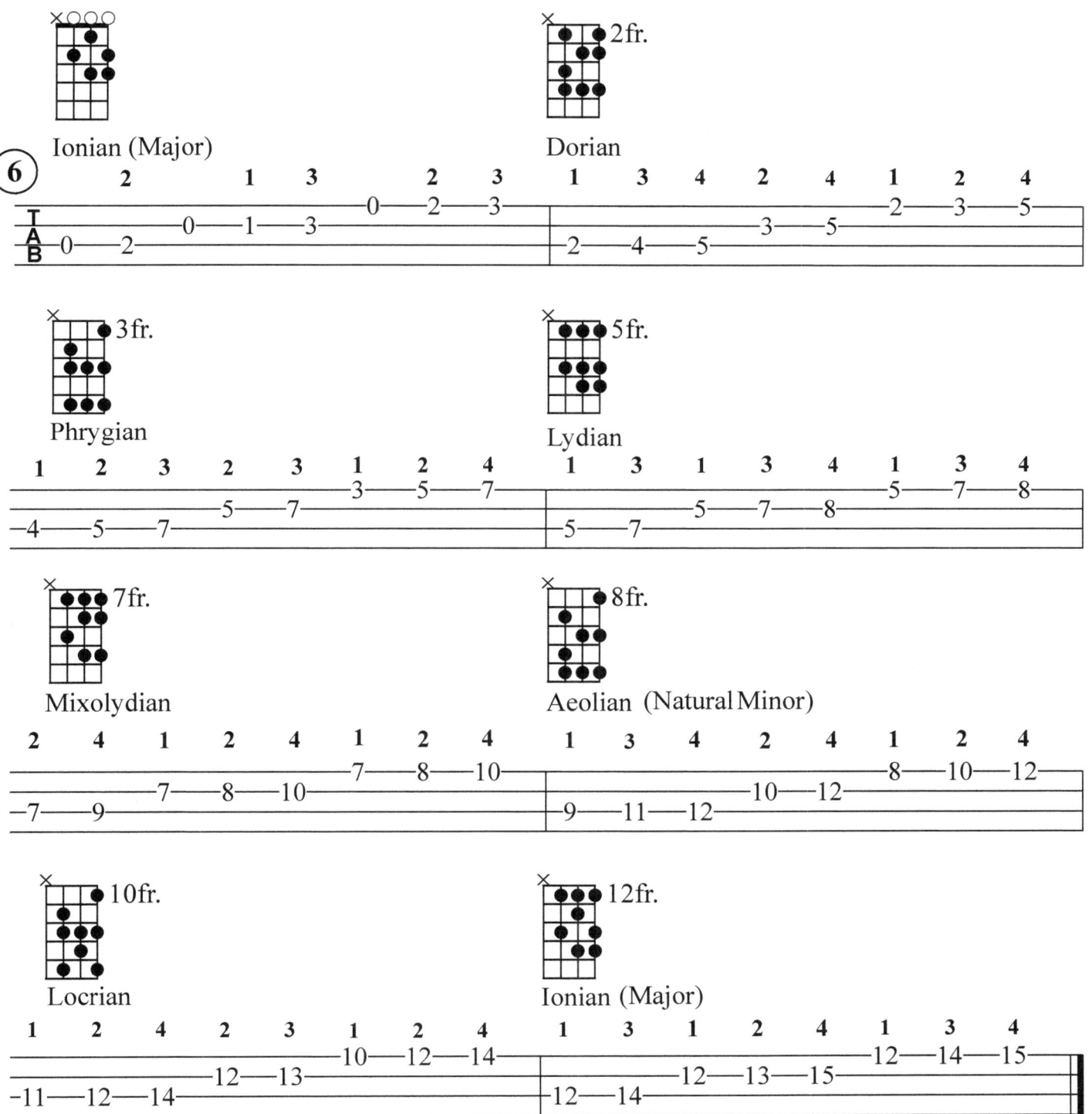

Campanella - Hand Shift Exercise

Alright, let's try something a little different. In this exercise, we will work on shifting your hand while you play an open string, creating an overlapping sound that allows the notes to vibrate together. This technique is called campanella.

In terms of composition, this little piece starts with a five-note riff and continually adds a note, creating longer phrases. Try to achieve a very fluid elbow motion with a steady rhythm. I have included the preferred right-hand fingering, but this piece can also be practiced with a pick.

Barre Strengthening Exercise

In exercise eight, we go back to barre strengthening. Make a barre and form the chord in the diagram with your first finger. Move the chord up one fret at a time and play the major scales. Memorize the finger pattern and play with the indicated right-hand fingering or a pick if you prefer.

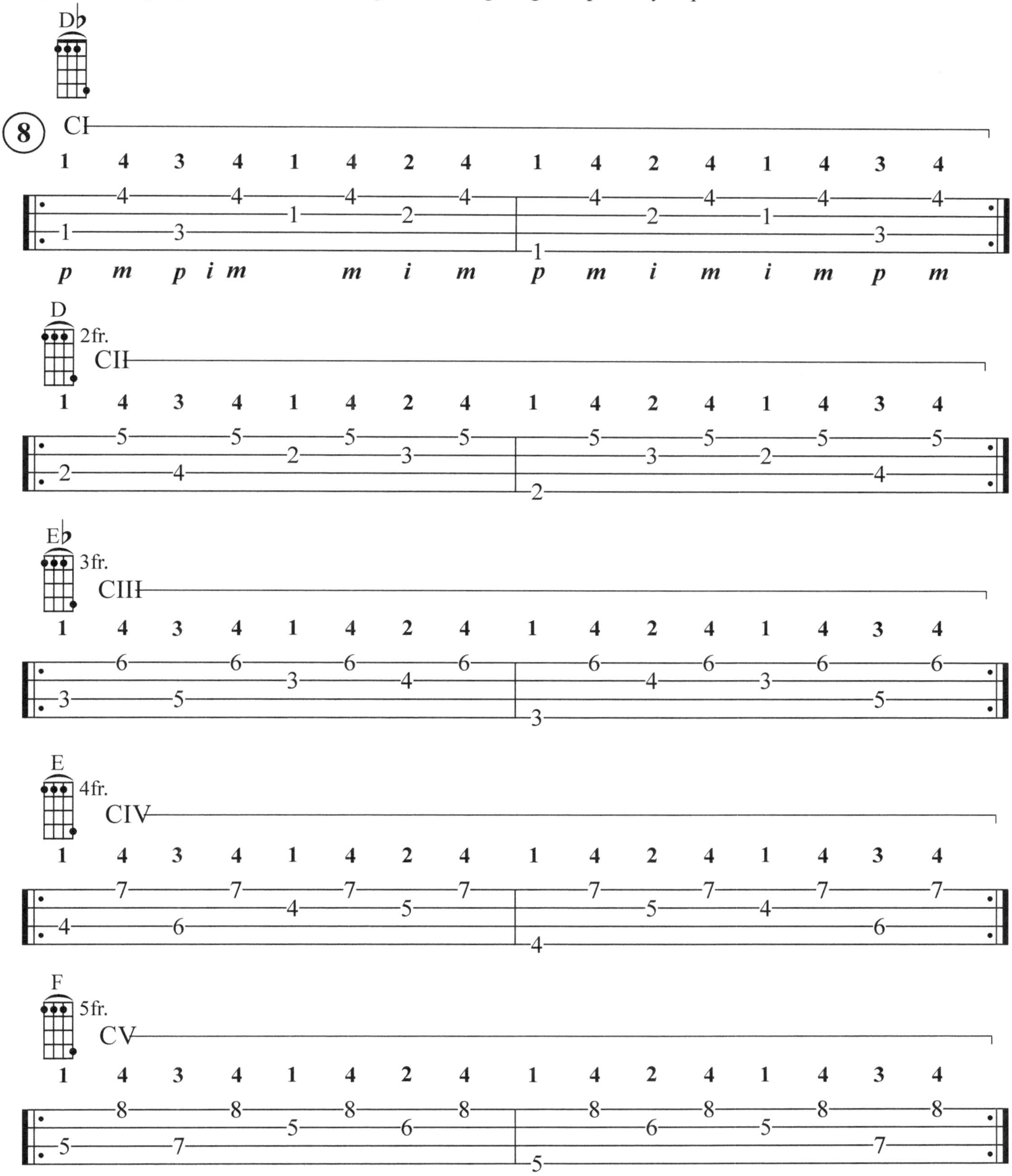

Scale, Chord and Arpeggio Exercises

Now, we will combine the major scale, chord, and arpeggio and play up the neck in every key. Again, you can play with a pick or follow along with the suggested right-hand fingering in C major.

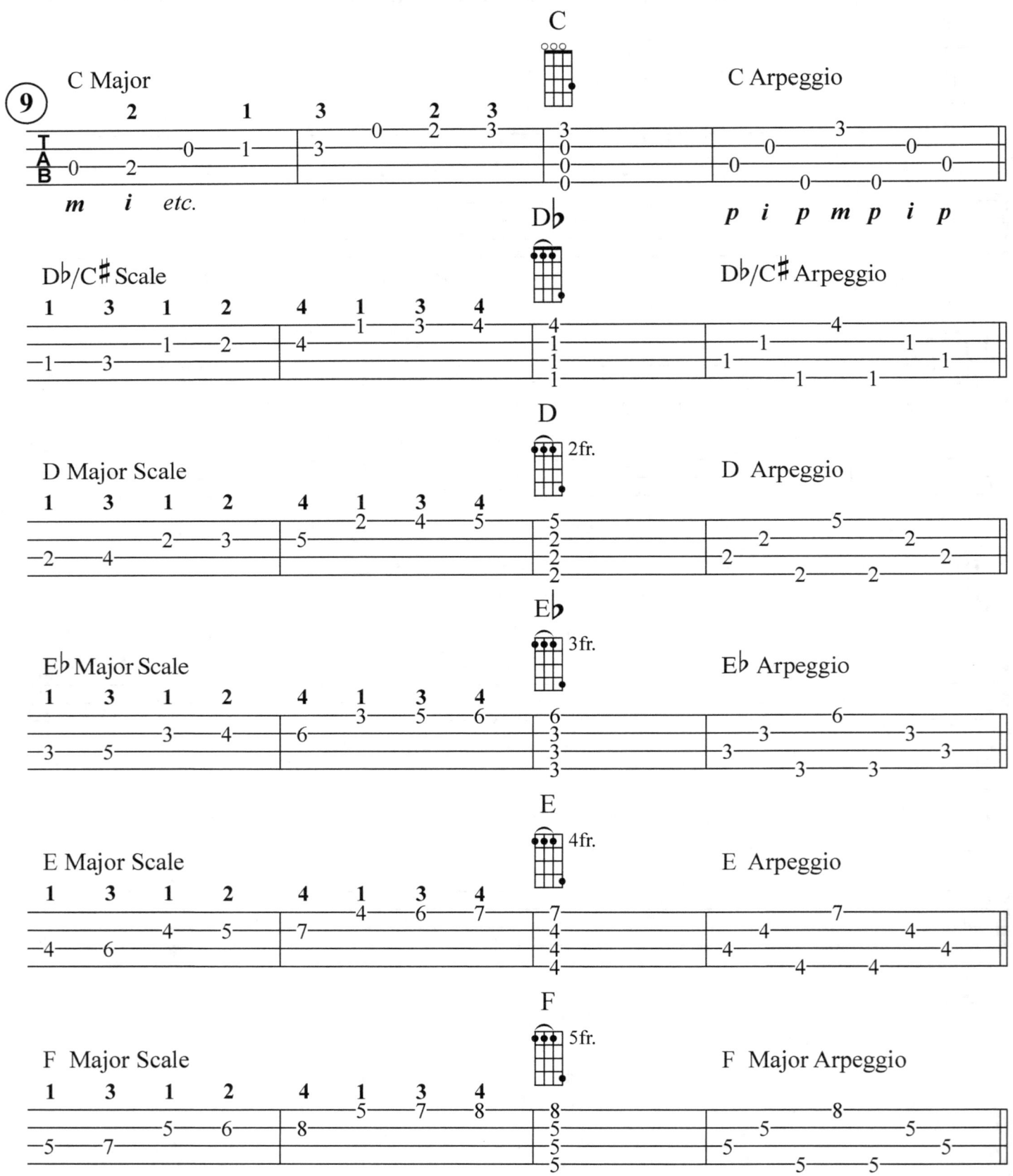

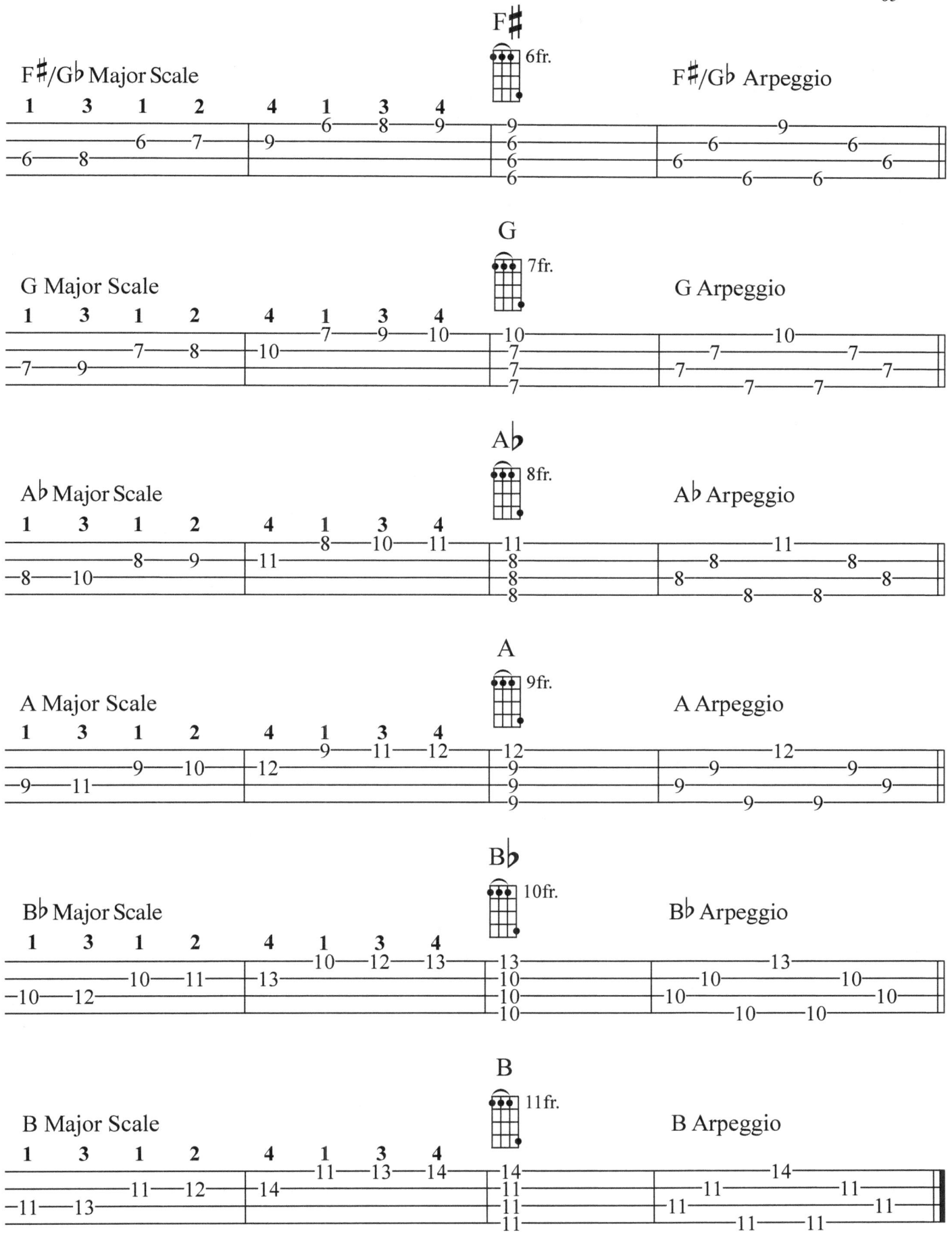

Major Chord Inversions - All Keys

In our last finger exercise, we will play each inversion of the major chord. An inversion rearranges the same notes in a different order. For example, a C chord has three notes: C, E and G. If C is the lowest sounding note, that is called **root position**. If E is the lowest sounding note, that is called **1st inversion** or C/E. If G is the lowest sounding note, it is called a **2nd inversion** chord or C/G.

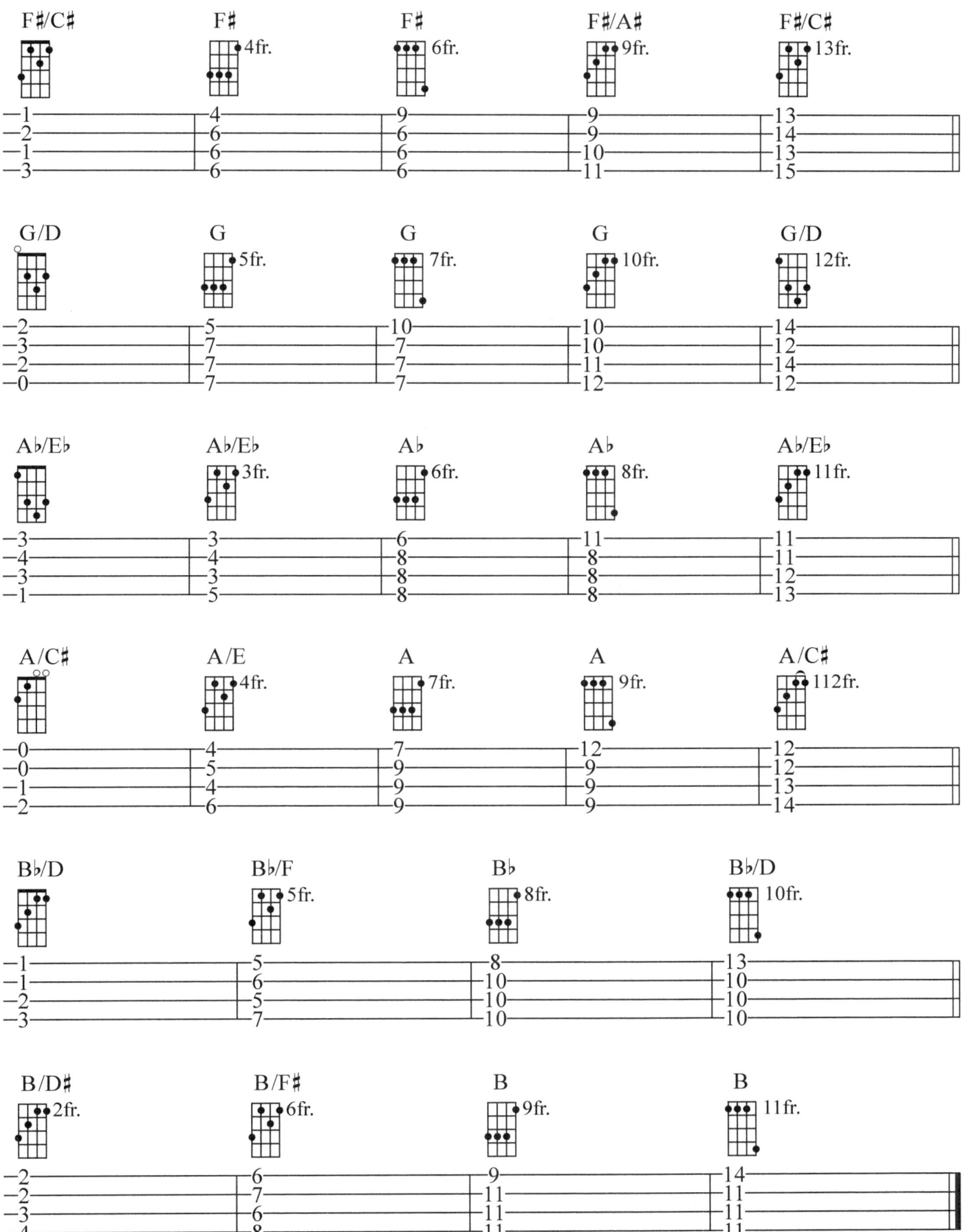

CHAPTER FIVE - THE ULTIMATE UKULELE CHORD WARM-UP

Introduction to Chord Theory

Most ukulele players play chords the majority of the time, so the next chapter will deal with an extensive set of warm-ups to improve your chord playing. We will get into tips for chord switching but begin with a quick overview of some basic music theory.

1) The Major Scale

We need to start with the Do Re Mi or major scale to understand chords. We will do our examples using the key of C. There are seven notes in the C major scale:

C	D	E	F	G	A	B
Do	Re	Mi	Fa	So	La	Ti

Now we will number each note starting with 1 on C:

C	D	E	F	G	A	B
1	2	3	4	5	6	7

And here's what it looks like in music notation:

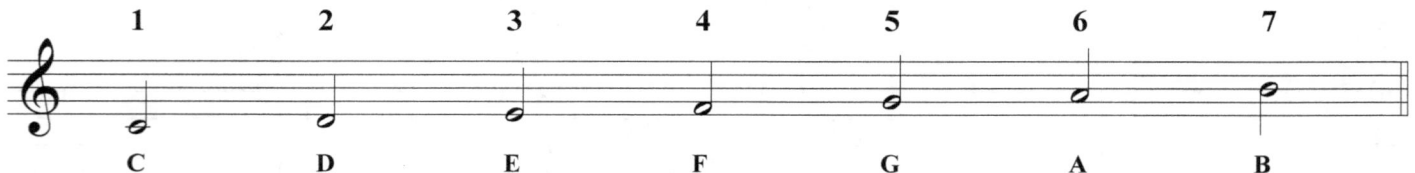

2) Triads

Next, we will build three-note chords called triads on each of the major scale's seven notes. To build a triad, skip every other note in the scale:

3) Major, Minor and Diminished Chords

Now, we have the seven triads from the major scale. These triads are called diatonic chords, meaning they are built from only notes within a scale (in our case, C major). Next, three types of triads are on the major scale: Major, minor, and diminished.

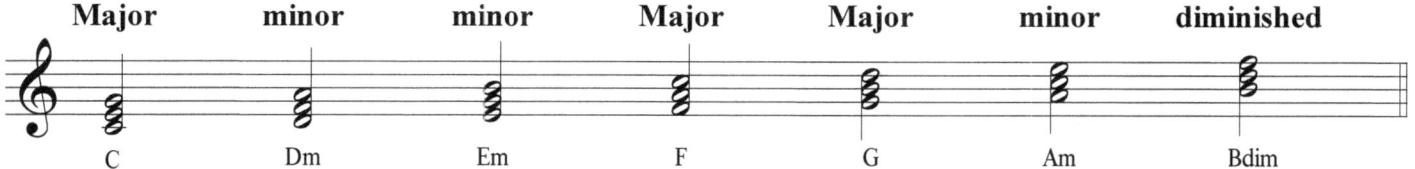

If you play the chords, you might be able to distinguish between the chords. The major sounds bright and happy, the minor sounds sad and dark, and the diminished sounds mysterious and unsettled.

4) Half and Whole Steps

The difference between the three chords lies in the distance between the notes or intervals. To understand intervals further, let's start with a few terms: half step and whole step.

<u>Half-Steps:</u>
The half-step is the closest note, either up or down on a string. On the ukulele, a half-step is one fret apart. For example, if you play the D (2nd fret - 3rd string) and then the E♭ one fret higher, that is a half-step. If you go down one fret and play the C♯, that is also a half-step.

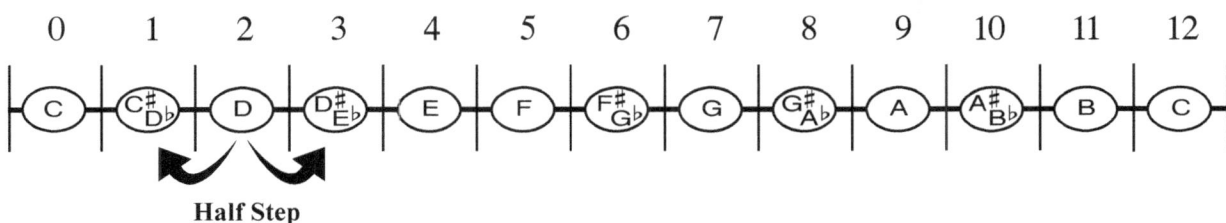

<u>Whole Steps</u>
The whole step is when you go up or down two frets. So, if you play the D note again and then the E two frets higher, that is a whole step. And if you go down two frets, you play the open C, which is a whole step lower.

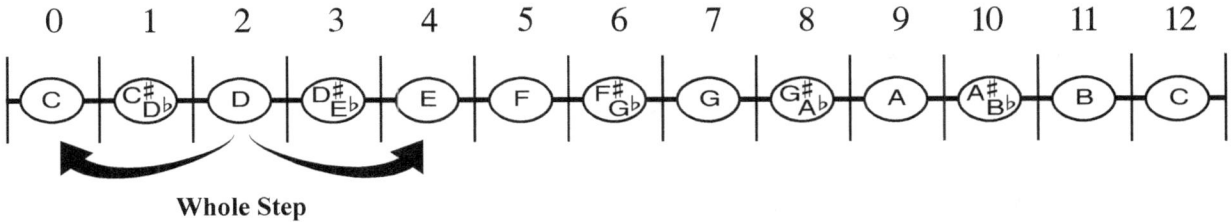

5) Intervals

Now, if we take a closer look at our three chords again (major, minor, diminished), we see there are three unique sets of half and whole steps to define the chord. For example, the C **major chord** (C-E-G) has 4 half steps followed by 3 half steps. Play the notes on your ukulele starting on the C (third string open) and count the half steps.

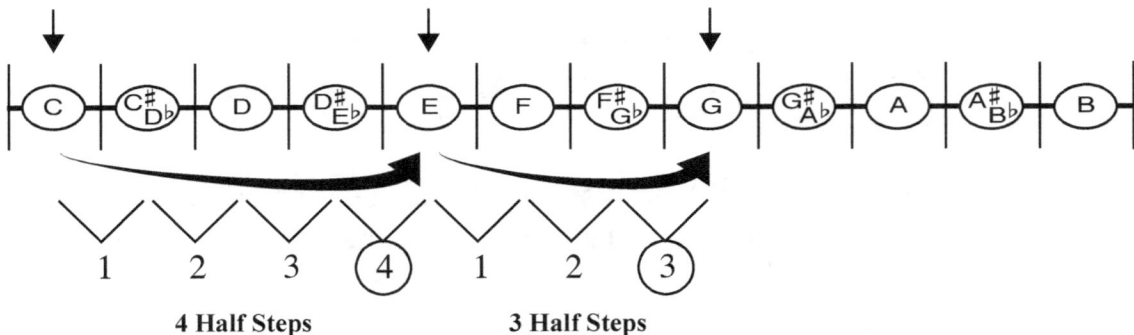

So, the major chord has 4-3 half steps. If we look at the **minor chord**, you will notice a different set of half steps. For example, a C minor chord (C-Eb-G) has 3 half steps followed by 4 half steps. The reverse of the major chord:

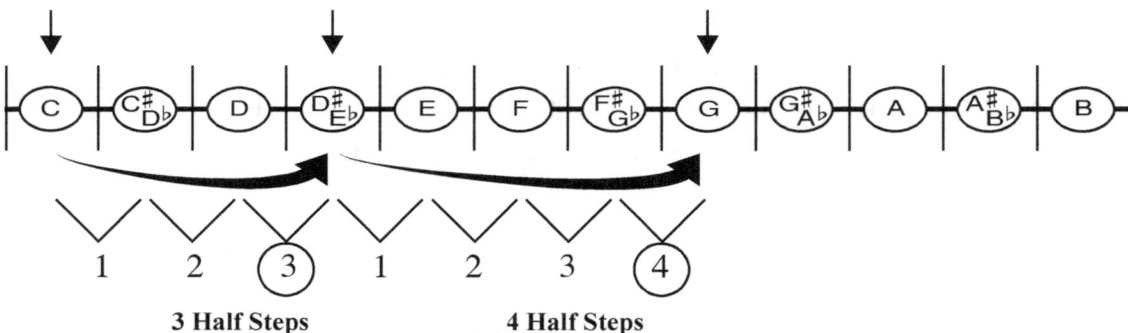

Finally, if we look at the **diminished chord** (C-Eb-Gb), we find there are two identical sets of 3 half steps:

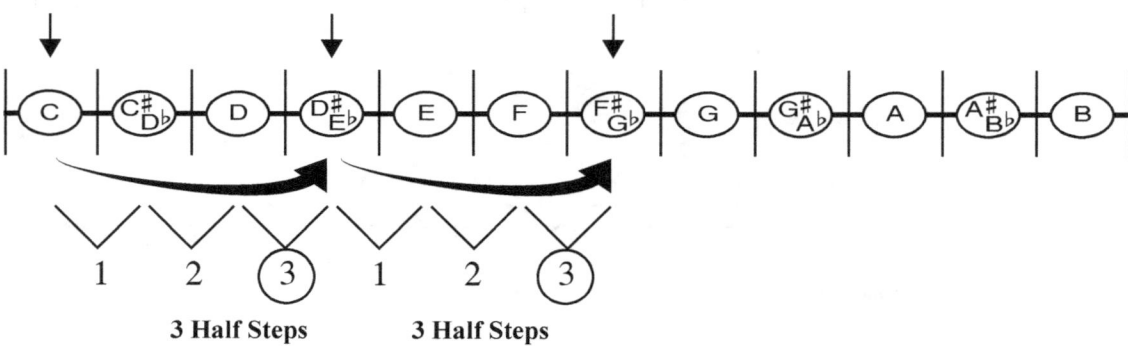

6) Chord Progressions

Now, you should have a basic understanding of diatonic triads. When we combine two or more chords, we get a chord progression. For our purposes, we will exclude the diminished chord because it is rarely used in popular music due to its ambiguity. So, that leaves us with *six* chords for our chord progression workout.

Ok, now let's make a chord progression using only two chords. How about C to F?

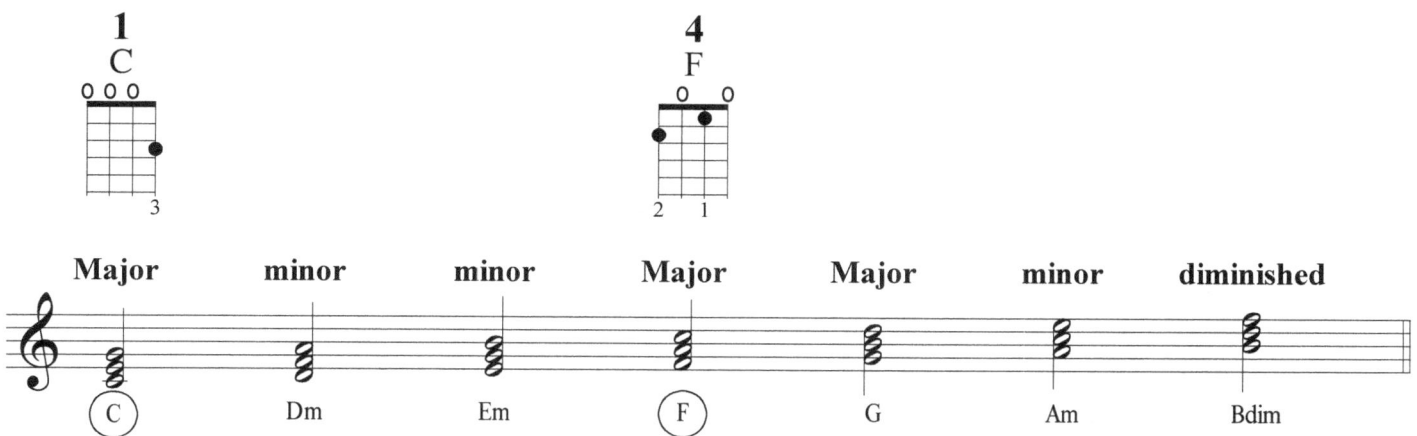

Remember, the C is the first chord in the key of C, and the F is the fourth. Musicians often simplify this and call the chord according to its number in the scale. So, c to F is: 1 - 4. We can add as many chords as you like. For example, a chord progression C, Am, F, G in numbers is 1-6m-4-5. Notice that the m is added to the 6, which is a minor chord. The upcoming chord workout will explore every chord progression in depth in a diatonic key.

There is much more to learn about chord progression in the study of harmony, but we will end the music theory here for our purposes.

"Theory is a means to an end." — unknown

7) Strumming Patterns

There are no fixed strumming patterns in the upcoming chord progression workout, so to begin, you can simply strum each chord once before switching to the next.

I've included 10 popular ukulele strumming patterns and 15 rhythm variations based on a sixteenth-note grid that you can apply if you prefer more structure. The blues and jazz section in Chapter Six also includes its own set of stylistic patterns for you to explore.

Tip: Start experimenting with strumming patterns once you can transition between chords smoothly. Create your own or try the ones provided.

10 Ukulele Strumming Patterns

Before we begin the chord progression workout, let's learn 10 of the most common ukulele strumming patterns. Here are a few ways to approach strumming on the ukulele: 1) with the index finger, 2) with a combination of the index finger for downstrokes and the thumb for upstrokes, and 3) with a pick. Whichever way you strum, remember to keep the counting in your head or say it out loud as you practice. I have indicated chords, but feel free to use whatever chords you prefer. You can apply these strumming patterns to the upcoming chord progression workouts.

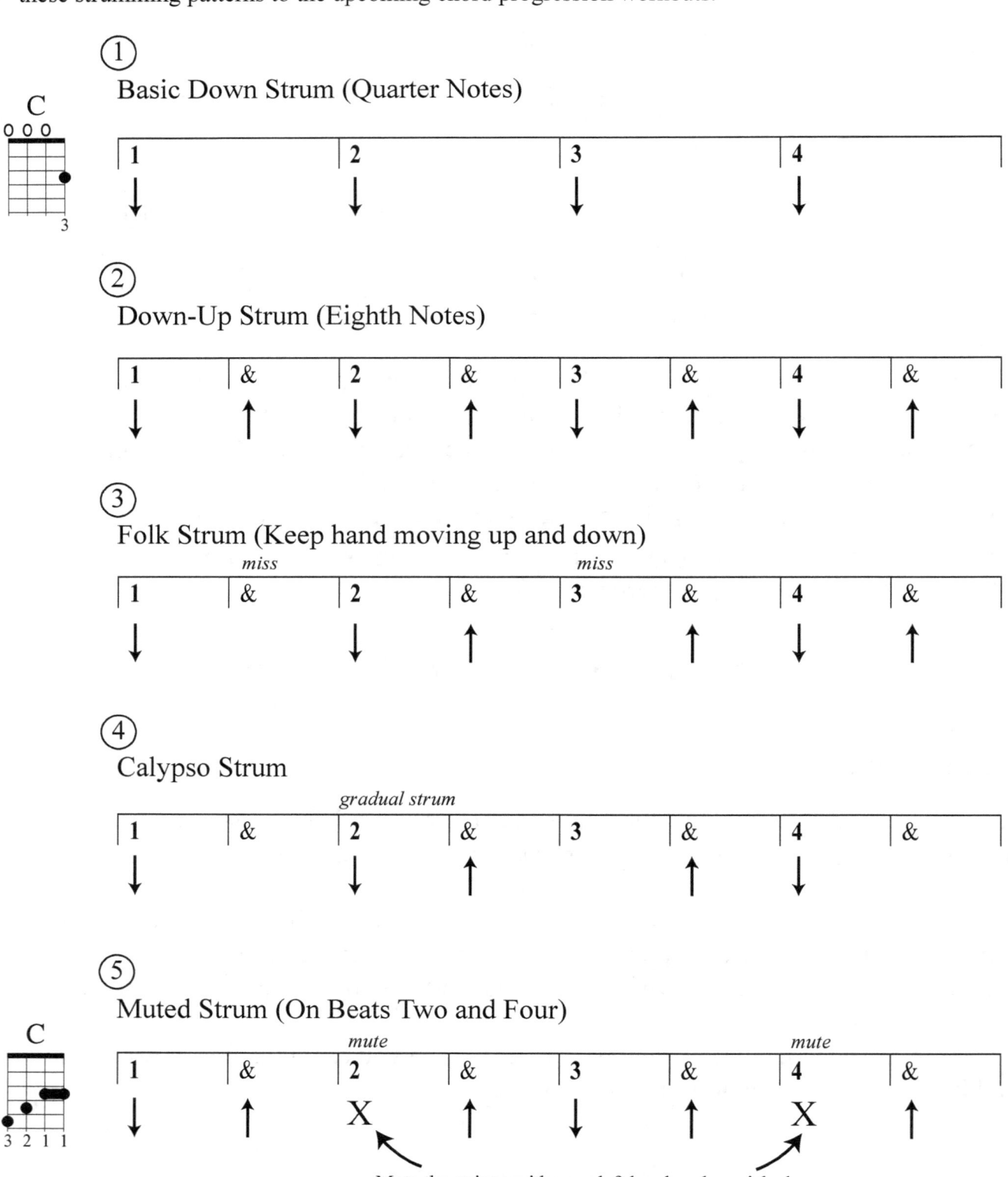

Mute the strings with your left hand or do a pick slap.

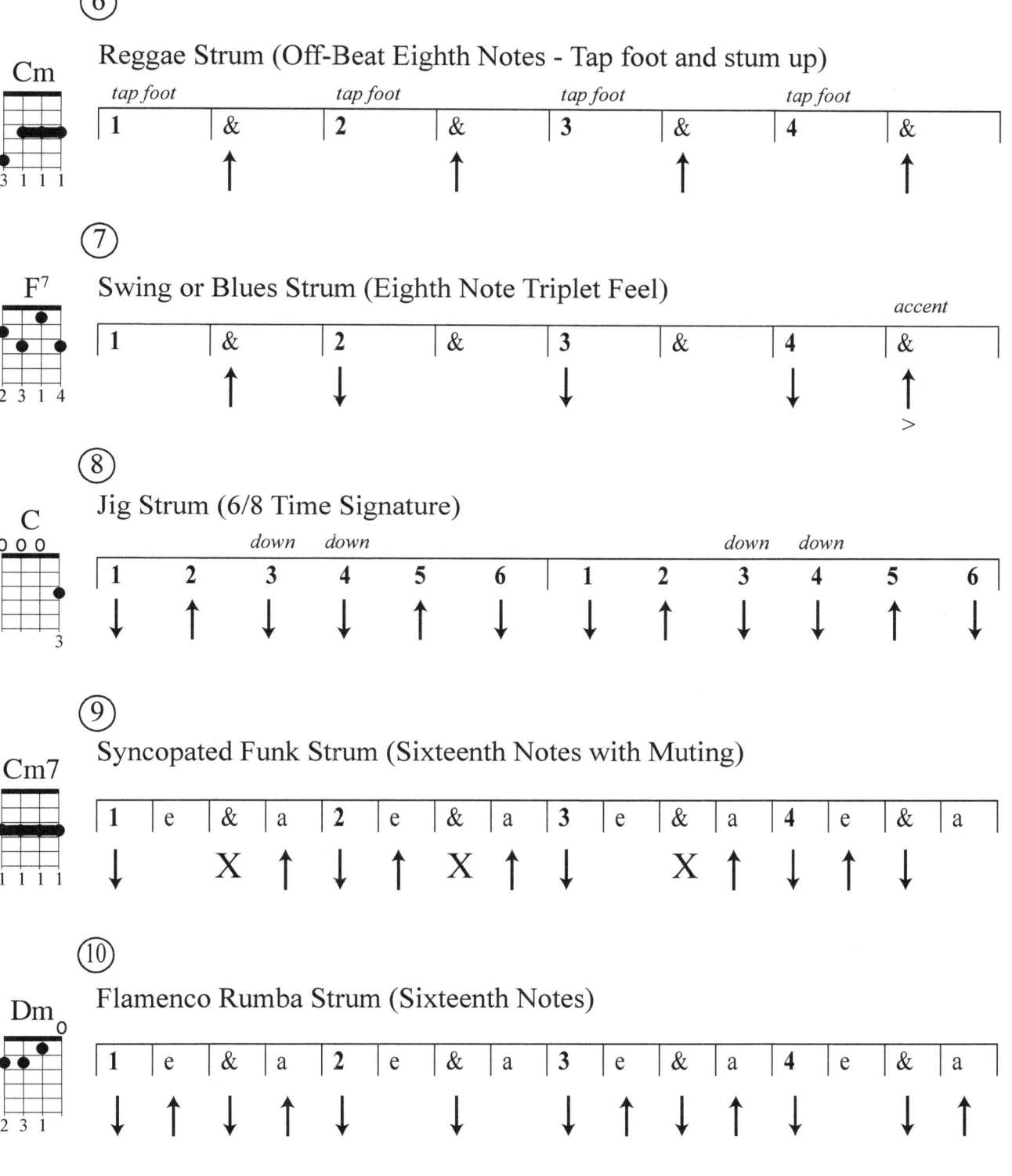

⑥

Reggae Strum (Off-Beat Eighth Notes - Tap foot and stum up)

Cm

⑦

Swing or Blues Strum (Eighth Note Triplet Feel)

F⁷

⑧

Jig Strum (6/8 Time Signature)

C

⑨

Syncopated Funk Strum (Sixteenth Notes with Muting)

Cm7

⑩

Flamenco Rumba Strum (Sixteenth Notes)

Dm

Steady Down Up Strumming Exercises

Most of the time, when you strum chords, you need to keep your arm swinging in a steady down-and-up motion. Becoming proficient with this technique takes practice, but it is essential to creating rhythmically accurate patterns. Play through each of the 15 patterns until you can complete them with a steady down-up motion **without stopping the arm movement**. You can play any chord or chord progression with these exercises; just focus on keeping your arm moving. I've included what the rhythmic notation looks like with a sixteenth and eighth-note subdivision.

	D ⊓	U ∨	D ⊓	U ∨	Sixteenth Note	Eighth Note
1.	↓	↑	↓	↑		
2.	↓	↑	↓			
3.	↓		↓	↑		
4.	↓	↑		↑		
5.		↑	↓	↑		
6.	↓	↑				
7.	↓		↓			
8.	↓			↑		
9.		↑	↓			
10		↑		↑		
11			↓	↑		
12.	↓					
13.		↑				
14.			↓			
15.				↑		

TIPS FOR PLAYING BETTER UKULELE CHORDS

Before we start the chord progression workout, let's review five essential tips for playing ukulele chords.

1) **Placement:** Where you place your finger in relation to the frets can greatly influence your tone's quality. A simple rule to remember is to keep your fingers close to the fret (whenever possible). I say 'whenever possible' because fingers can sometimes get in each other's way, especially given how close the frets are and how tight the chords are. To understand placement, let's have another look at how the note is produced:

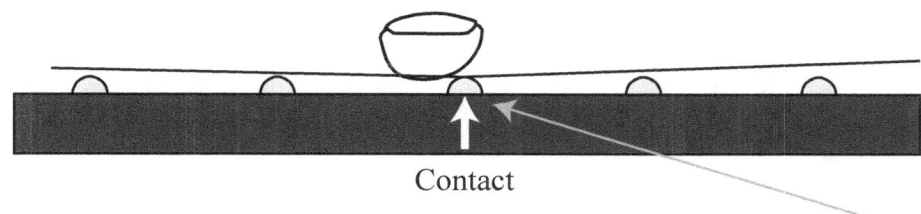

Contact

It doesn't matter where you place your finger between the frets because the note is stopped at the fret.

You will hear a buzzing or "fret rattle" when you don't create good contact with the fret, as shown in the diagram below:

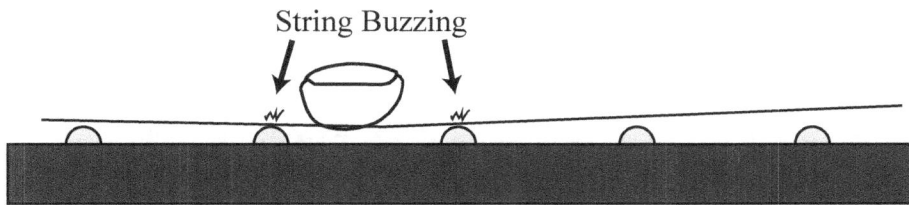

String Buzzing

Before leaving this topic, I should emphasize that playing single notes differs from playing chords with several fingers. Many chords require different leverage points, cramped finger placements and unusual wrist positions. So, keeping the fingers close to the fret is not always possible. In this case, you must apply more force on the string to prevent buzzing and poor tone.

2) **Reposition:** If you are still hearing muted, buzzing or poor-quality notes, reposition your wrist until all notes ring. Sometimes, the repositioning will be slight, but often, you must move the arm and wrist quite dramatically until the notes ring clear. One way to check is to play one string at a time until each note rings clearly. If the chord sounds good, take note of your wrist position and move on to another chord. Try this exercise to improve your repositioning accuracy:

1. **Play any chord,**
2. **Take your hand off the ukulele,**
3. **Shake your wrist,**
4. **Play the chord again.**

*Eventually, you will develop muscle memory and position the chord consistently.

3) Curve your fingers and wrist to avoid the strings underneath and above. Note: Avoiding the strings sometimes requires a dramatic arm and wrist position out in front of the neck. Many beginners don't realize their chords are buzzing because their wrist are 1) relaxed or 2) curved enough to produce clean, clear notes. As in tip two, reposition your arm/wrist/hand and curve the fingers until each note rings clearly.

Wrist is not curved enough.

Fingers are not curved enough.

Fingers are touching other strings.

Wrist nicely curved.

Fingers curved to avoid strings.

Thumb balanced with fingers.

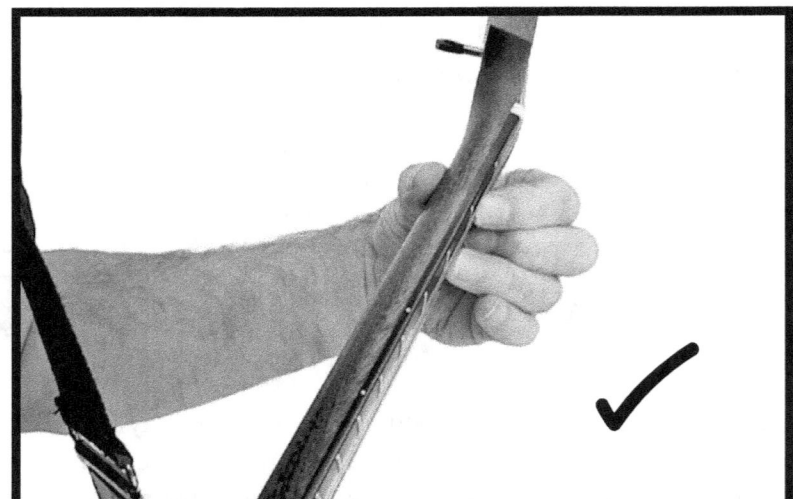

4) Hover and Drop: If you watch advanced ukulele and guitar players, you will notice that they often drop all their fingers in one motion when they play a chord. If you were to watch them playing chords in slow motion, you would see a two-step approach:

    i) **Hover the fingers** over the strings in the chord shape, and
    ii) **Land the fingers together** according to the rhythm of the chord changes.

This two-step approach generally develops naturally with lots of practice. Some tips that could help are:

1) Memorize all the chords needed in the song you are working on.
2) Adapt the exercise from number 2 (reposition) to work on hovering and landing fingers.
3) Practice slowly with a metronome and only increase speed when your chords sound clearly and in rhythm.

5) Preparation: Start forming the next chord slightly before the beat to ensure a smooth transition when playing chord progressions. Since it's nearly impossible to switch chords exactly on the beat, early preparation is essential to maintain a steady rhythm. In other words, think ahead to the next chord before you play it.

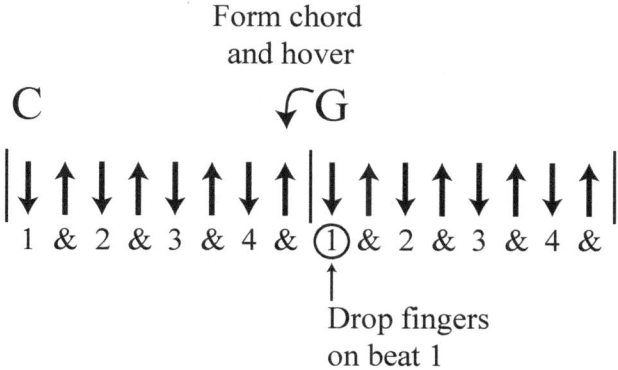

Keep these in mind while practicing:

1)   Maintain a steady strumming rhythm even if open or muted strings sound as you prepare a chord.
2)   As previously stated, memorize the chords and practice with a recording of the song or metronome.
3)   Identify the time signature and count carefully to land each chord (not too early or too late).

Summary

Playing chords is an essential part of all music on the ukulele, and it takes time and consistent practice. As you improve, try to identify any issues and occasionally record and listen to yourself to track your progress. Here is a summary of the five chord tips to remember:

(**1**) Keep your fingers close to the frets to avoid buzzing.

(**2**) Reposition your wrist so all the strings ring clearly.

(**3**) Curve your fingers so the strings above and below are not muffled.

(**4**) Hover the fingers over the chord shape and drop the fingers simultaneously.

(**5**) Prepare for the next chord so the chord lands on the beat.

"If your chords don't ring true, don't press harder—reposition smarter."

Let's Get to Work!

It's time to dive in and master those chord changes. You're about to see a lot of numbers in the next few pages, but don't let that intimidate you! Once you've played through all these chord progressions, you'll have covered the foundations behind nearly every song ever written.
Start by playing each chord once, then switch to the next chord. Once the transitions feel smooth and the tone is clean, apply some of the previous strumming patterns to bring the progressions to life.

The Ultimate Two Chord Progression Workout - **Key of C**

We'll begin with all the two-chord progressions in the key of C. Using the diatonic chords (excluding the diminished), there are 30 possible combinations. Each chord is shown in two shapes, but feel free to use any voicings you prefer. Start with a single strum per chord, and aim for smooth, accurate changes. Once that feels comfortable, add strumming patterns. As you work through the pages, note which transitions need work and prioritize those.

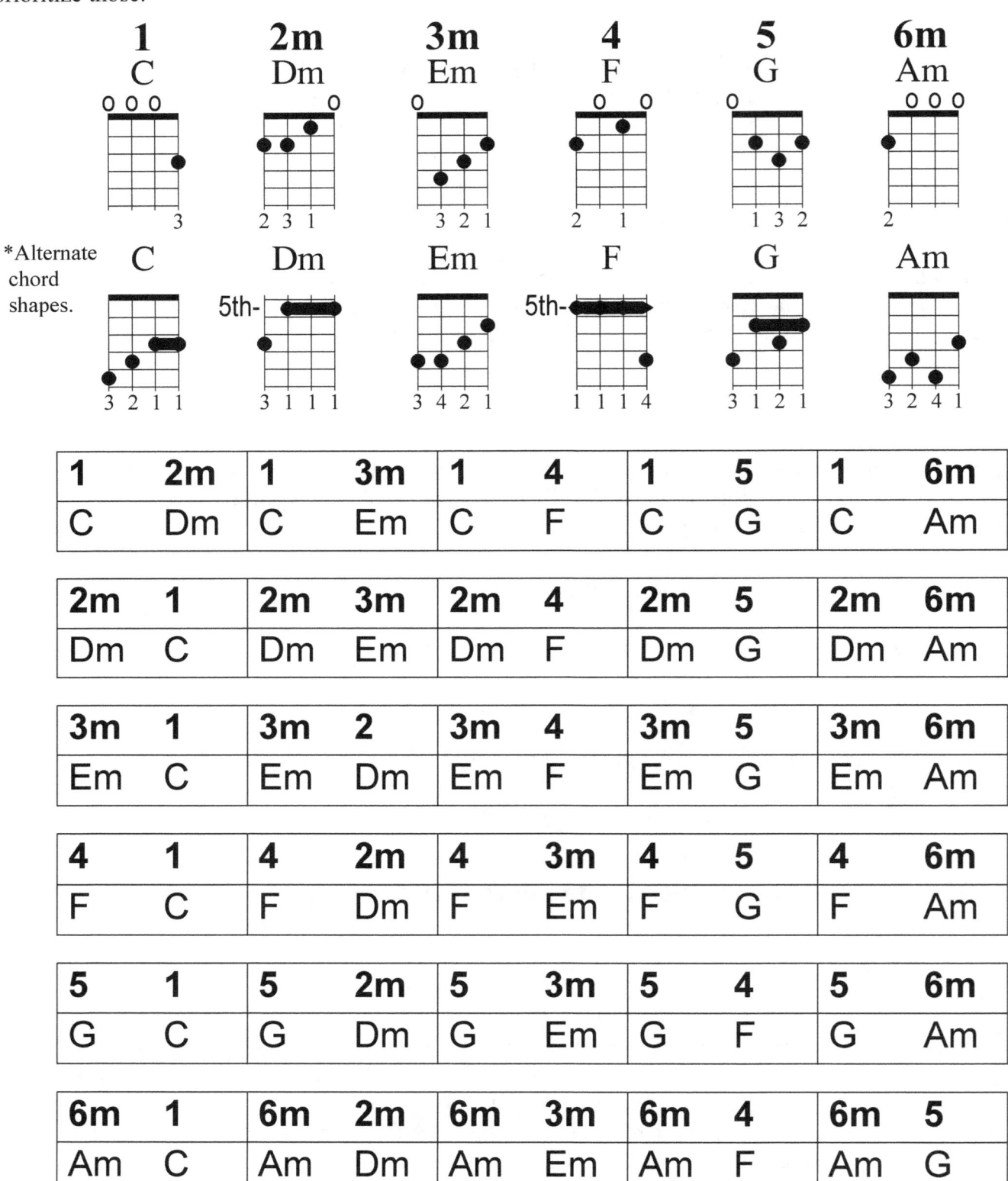

1	2m	1	3m	1	4	1	5	1	6m
C	Dm	C	Em	C	F	C	G	C	Am

2m	1	2m	3m	2m	4	2m	5	2m	6m
Dm	C	Dm	Em	Dm	F	Dm	G	Dm	Am

3m	1	3m	2	3m	4	3m	5	3m	6m
Em	C	Em	Dm	Em	F	Em	G	Em	Am

4	1	4	2m	4	3m	4	5	4	6m
F	C	F	Dm	F	Em	F	G	F	Am

5	1	5	2m	5	3m	5	4	5	6m
G	C	G	Dm	G	Em	G	F	G	Am

6m	1	6m	2m	6m	3m	6m	4	6m	5
Am	C	Am	Dm	Am	Em	Am	F	Am	G

The Ultimate Two Chord Progression Workout - **Key of G**

Here are all the two chord progressions in the key of G. Again, mix and match any of the chords you know and apply the strumming patterns when the changes are smooth and precise. As you work through the chord progressions, see if you can remember what diatonic chord number you are playing. Instead of thinking, play a G to Am, say to yourself 1 going to 2m.

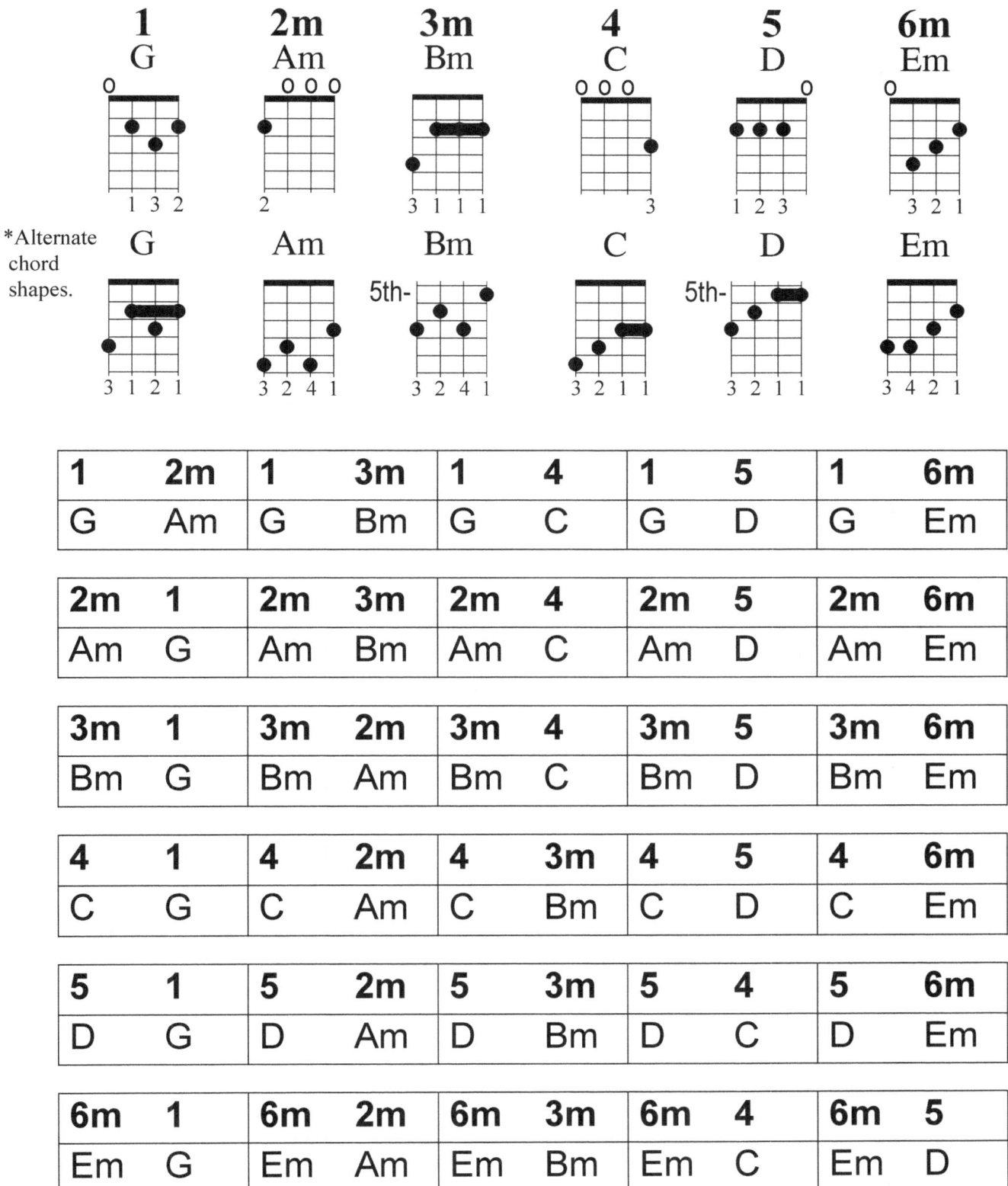

1	2m	1	3m	1	4	1	5	1	6m
G	Am	G	Bm	G	C	G	D	G	Em

2m	1	2m	3m	2m	4	2m	5	2m	6m
Am	G	Am	Bm	Am	C	Am	D	Am	Em

3m	1	3m	2m	3m	4	3m	5	3m	6m
Bm	G	Bm	Am	Bm	C	Bm	D	Bm	Em

4	1	4	2m	4	3m	4	5	4	6m
C	G	C	Am	C	Bm	C	D	C	Em

5	1	5	2m	5	3m	5	4	5	6m
D	G	D	Am	D	Bm	D	C	D	Em

6m	1	6m	2m	6m	3m	6m	4	6m	5
Em	G	Em	Am	Em	Bm	Em	C	Em	D

The Ultimate Two Chord Progression Workout - **Key of F**

Our final set of two-chord progressions is in the key of F. Once you've worked through this page, the next step is to transpose these progressions into other keys. Use the chord numbers as a guide and apply them to the diatonic chords in all 12 keys (see the following pages). For additional voicings, refer to the chord library in the reference section.

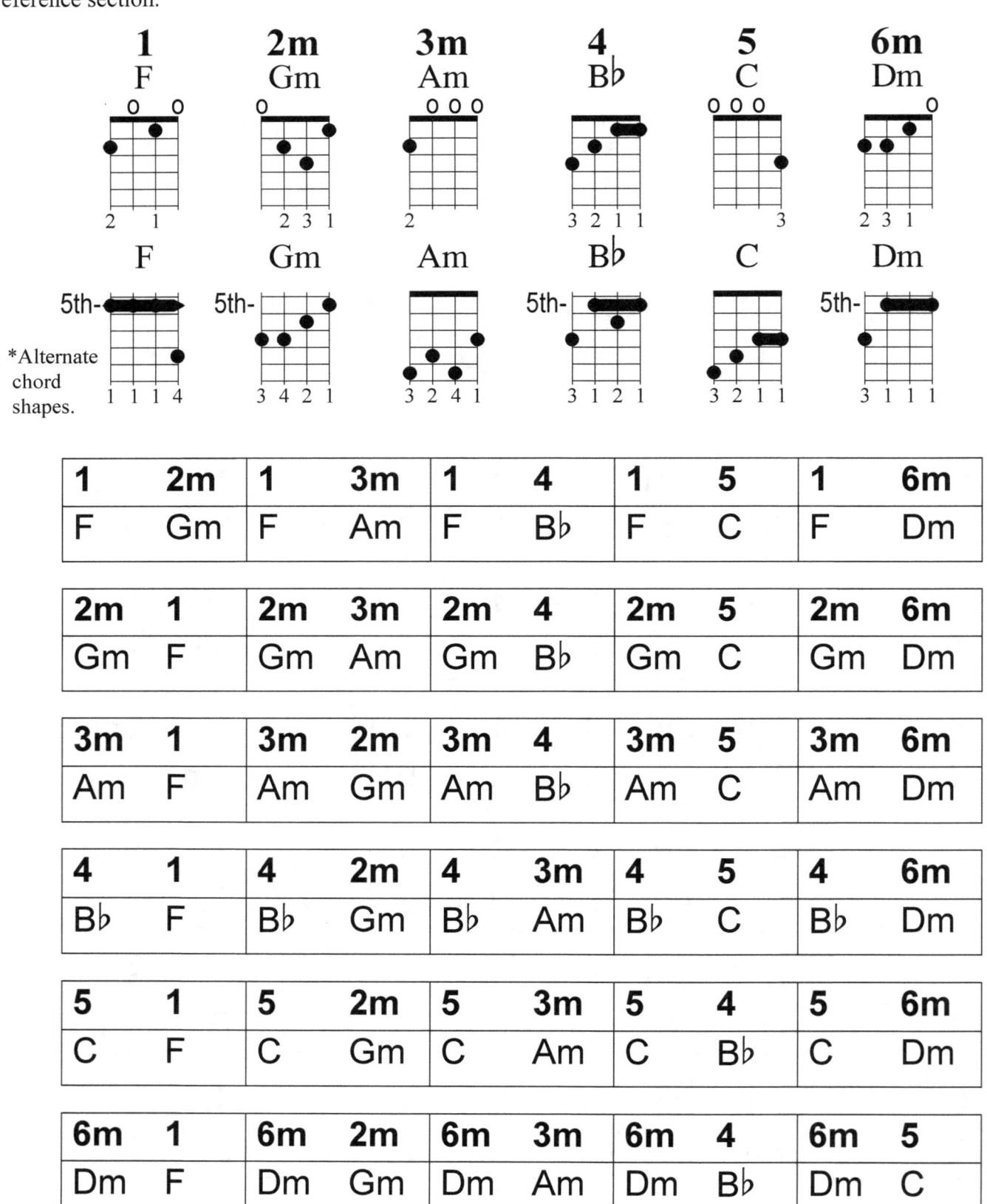

1	2m	1	3m	1	4	1	5	1	6m
F	Gm	F	Am	F	B♭	F	C	F	Dm

2m	1	2m	3m	2m	4	2m	5	2m	6m
Gm	F	Gm	Am	Gm	B♭	Gm	C	Gm	Dm

3m	1	3m	2m	3m	4	3m	5	3m	6m
Am	F	Am	Gm	Am	B♭	Am	C	Am	Dm

4	1	4	2m	4	3m	4	5	4	6m
B♭	F	B♭	Gm	B♭	Am	B♭	C	B♭	Dm

5	1	5	2m	5	3m	5	4	5	6m
C	F	C	Gm	C	Am	C	B♭	C	Dm

6m	1	6m	2m	6m	3m	6m	4	6m	5
Dm	F	Dm	Gm	Dm	Am	Dm	B♭	Dm	C

DIATONIC CHORDS IN ALL KEYS

We have worked with the keys of C, F and G but there are 12 sounding keys in total. Here are the diatonic chords in all keys.

82

KEY OF D

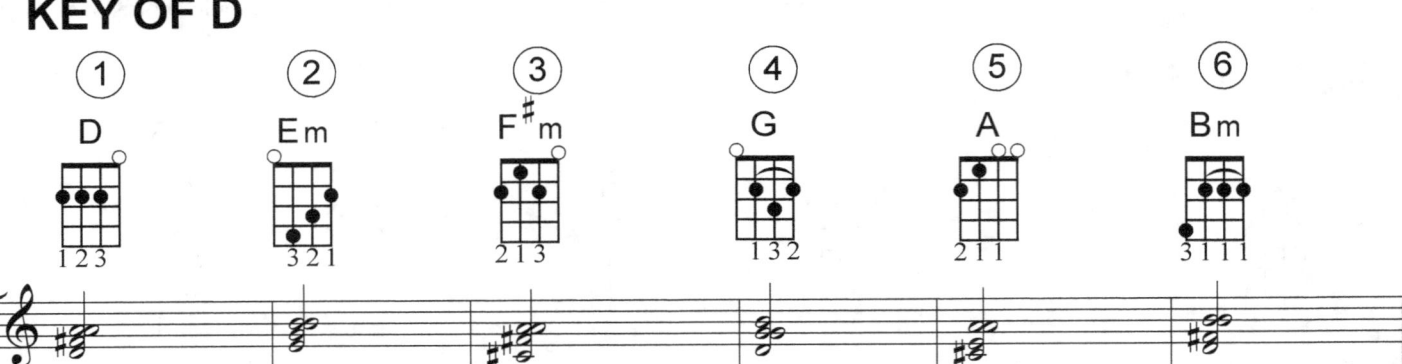

KEY OF A

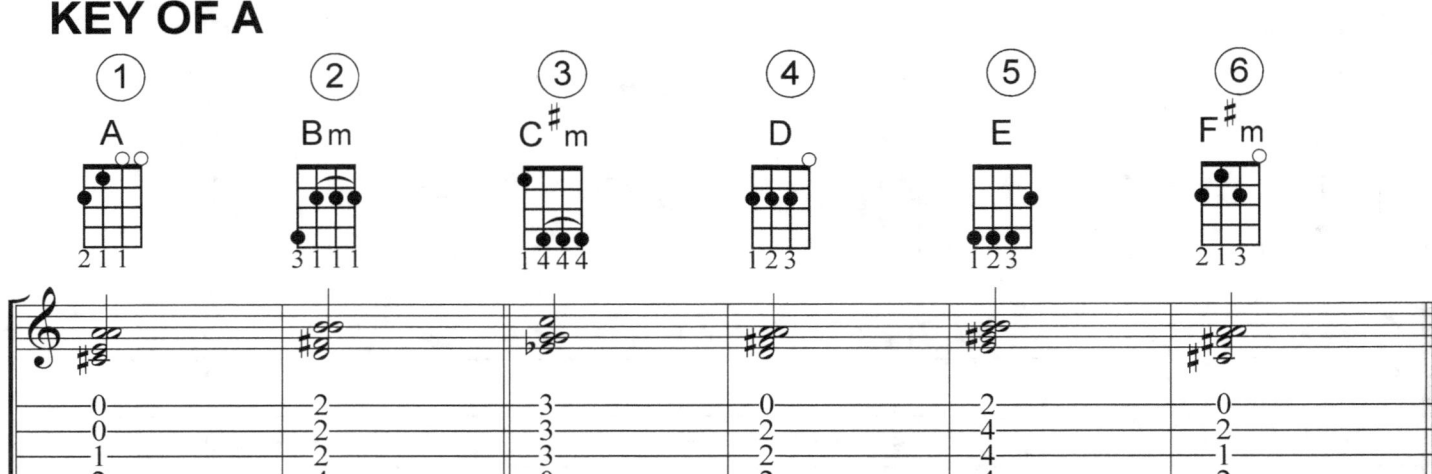

KEY OF E

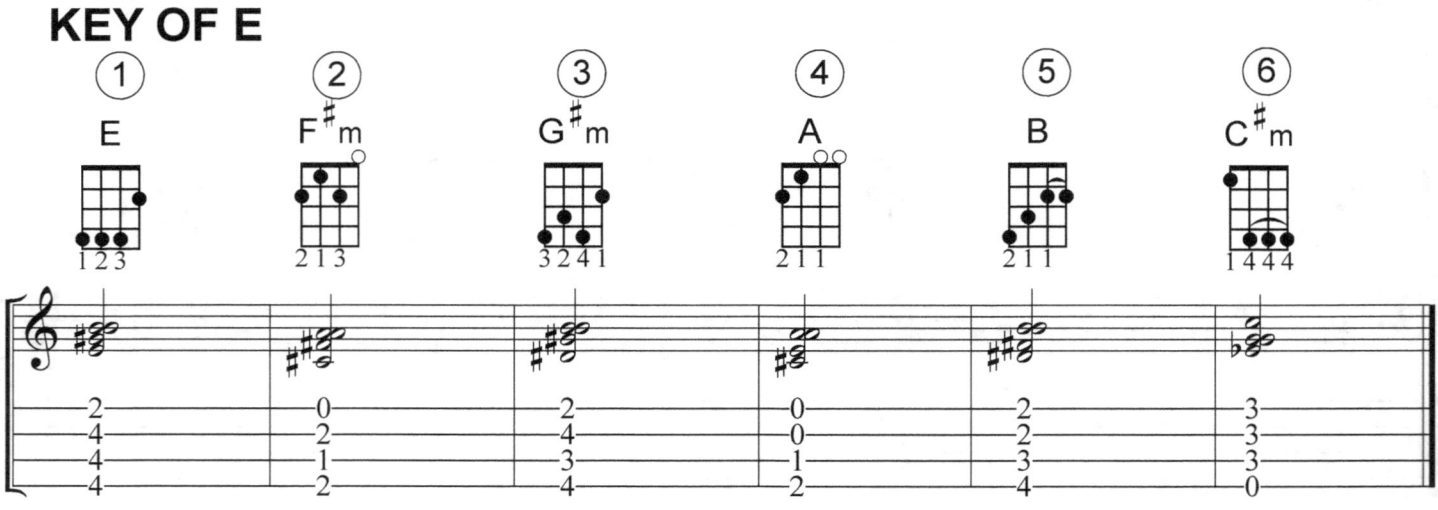

KEY OF B

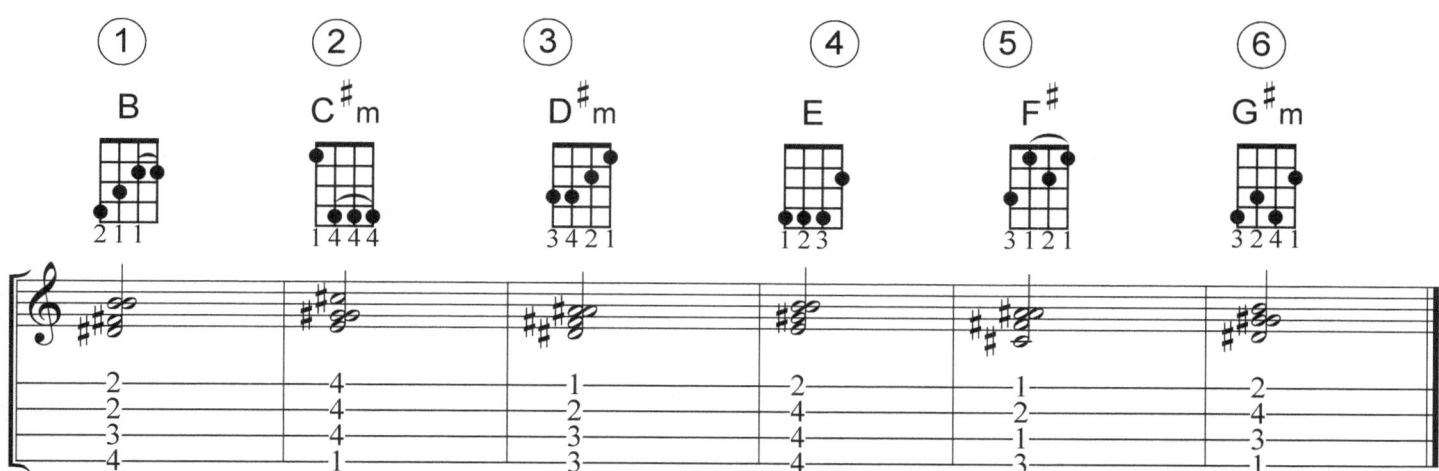

KEY OF F♯ or G♭

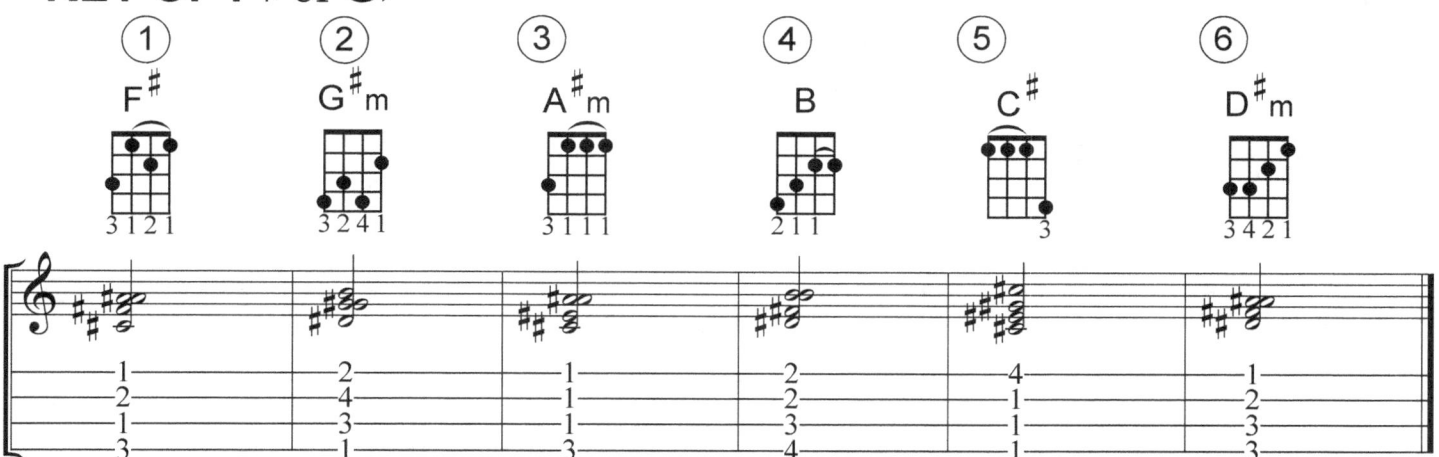

KEY OF C♯ or D♭

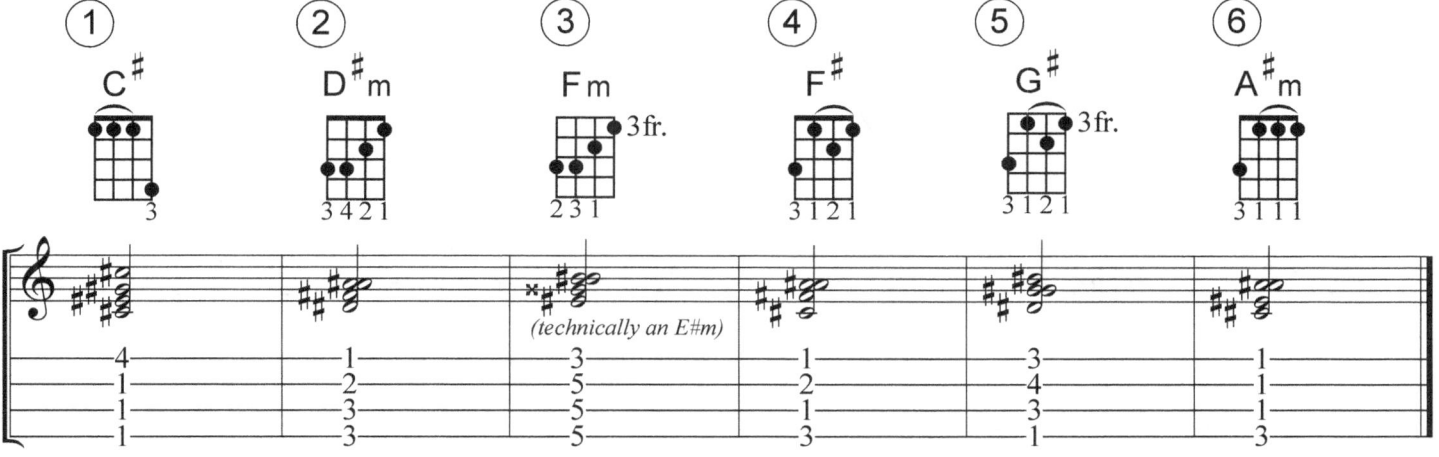

KEY OF A♭

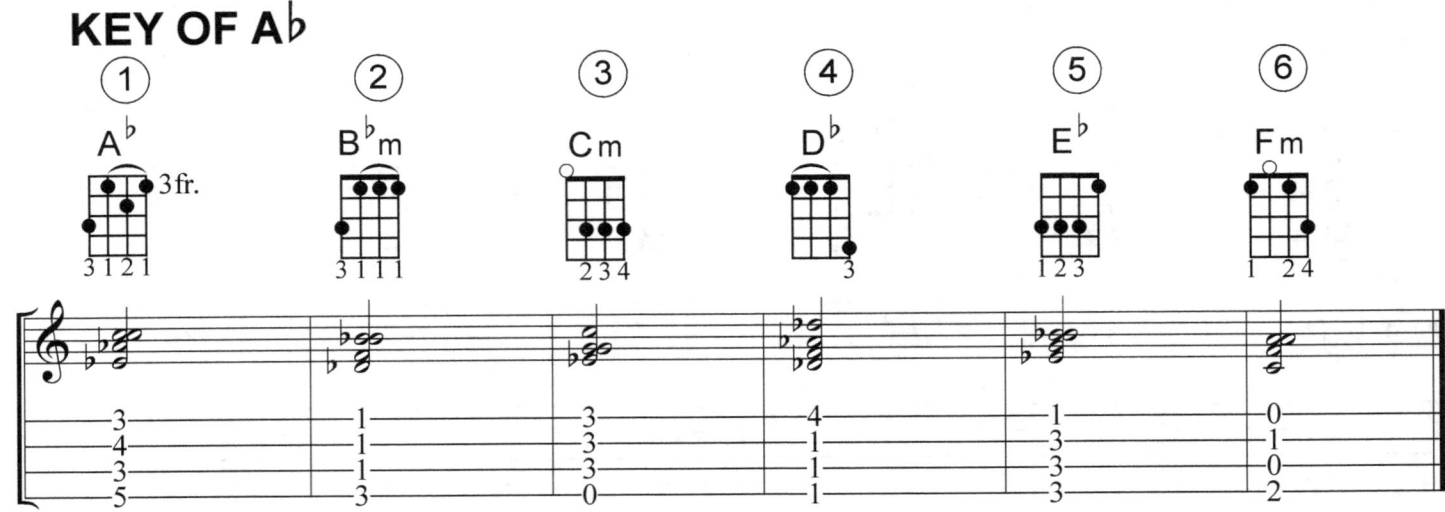

KEY OF E♭

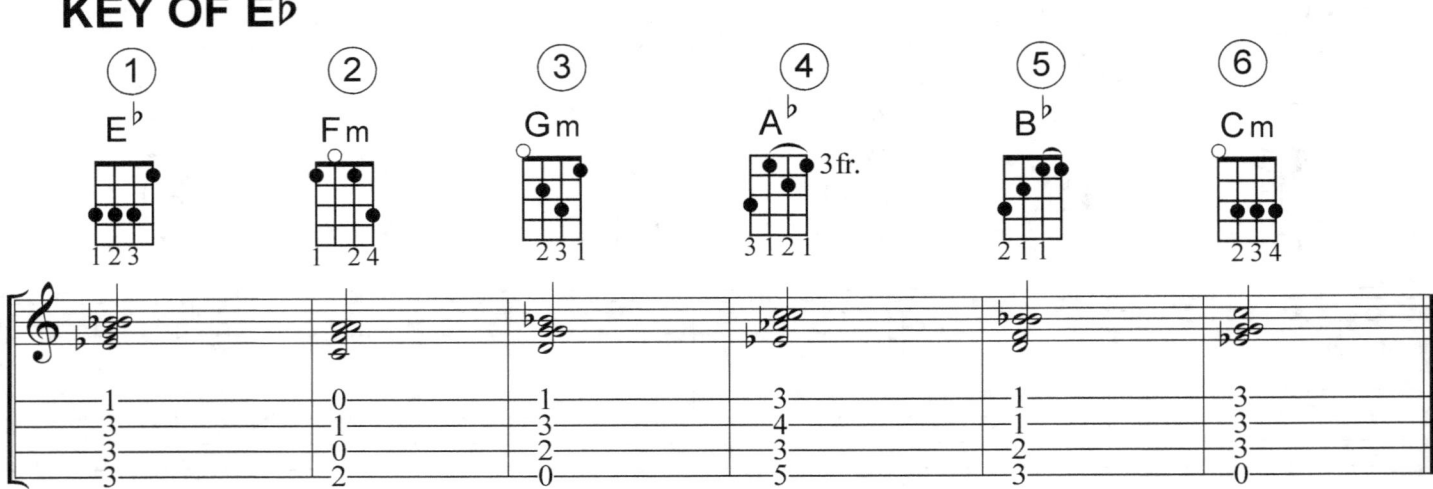

KEY OF B♭

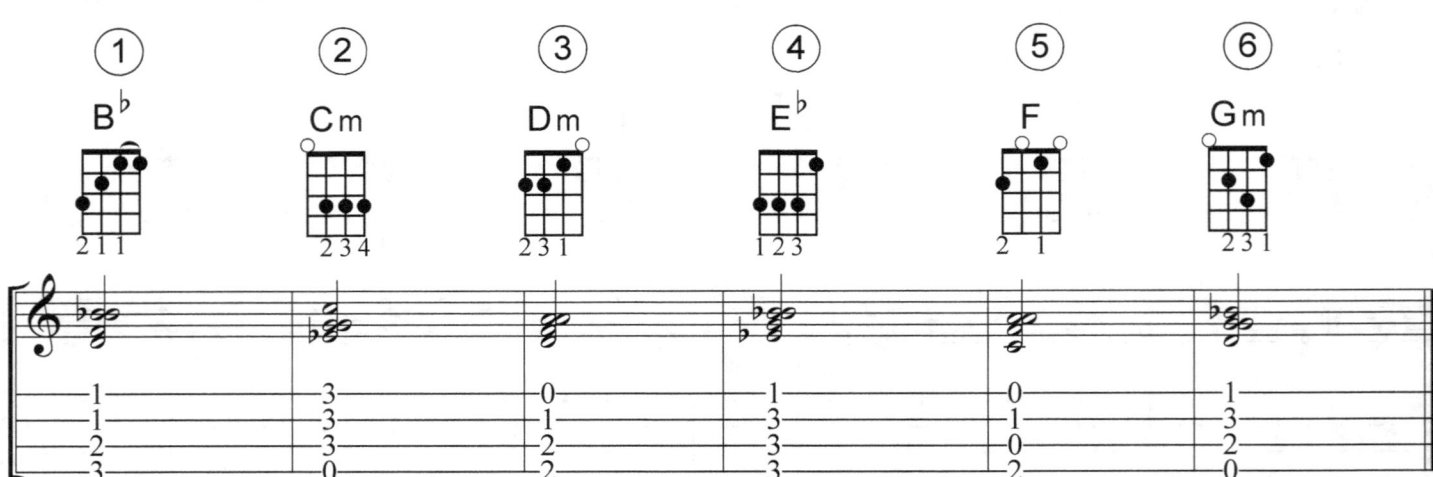

The Ultimate Three Chord Progression Workout in C

So far, we have played chord progressions with two chords, but most songs have more than two. The next exercise goes through all the three chord possibilities in the key of C. To make the most of this exercise, transpose to other keys using the diatonic chord numbers. For example, the first chord progression is 1-2-3. If you play this in G, the chords would be G-1, Am-2 and Bm-3.

1	2m	3m	1	2m	4	1	2m	5	1	2m	6m	1	3m	2m
C	Dm	Em	C	Dm	F	C	Dm	G	C	Dm	Am	C	Em	Dm

1	3m	4	1	3m	5	1	3m	6m	1	4	2m	1	4	3m
C	Em	F	C	Em	G	C	Em	Am	C	F	Dm	C	F	Em

1	4	5	1	4	6m	1	5	2m	1	5	3m	1	5	4
C	F	G	C	F	Am	C	G	Dm	C	G	Em	C	G	F

1	5	6m	1	6m	2m	1	6m	3m	1	6m	4	1	6m	5
C	G	Am	C	Am	Dm	C	Am	Em	C	Am	F	C	Am	G

2m	1	3m	2m	1	4	2m	1	5	2m	1	6m	2m	3m	1
Dm	C	Em	Dm	C	F	Dm	C	G	Dm	C	Am	Dm	Em	C

2m	3m	4	2m	3m	5	2m	3m	6m	2m	4	1	2m	4	3m
Dm	Em	F	Dm	Em	G	Dm	Em	Am	Dm	F	C	Dm	F	Em

2m	4	5	2m	4	6m	2m	5	1	2m	5	3m	2m	5	4
Dm	F	G	Dm	F	Am	Dm	G	C	Dm	G	Em	Dm	G	F

2m	5	6m	2m	6m	1	2m	6m	3m	2m	6m	4	2m	6m	5
Dm	G	Am	Dm	Am	C	Dm	Am	Em	Dm	Am	F	Dm	Am	G

3m	1	2m	3m	1	4	3m	1	5	3m	1	6m	3m	2m	1
Em	C	Dm	Em	C	F	Em	C	G	Em	C	Am	Em	Dm	C

3m	2m	4	3m	2m	5	3m	2m	6m	3m	4	1	3m	4	2m
Em	Dm	F	Em	Dm	G	Em	Dm	Am	Em	F	C	Em	F	Dm

3m	4	5	3m	4	6m	3m	5	1	3m	5	2m	3m	5	4
Em	F	G	Em	F	Am	Em	G	C	Em	G	Dm	Em	G	F

3m	5	6m	3m	6m	1	3m	6m	2m	3m	6m	4	3m	6m	5
Em	G	Am	Em	Am	C	Em	Am	Dm	Em	Am	F	Em	Am	G

4	1	2m	4	1	3m	4	1	5	4	1	6m	4	2m	1
F	C	Dm	F	C	Em	F	C	G	F	C	Am	F	Dm	C

4	2m	3m	4	2m	5	4	2m	6m	4	3m	1	4	3m	2m
F	Dm	Em	F	Dm	G	F	Dm	Am	F	Em	C	F	Em	Dm

4	3m	5	4	3m	6m	4	5	1	4	5	2m	4	5	3m
F	Em	G	F	Em	Am	F	G	C	F	G	Dm	F	G	Em

4	5	6m	4	6m	1	4	6m	2m	4	6m	3m	4	6m	5
F	G	Am	F	Am	C	F	Am	Dm	F	Am	Em	F	Am	G

5	1	2m	5	1	3m	5	1	4	5	1	6m	5	2m	1
G	C	Dm	G	C	Em	G	C	F	G	C	Am	G	Dm	C

5	2m	3m	5	2m	4	5	2m	6 m	5	3m	1	5	3m	2m
G	Dm	Em	G	Dm	F	G	Dm	Am	G	Em	C	G	Em	Dm

5	3m	4	5	3m	6m	5	4	1	5	4	2m	5	4	3m
G	Em	F	G	Em	Am	G	F	C	G	F	Dm	G	F	Em

5	4	6m	5	6m	1	5	6m	2m	5	6m	3m	5	6m	4
G	F	Am	G	Am	C	G	Am	Dm	G	Am	Em	G	Am	F

6m	1	2m	6m	1	3m	6m	1	4	6m	1	5	6m	2m	1
Am	C	Dm	Am	C	Em	Am	C	F	Am	C	G	Am	Dm	C

6m	2m	3m	6m	2m	4	6m	2m	5	6m	3m	1	6m	3m	2m
Am	Dm	Em	Am	Dm	F	Am	Dm	G	Am	Em	C	Am	Em	Dm

6m	3m	4	6m	3m	5	6m	4	1	6m	4	2m	6m	4	3m
Am	Em	F	Am	Em	G	Am	F	C	Am	F	Dm	Am	F	Em

6m	4	5	6m	5	1	6m	5	2m	6m	5	3m	6m	5	4
Am	F	G	Am	G	C	Am	G	Dm	Am	G	Em	Am	G	F

The Ultimate Four Chord Progression Workout

I'm sure your chord changing must be vastly improved if you have worked through all the two and three chord progressions. There is probably no need to continue, but we should include the four chord progressions to be complete. As you can imagine, there are many possibilities – 360, to be exact! To review, I have included the chords in C major with a few examples of four chord progressions in C:

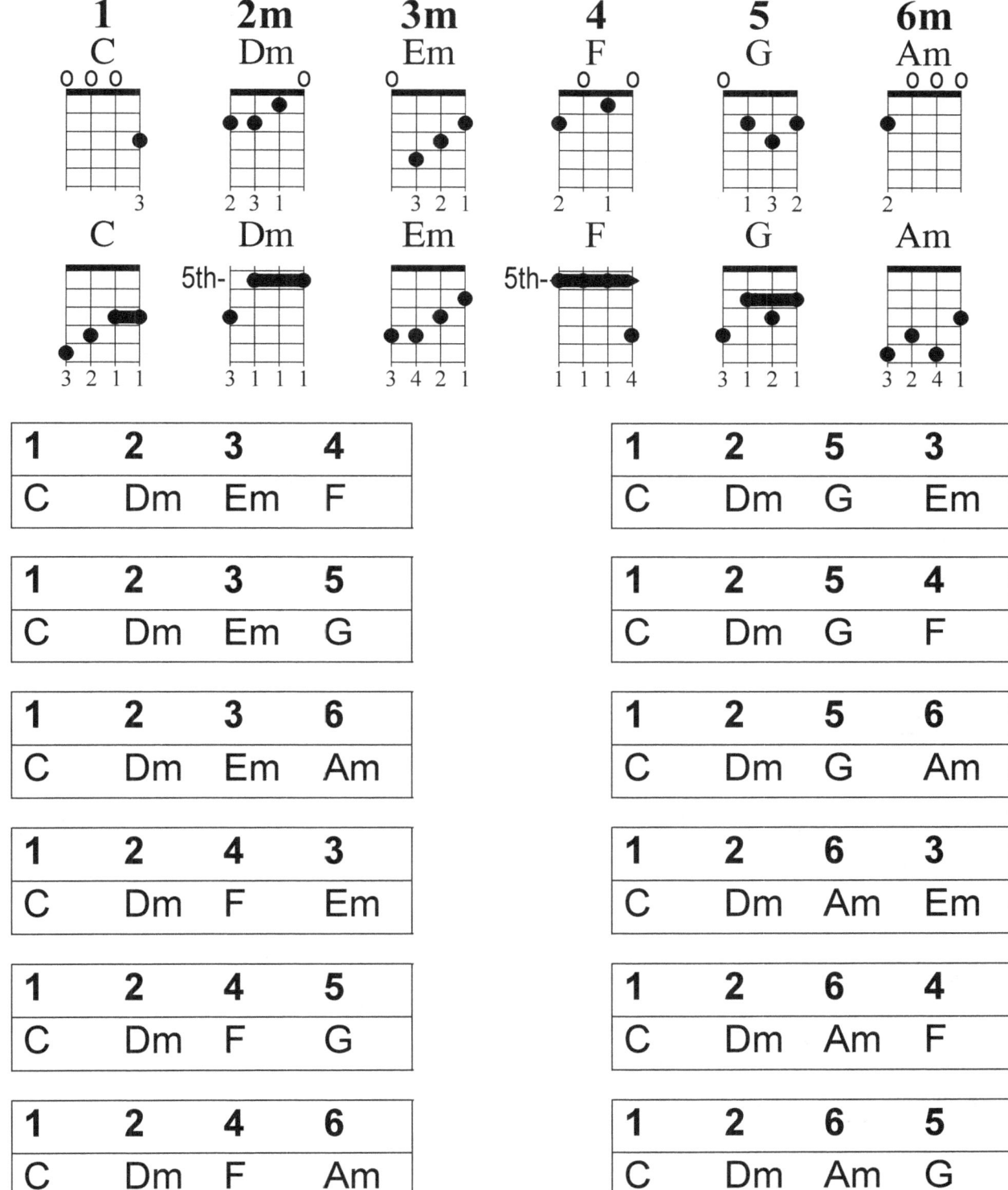

The following four-chord progressions might look confusing, but if you play each progression, you will have played all the four-chord diatonic progressions available. I have included a little black dot to help keep your place in this maze of numbers. You can transpose them into any key or use them for songwriting.

1-2m-3m-4	1-4-5-3m	2m-1-3m-6m	2m-4-6m-1
1-2m-3m-5 •	1-4-5-6m	2m-1-4-3m •	2m-4-6m-3m
1-2m-3m-6m	1-4-6m-2m	2m-1-4-5	2m-4-6m-5
1-2m-4-3m •	1-4-6m-3m	2m-1-4-6m •	2m-5-1-3m
1-2m-4-5	1-4-6m-5	2m-1-5-3m	2m-5-1-4
1-2m-4-6m •	1-5-2m-3m	2m-1-5-4 •	2m-5-1-6m
1-2m-5-3m	1-5-2m-4	2m-1-5-6m	2m-5-3m-1
1-2m-5-4 •	1-5-2m-6m	2m-1-6m-3m •	2m-5-3m-4
1-2m-5-6m	1-5-3m-2m	2m-1-6m-4	2m-5-3m-6m
1-2m-6m-3m •	1-5-3m-4	2m-1-6m-5 •	2m-5-4-1
1-2m-6m-4	1-5-3m-6m	2m-3m-1-4	2m-5-4-3m
1-2m-6m-5 •	1-5-4-2m	2m-3m-1-5 •	2m-5-4-6m
1-3m-2m-4	1-5-4-3m	2m-3m-1-6m	2m-5-6m-1
1-3m-2m-5 •	1-5-4-6m	2m-3m-4-1 •	2m-5-6m-3m
1-3m-2m-6m	1-5-6m-2m	2m-3m-4-5	2m-5-6m-4
1-3m-4-2m •	1-5-6m-3m	2m-3m-4-6m •	2m-6m-1-3m
1-3m-4-5	1-5-6m-4	2m-3m-5-1	2m-6m-1-4
1-3m-4-6m •	1-6m-2m-3m	2m-3m-5-4 •	2m-6m-1-5
1-3m-5-2m	1-6m-2m-4	2m-3m-5-6m	2m-6m-3m1
1-3m-5-4 •	1-6m-2m-5	2m-3m-6m-1 •	2m-6m-34
1-3m-5-6m	1-6m-3m-2m	2m-3m-6m-4	2m-6m-3m-5
1-3m-6m-2m •	1-6m-3m-4	2m-3m-6m-5 •	2m-6m-4-1
1-3m-6m-4	1-6m-3m-5	2m-4-1-3m	2m-6m-4-3m
1-3m-6m-5 •	1-6m-4-2m	2m-4-1-5 •	2m-6m-4-5
1-4-2m-3m	1-6m-4-3m	2m-4-11-6m	2m-6m-5-1
1-4-2m-5 •	1-6m-4-5	2m-4-3m-1 •	2m-6m-5-3m
1-4-2m-6m	1-6m-5-2m	2m-4-3m-5	2m-6m-5-4
1-4-3m-2m •	1-6m-5-3m	2m-4-3m-6m •	3m-1-2m-4
1-4-3m-5	1-6m-5-4	2m-4-5-1	3m-1-2m-5
1-4-3m-6m •	2m-1-3m-4	2m-4-5-3m •	3m-1-2m-6m
1-4-5-2m	2m-1-3m-5	2m-4-5-6m	3m-1-4-2m

3_m-1-4-5		3_m-4-6_m-5	4-1-5-2_m		4-5-1-3_m
3_m-1-4-6_m	●	3_m-5-1-2_m	4-1-5-3_m	●	4-5-1-6_m
3_m-1-5-2_m		3_m-5-1-4	4-1-5-6_m		4-5-2_m-1
3_m-1-5-4	●	3_m-5-1-6_m	4-1-6_m-2_m	●	4-5-2_m-3_m
3_m-1-5-6_m		3_m-5-2_m-1	4-1-6_m-3_m		4-5-2_m-6_m
3_m-1-6_m-2_m	●	3_m-5-2_m-4	4-1-6_m-5	●	4-5-3_m-1
3_m-1-6_m-4		3_m-5-2_m-6_m	4-2_m-1-3_m		4-5-3_m-2_m
3_m-1-6_m-5	●	3_m-5-4-1	4-2_m-1-5	●	4-5-3_m-6_m
3_m-2_m-1-4		3_m-5-4-2_m	4-2_m-1-6_m		4-5-6_m-1
3_m-2_m-1-5	●	3_m-5-4-6_m	4-2_m-3_m-1	●	4-5-6_m-2_m
3_m-2_m-1-6_m		3_m-5-6_m-1	4-2_m-3_m-5		4-5-6_m-3_m
3_m-2_m-4-1	●	3_m-5-6_m-2_m	4-2_m-3_m-6_m	●	4-6_m-1-2_m
3_m-2_m-4-5		3_m-5-6_m-4	4-2_m-5-1		4-6_m-1-3_m
3_m-2_m-4-6_m	●	3_m-6_m-1-2_m	4-2_m-5-3_m	●	4-6_m-1-5
3_m-2_m-5-1		3_m-6_m-1-4	4-2_m-5-6_m		4-6_m-2_m-1
3_m-2_m-5-4	●	3_m-6_m-1-5	4-2_m-6_m-1	●	4-6_m-2_m-3_m
3_m-2_m-5-6_m		3_m-6_m-2_m-1	4-2_m-6_m-3_m		4-6_m-2_m-5
3_m-2_m-6_m-1	●	3_m-6_m-2_m-4	4-2_m-6_m-5	●	4-6_m-3_m-1
3_m-2_m-6_m-4		3_m-6_m-2_m-5	4-3_m-1-2_m		4-6_m-3_m-2_m
3_m-2_m-6_m-5	●	3_m-6_m-4-1	4-3_m-1-5	●	4-6_m-3_m-5
3_m-4-1-2_m		3_m-6_m-4-2_m	4-3_m-1-6_m		4-6_m-5-1
3_m-4-1-5	●	3_m-6_m-4-5	4-3_m-2_m-1	●	4-6_m-5-2_m
3_m-4-1-6_m		3_m-6_m-5-1	4-3_m-2_m-5		4-6_m-5-3_m
3_m-4-2_m-1	●	3_m-6_m-5-2_m	4-3_m-2_m-6_m	●	5-1-$2_m$$3_m$
3_m-4$2_m$-5		3_m-6_m-5-4	4-3_m-5-1		5-1-2_m4
3_m-4-2_m-6_m	●	4-1-$2_m$$3_m$	4-3_m-5-2_m	●	5-1-$2_m$$6_m$
3_m-4-5-1		4-1-2_m5	4-3_m-5-6_m		5-1-3_m-2_m
3_m-4-5-2_m	●	4-1-$2_m$$6_m$	4-3_m-6_m-1	●	5-1-3_m-4
3_m-4-5-6_m		4-1-3_m-2_m	4-3_m-6_m-2_m		5-1-3_m-6_m
3_m-4-6_m-1	●	4-1-3_m-5	4-3_m-6_m-5	●	5-1-4-2_m
3_m-4-6_m-2_m		4-1-3_m-6_m	4-$5$1-2_m		5-1-4-3_m

5-1-4-6m		5-4-2m-1	6m-1-5-3m		6m-4-2m-5
5-1-6m-2m	•	5-4-2m-3m	6m-1-5-4	•	6m-4-3m-1
5-1-6m-3m		5-4-2m-6m	6m-2m-1-3m		6m-4-3m-2m
5-1-6m-4	•	5-4-3m-1	6m-2m-1-4	•	6m-4-3m-5
5-2m-1-3m		5-4-3m-2m	6m-2m-1-5		6m-4-5-1
5-2m-1-4	•	5-4-3m-6m	6m-2m-3m-1	•	6m-4-5-2m
5-2m-1-6m		5-4-6m-1	6m-2m-3m-4		6m-4-5-3m
5-2m-3m-1	•	5-4-6m-2m	6m-2m-3-5	•	6m-5-1-2m
5-2m-3m-4		5-4-6m-3m	6m-2m-4-1		6m-5-1-3m
5-2m-3m-6m	•	5-6m-1-2m	6m-2m-4-3m	•	6m-5-1-4
5-2m-4-1		5-6m-1-3m	6m-2m-4-5		6m-5-2m-1
5-2m-4-3m	•	5-6m-1-4	6m-2m-5-1	•	6m-5-2m-3m
5-2m-4-6m		5-6m-2m-1	6m-2m-5-3m		6m-5-2m-4
5-2m-6m-1	•	5-6m-2m-3m	6m-2m-54	•	6m-5-3m-1
5-2m-6m-3m		5-6m-2-4	6m-3m-1-2m		6m-5-3m-2m
5-2m-6m-4	•	5-6m-3m-1	6m-3m-1-4	•	6m-5-3m-4
5-3m-1-2m		5-6m-3m-2m	6m-3m-1-5		6m-5-4-1
5-3m-1-4	•	5-6m-3m-4	6m-3m-2m-1	•	6m-5-4-2m
5-3m-1-6m		5-6m-4-1	6m-3m-2m-4		6m-5-4-3m
5-3m-2m-1	•	5-6m-4-2m	6m-3m-2m-5	•	
5-3m-2m-4		5-6m-4-3m	6m-3m-4-1		
5-3m-2m-6m	•	6m-1-2m-3m	6m-3m-4-2m	•	
5-3m-4-1		6m-1-2m-4	6m-3m-4-5		
5-3m-4-2m	•	6m-1-2m-5	6m-3m-5-1	•	
5-3m-4-6m		6m-1-3m-2m	6m-3m-5-2m		
5-3m-6m-1	•	6m-1-3m-4	6m-3m-5-4	•	
5-3m-6m-2m		6m-1-3m-5	6m-4-1-2m		
5-3m-6m-4	•	6m-1-4-2m	6m-4-1-3m	•	
5-4-1-2m		6m-1-4-3m	6m-4-1-5		
5-4-1-3m	•	6m-1-4-5	6m-4-2m-1	•	
5-4-1-6m		6m-1-5-2m	6m-4-2m-3m		

CHAPTER SIX - BLUES AND JAZZ CHORDS

So far, we've focused on the diatonic chords commonly used in popular music. Now, we'll shift our attention to blues and jazz chord progressions.

Many of you may already be familiar with the blues. For those who aren't, we'll start with a brief overview, focusing on the 12-bar blues form and a few common variations. Here's the basic 12-bar blues in C, built on the I–IV–V chord functions similar to the diatonic progressions we've practiced. The main difference is that blues often uses dominant seventh chords, like C7, F7, and G7.

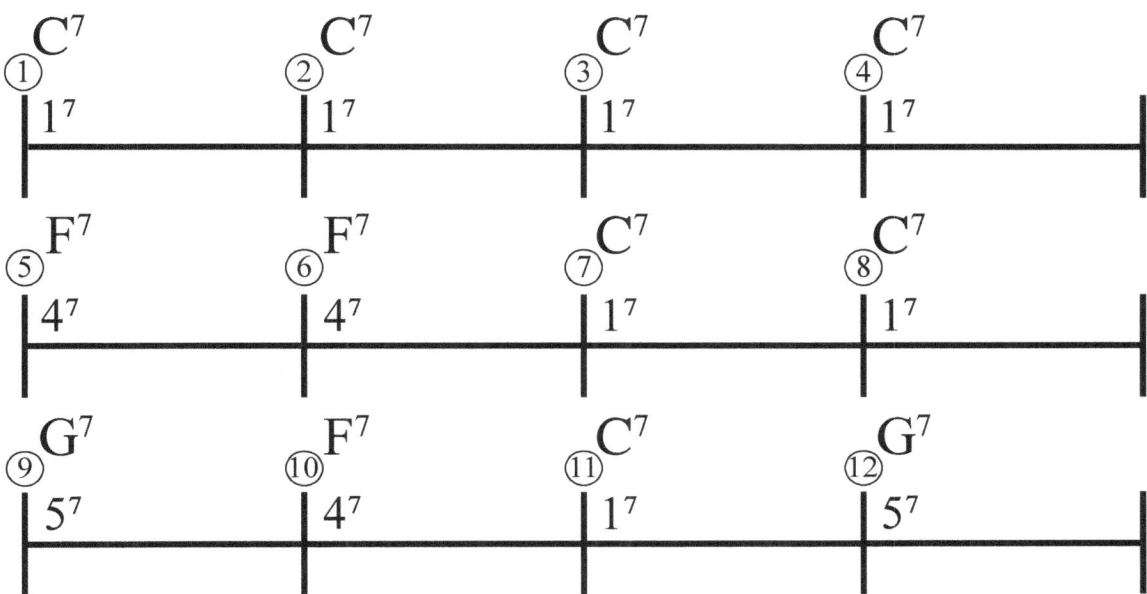

You may also see chord substitutions, such as replacing F7 with F9. While the fingerings change, the function of the chord remains the same (in this case, dominant). These substitutions are typical in blues and jazz styles and help add color to your progressions.

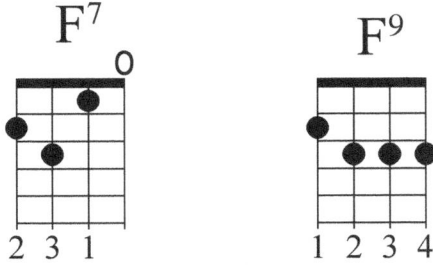

There are many styles and variations in blues and jazz, but the exercises in this section will give you a solid foundation.

Blues and Jazz Rhythms

One final point: blues and jazz are often played with a *swing* or *shuffle* rhythm. Playing with a blues shuffle or jazz swing means the beat isn't evenly divided like in straight eighth notes. Instead, there is a long/short galop to the feel. The blues/jazz feel comes from dividing each beat into three parts, which you know as triplets. So, you play the first note longer and the second shorter, roughly following a 66/34% split.

Now, there are different swing levels, meaning it could be 60/40 or 70/30. Nevertheless, the idea is to play the first note longer than the second note shorter:

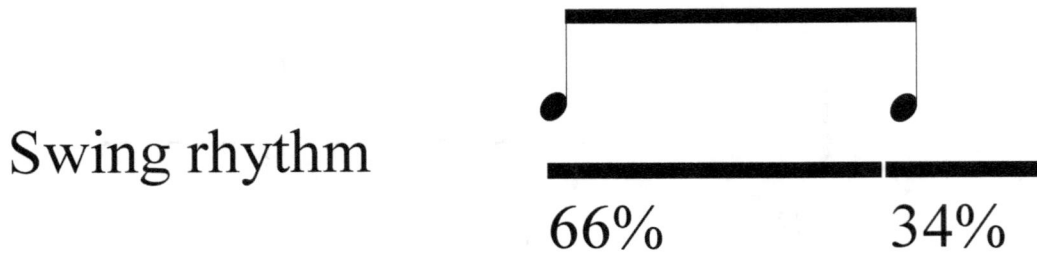

Swing rhythm 66% 34%

Often, the words "swing" or "shuffle" are used in sheet music with two eighth notes and an equal sign showing two triplet eighth notes:

Swing! ♫ = ♩♪

Just as a visual reference, a straight rhythm, as opposed to a swing rhythm, is played evenly or 50/50:

Straight rhythm 50% 50%

Before we move on to the blues and jazz chord progressions, let's learn some typical strumming patterns you can apply to the chord progressions in this section.

BLUES STRUMMING PATTERNS

Here are twenty blues strumming patterns you can apply to some of the upcoming blues chord progressions. Refer to the "How to Read Rhythms" section if needed and listen to the audio online. The symbols below indicate the strumming techniques used in this section:

Down ⊓   Up ∨   Mute **X**   Accent >

1. Down / Up Shuffle Pattern. Triplets

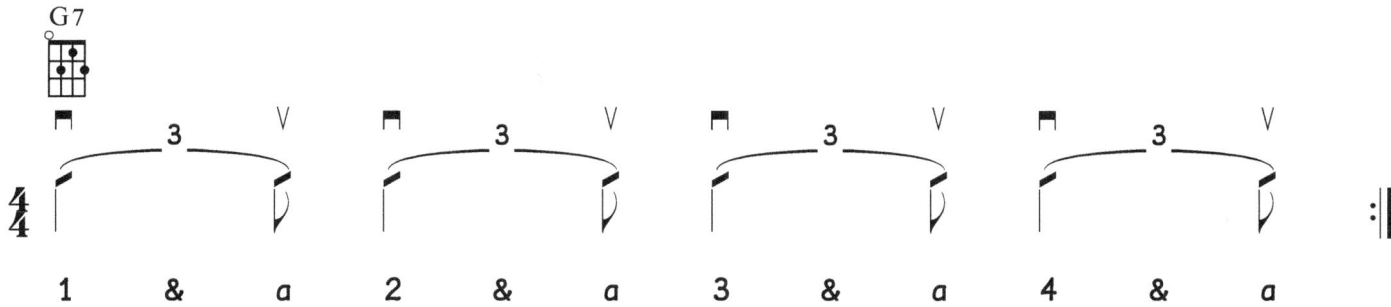

2. Down / Up Shuffle Pattern. Triplets - Accent 2nd & 4th Beat

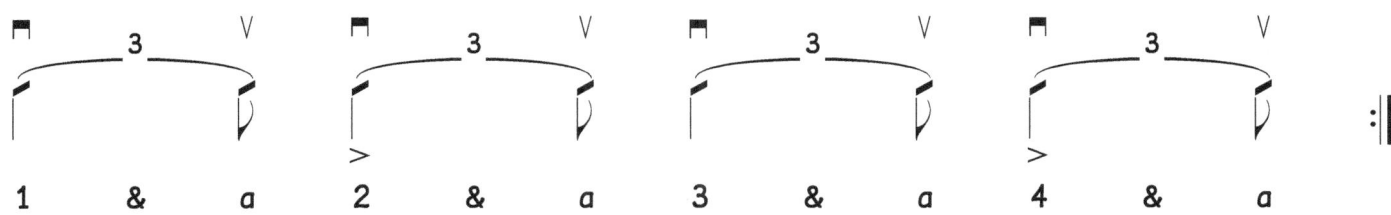

3. Down / Up Shuffle Pattern. Mute then Up Stroke

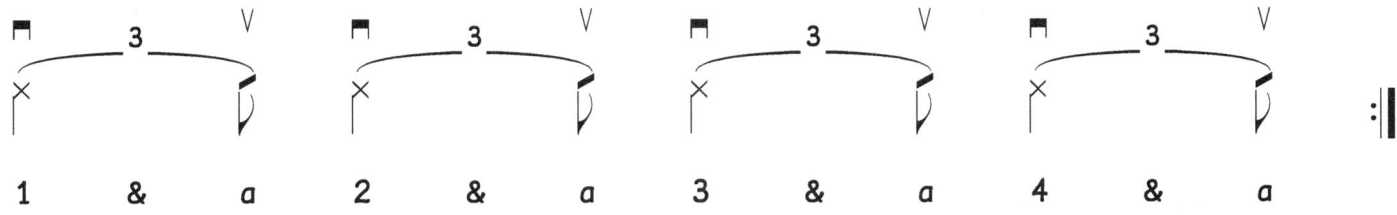

4. Down / Up Shuffle Pattern. Tied Note - Don't Strum on 3rd Beat

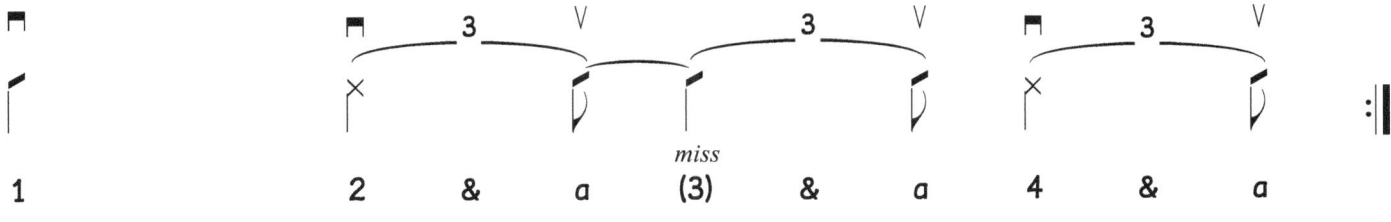

5. Straight or Shuffle Pattern #1

6. Straight or Shuffle Pattern #2

7. Straight or Shuffle Pattern #3

8. Straight or Shuffle Pattern #4

9. Straight or Shuffle Pattern #5

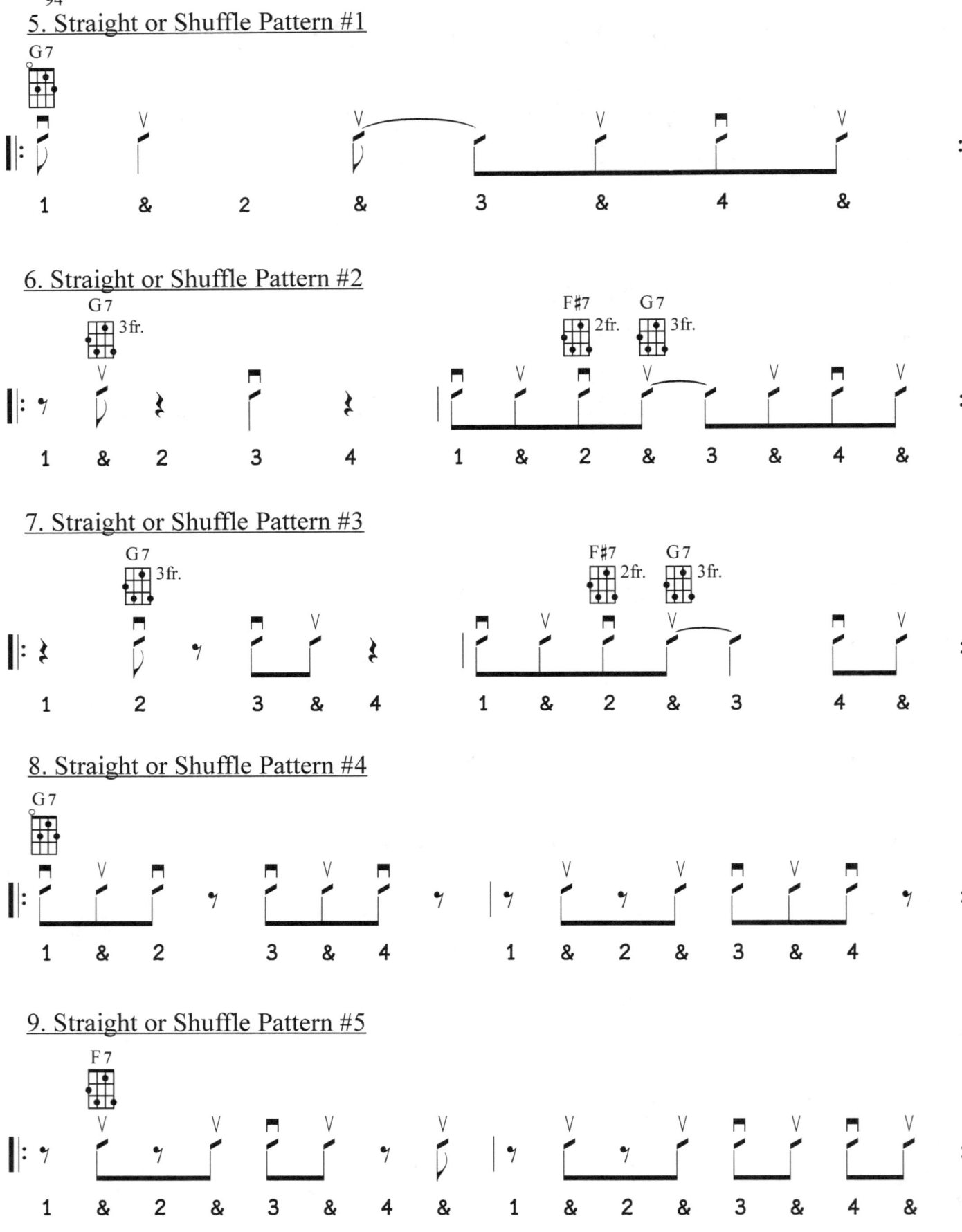

10. Blues Rock #1 (play with a straight rhythm)

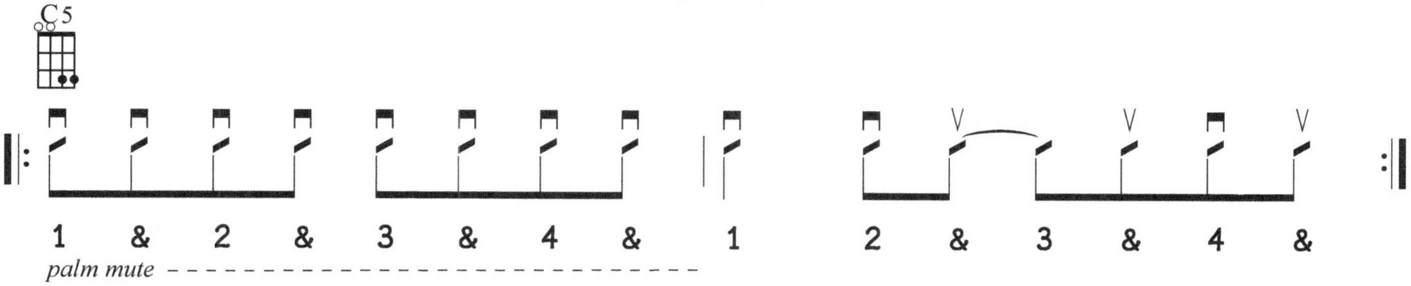

C5

1 & 2 & 3 & 4 & | 1 2 & 3 & 4 &

palm mute –

11. Blues Rock #2

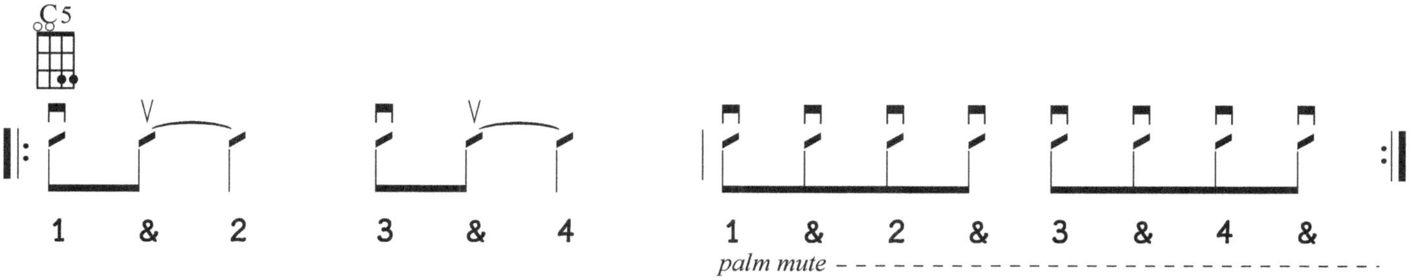

C5

1 & 2 3 & 4 | 1 & 2 & 3 & 4 &

palm mute –

12. Blues Rock #3

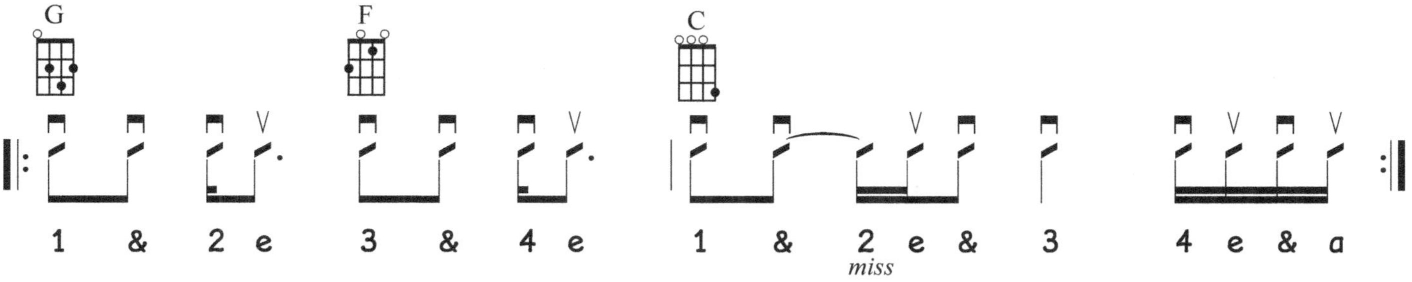

G   F   C

1 & 2 e 3 & 4 e | 1 & 2 e & 3 4 e & a

miss

13. Blues (50's) Rock #4

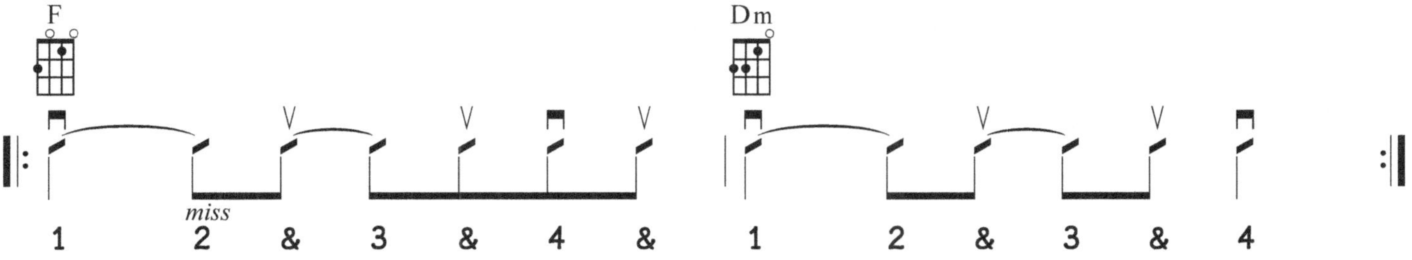

F   Dm

1 2 & 3 & 4 & | 1 2 & 3 & 4

miss

14. Blues (50's) Rock #5

F

1 2 & 3 4 | 1 2 & 3 4

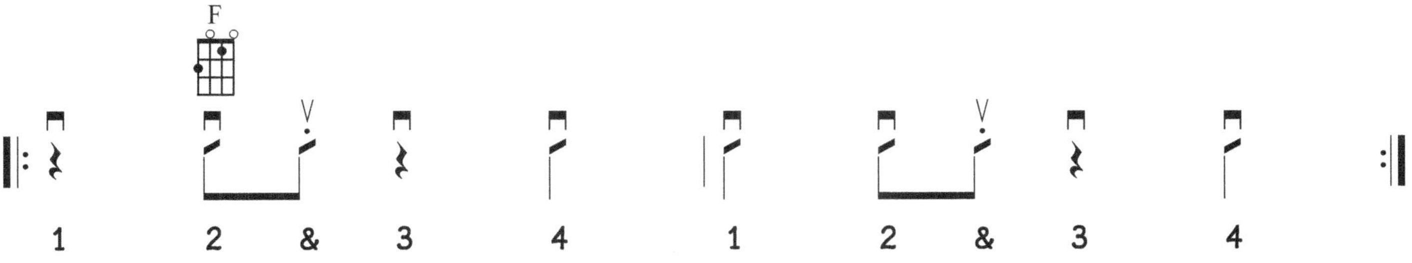

96

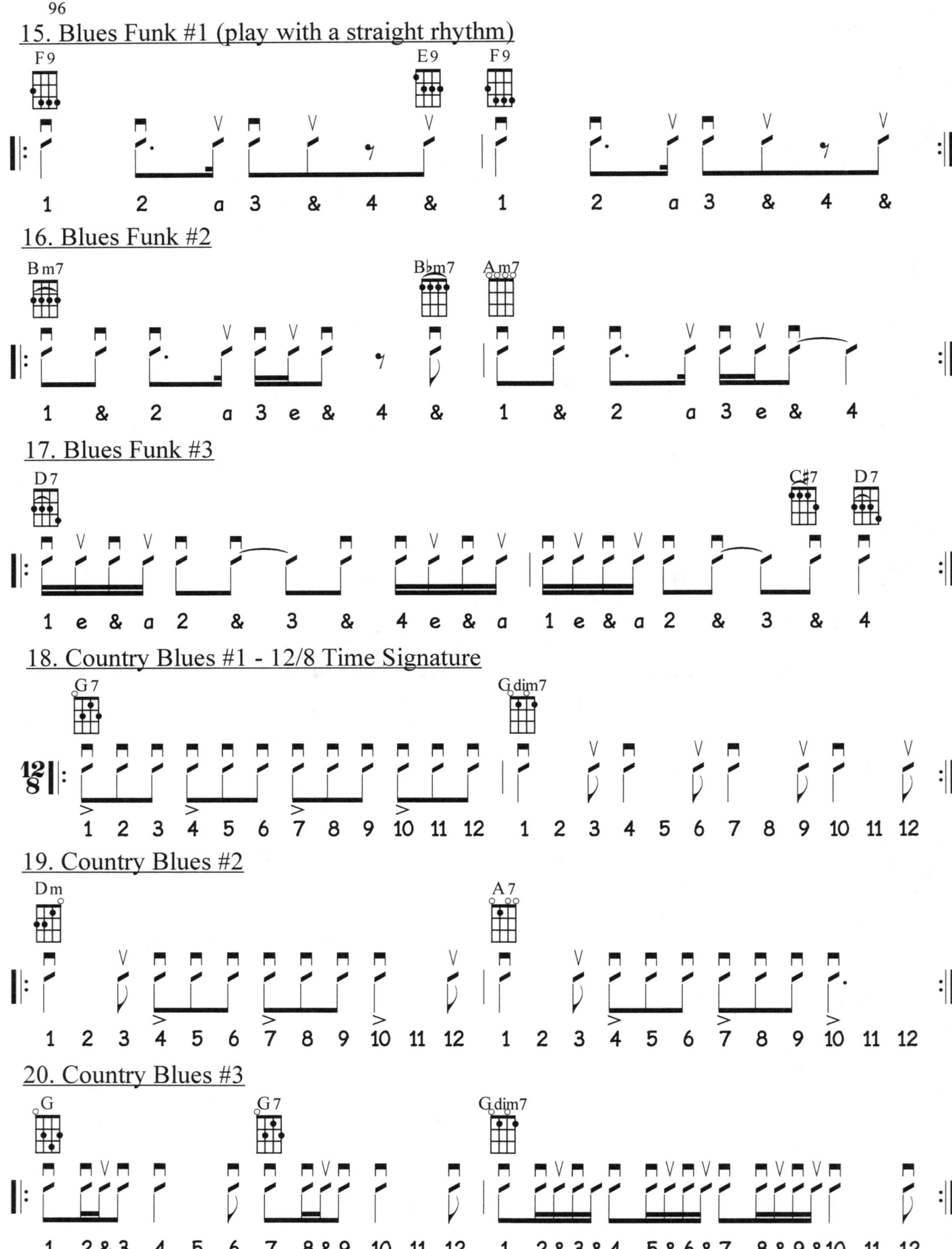

Basic 12 Bar Blues Progressions

Let's start with a few easy 12-bar blues chord progressions.

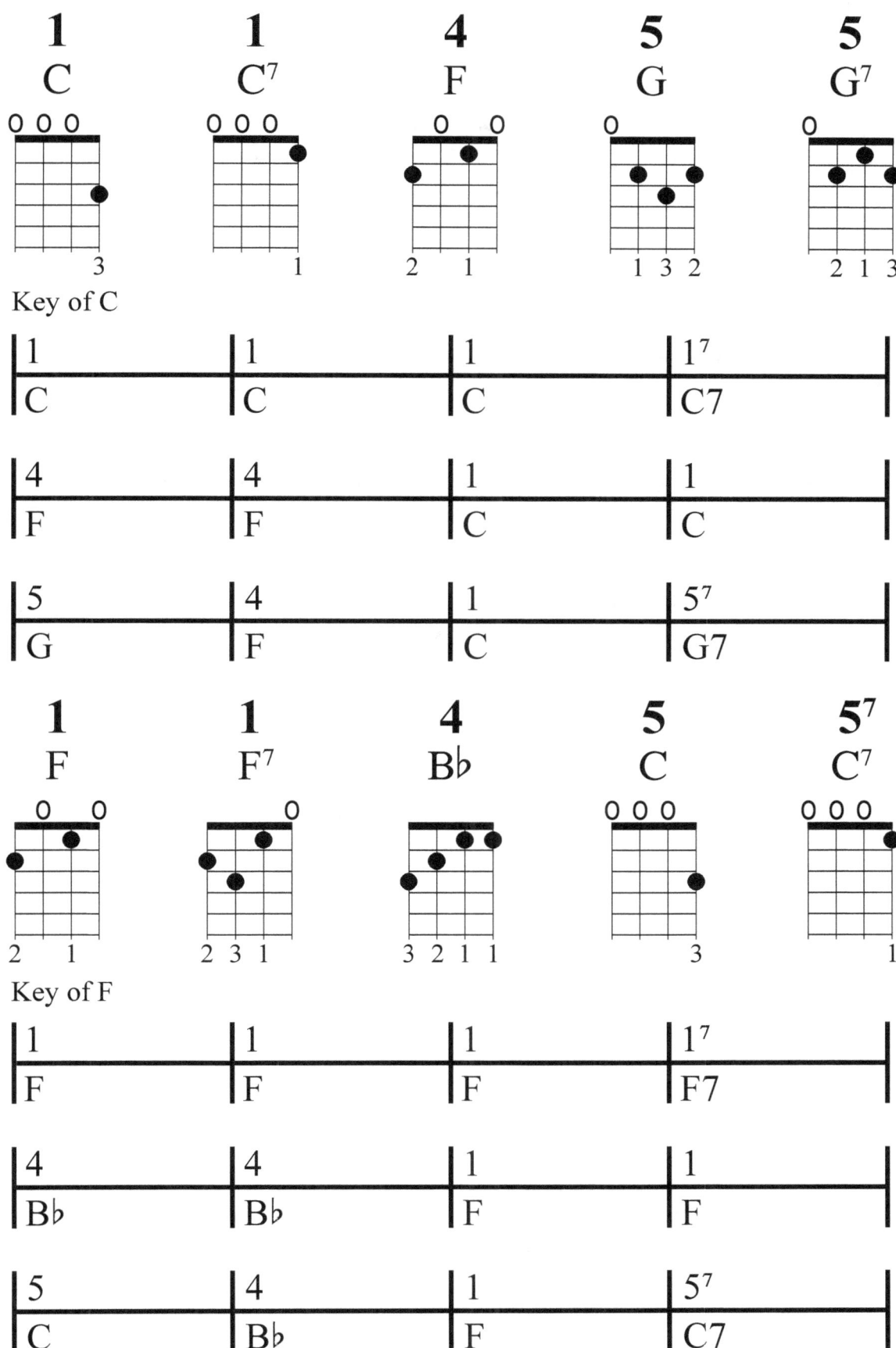

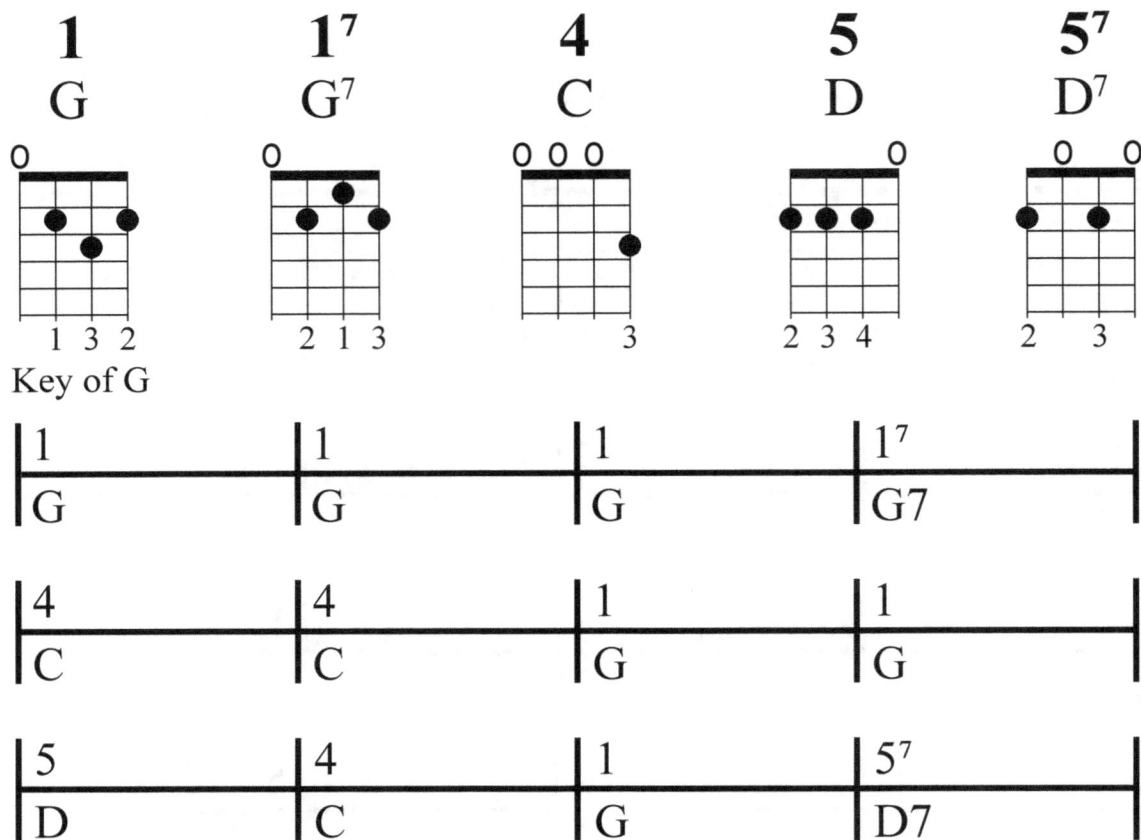

Now you can try. How about a 12-bar blues in the key of D, or maybe Bb?

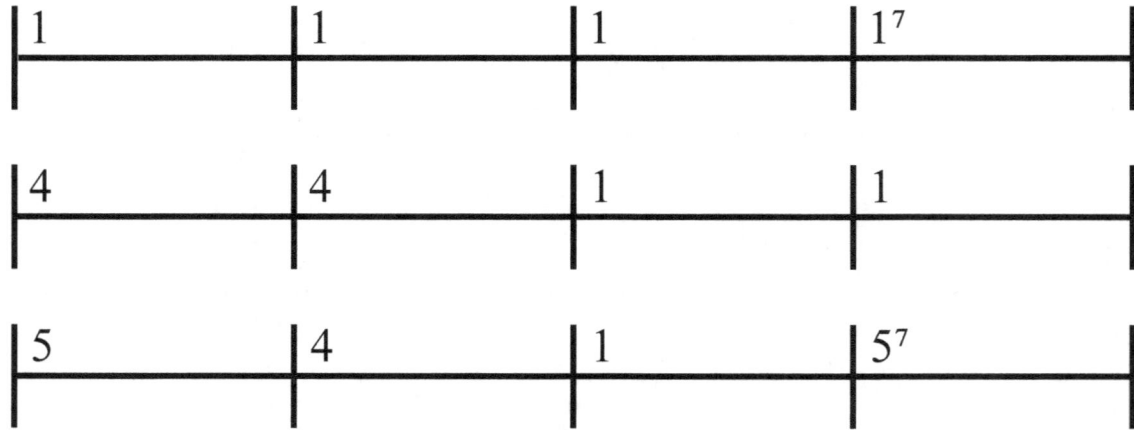

12 Bar Blues Progressions

Now, we will add more variety by expanding the chord selection and complexity of the 12-bar blues.

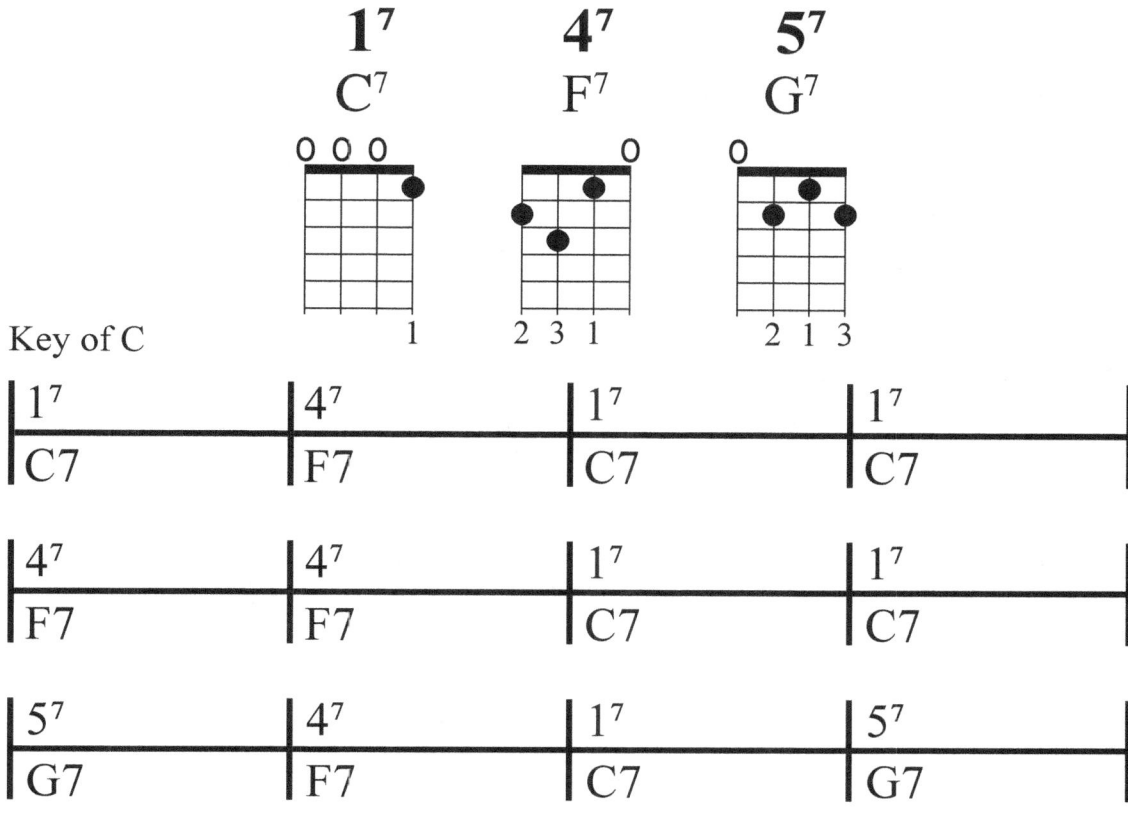

Key of C

1^7	4^7	1^7	1^7
C7	F7	C7	C7

4^7	4^7	1^7	1^7
F7	F7	C7	C7

5^7	4^7	1^7	5^7
G7	F7	C7	G7

This version of the 12 bar blues in F has several chord shapes you can choose from.

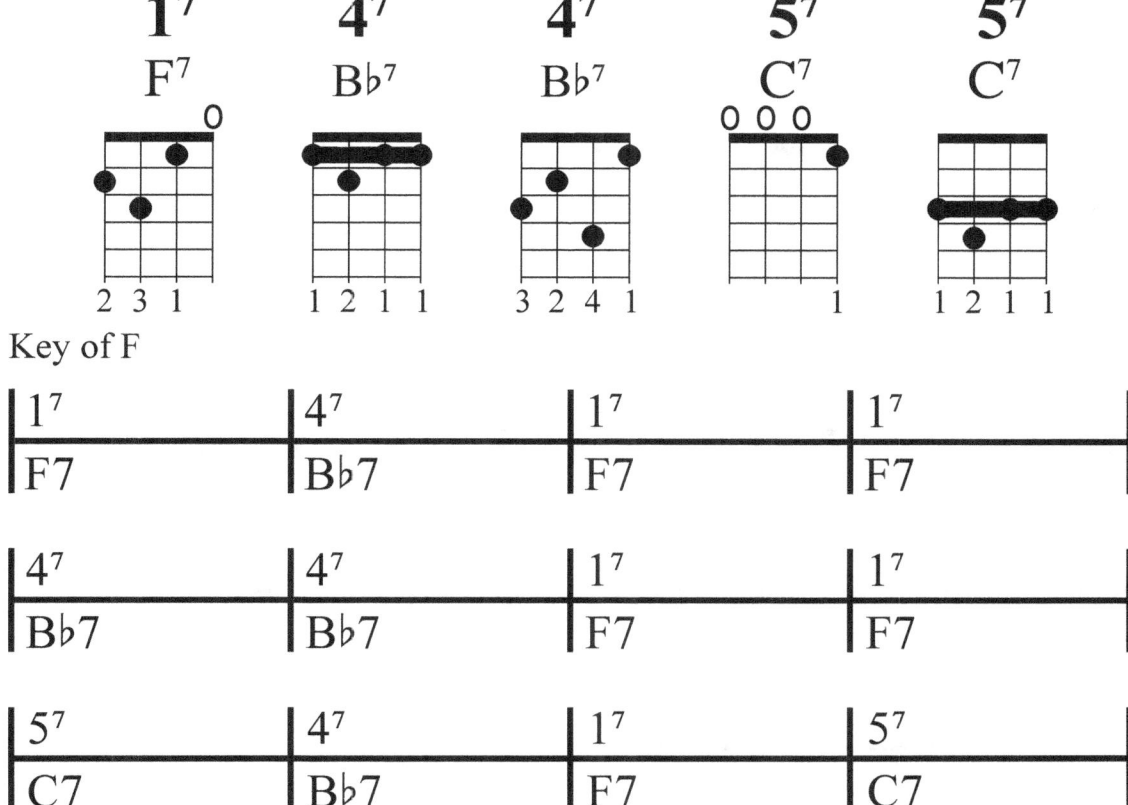

Key of F

1^7	4^7	1^7	1^7
F7	B♭7	F7	F7

4^7	4^7	1^7	1^7
B♭7	B♭7	F7	F7

5^7	4^7	1^7	5^7
C7	B♭7	F7	C7

In this version of the 12-bar blues, you can choose from several chord shapes and add a chromatic passing chord (D♭7) in the ninth measure.

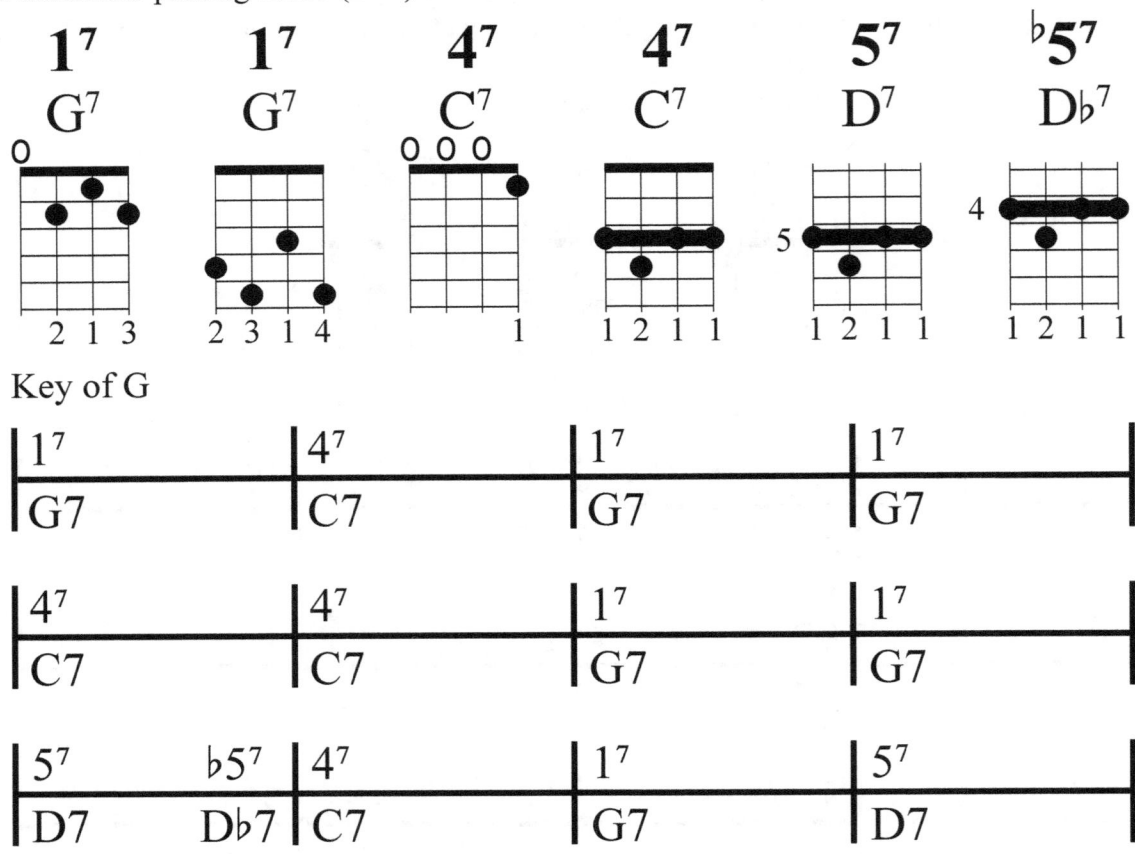

Key of G

1^7	4^7	1^7	1^7
G7	C7	G7	G7

4^7	4^7	1^7	1^7
C7	C7	G7	G7

5^7 $♭5^7$	4^7	1^7	5^7
D7 D♭7	C7	G7	D7

In our next 12 bar blues in C, we will substitute some of the the 7th chords with 9ths and add another chromatic passing chord (G♭9).

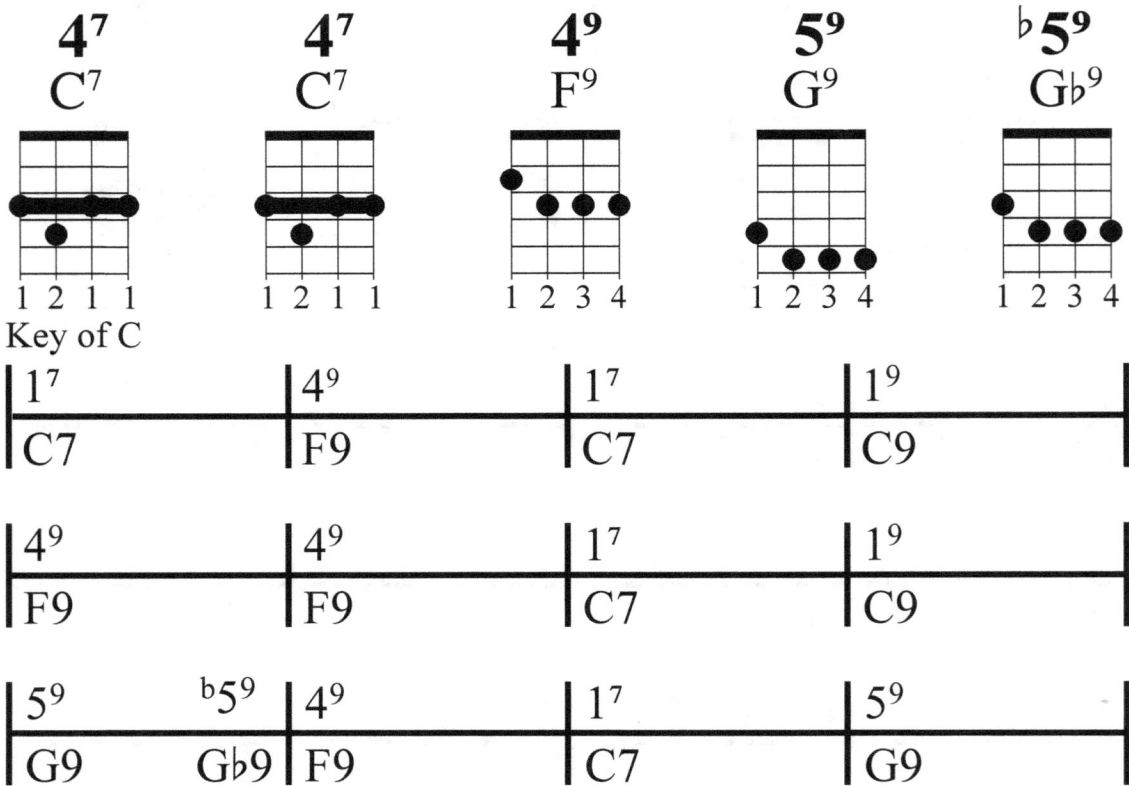

Key of C

1^7	4^9	1^7	1^9
C7	F9	C7	C9

4^9	4^9	1^7	1^9
F9	F9	C7	C9

5^9 $♭5^9$	4^9	1^7	5^9
G9 G♭9	F9	C7	G9

Jazz Blues - Next, we have a 12 bar jazz blues. The jazz progressions use alterations and substitutions for the dominant 7th chords.

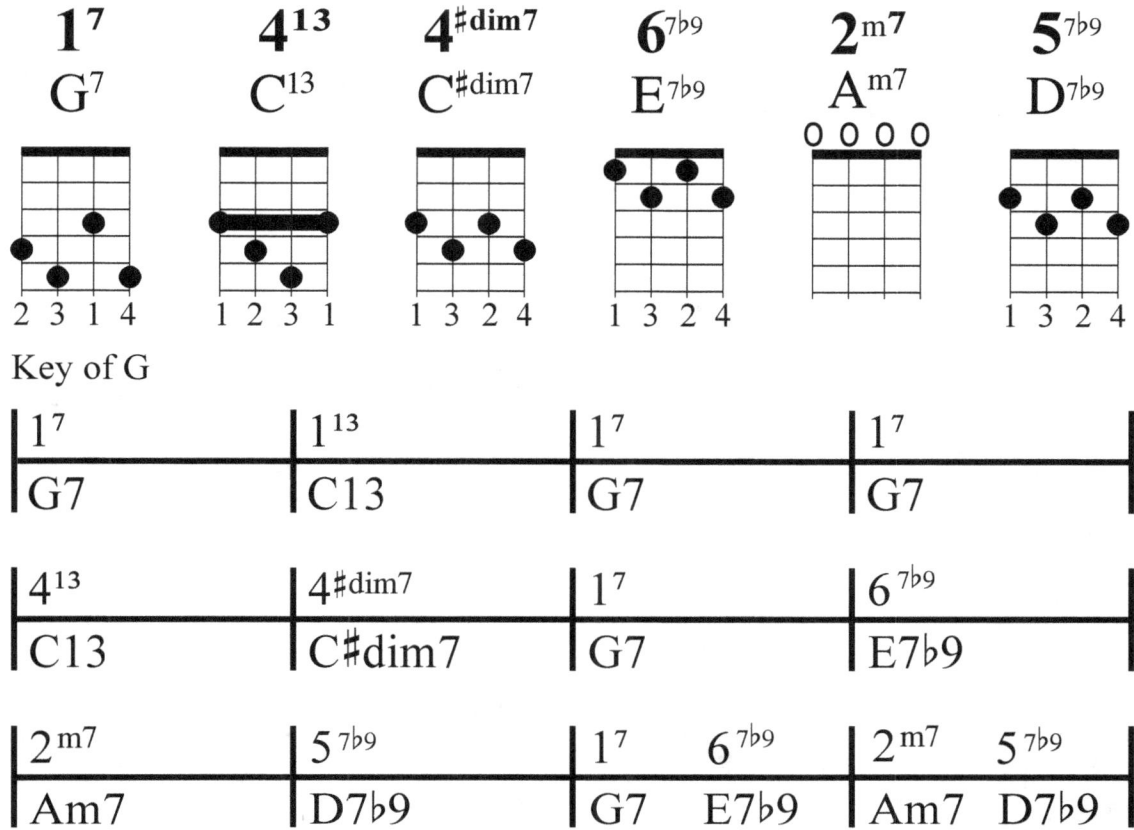

Key of G

1^7	1^{13}	1^7	1^7
G7	C13	G7	G7

4^{13}	$4^{\sharp dim7}$	1^7	$6^{7\flat9}$
C13	C#dim7	G7	E7♭9

2^{m7}	$5^{7\flat9}$	1^7 $6^{7\flat9}$	2^{m7} $5^{7\flat9}$
Am7	D7♭9	G7 E7♭9	Am7 D7♭9

Minor Blues - In our last variation on the 12 bar blues, we will shift to the key of C minor.

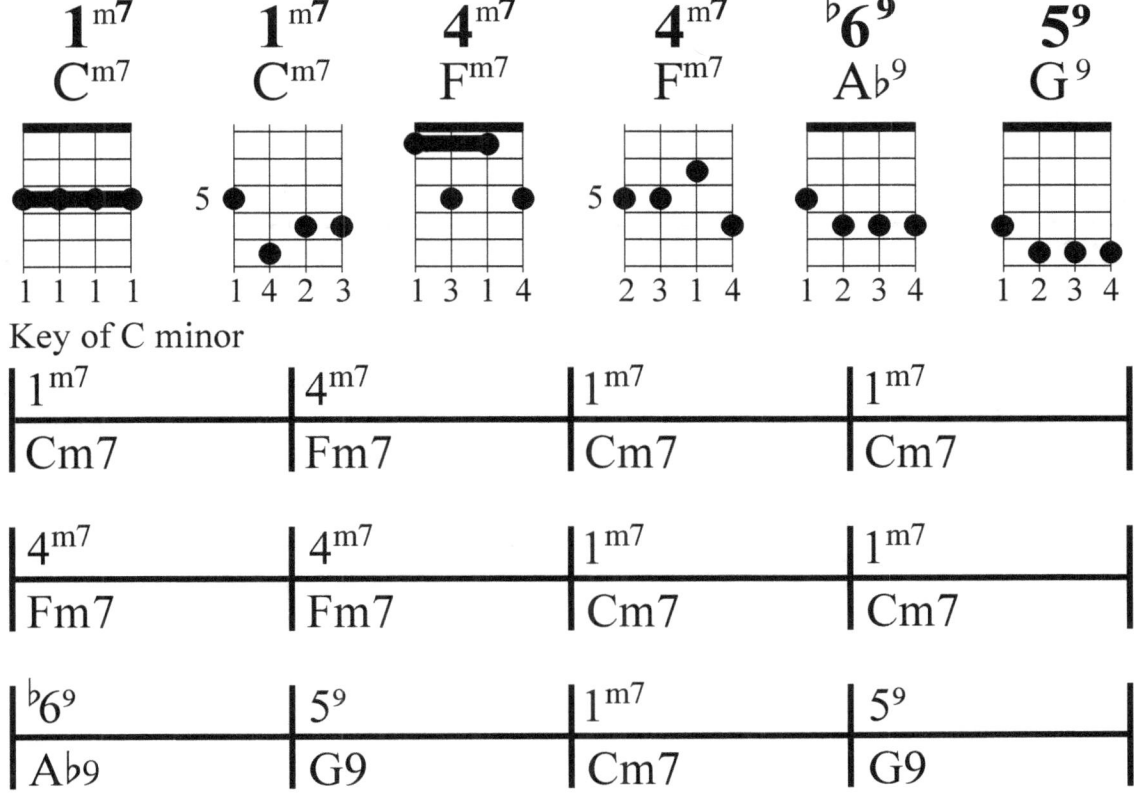

Key of C minor

1^{m7}	4^{m7}	1^{m7}	1^{m7}
Cm7	Fm7	Cm7	Cm7

4^{m7}	4^{m7}	1^{m7}	1^{m7}
Fm7	Fm7	Cm7	Cm7

$^\flat6^9$	5^9	1^{m7}	5^9
A♭9	G9	Cm7	G9

Circle of Fourths and Fifths Chord Progression

Here is a standard chord progression that jazz musicians practice. If you play from start to finish, you will be playing chords a perfect fourth apart; if you practice in reverse (finish to start), you will be playing chords a perfect fifth apart.

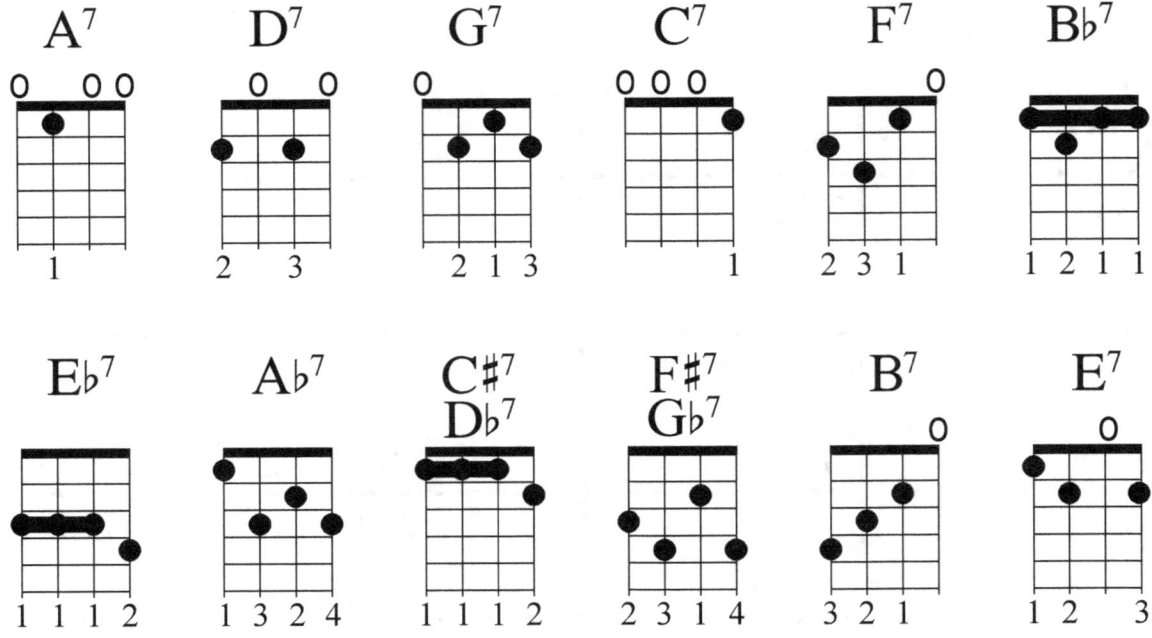

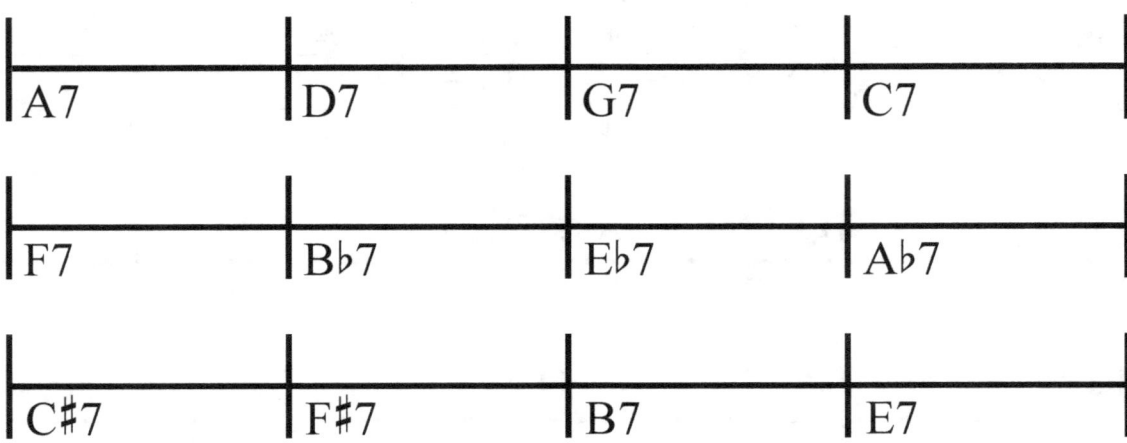

Jazz Chord Progressions - "Rhythm Changes"

Here is a well-known jazz chord progression in the key of C and F, often referred to as "Rhythm Changes."
The progression is similar to the song "I Got Rhythm" by George Gershwin. Use a swing rhythm.

Rhythm Changes in C

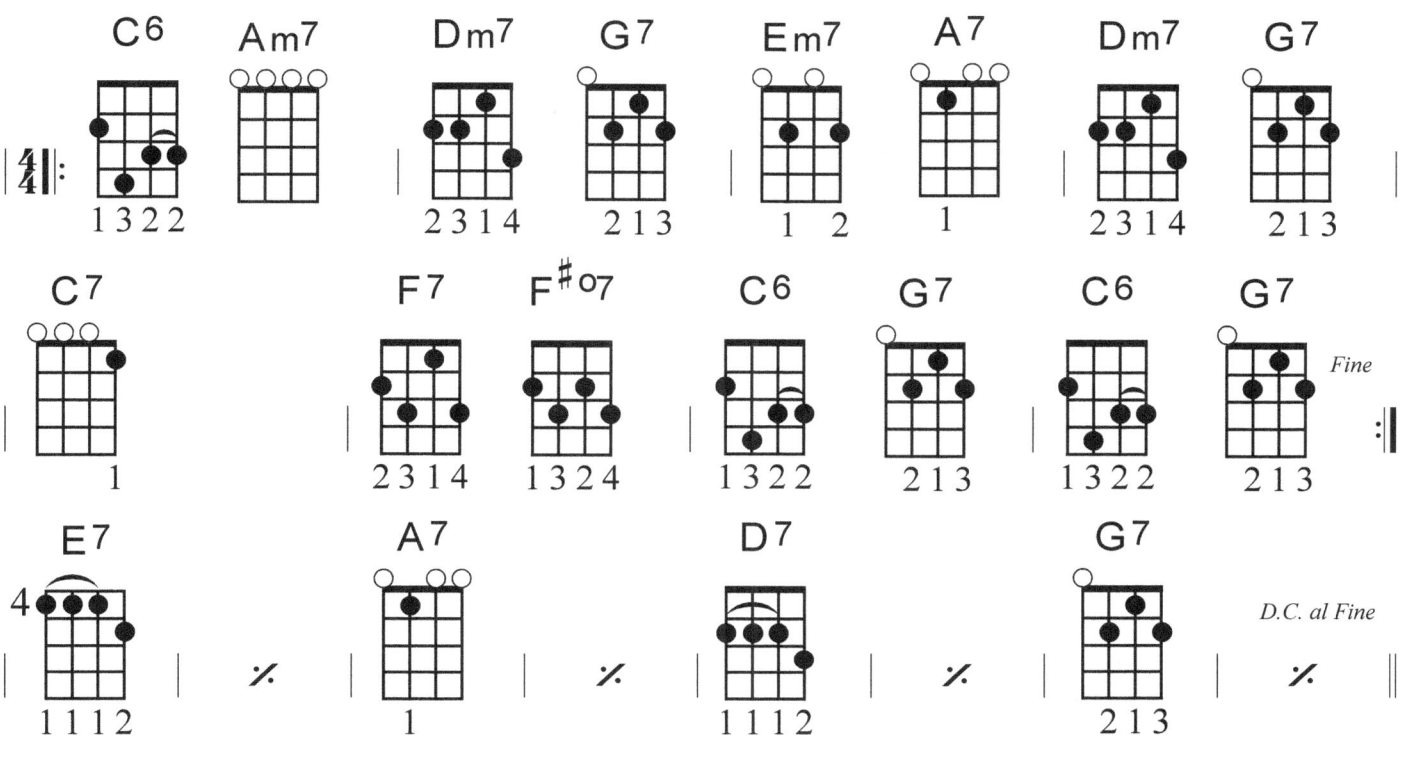

Rhythm Changes in F

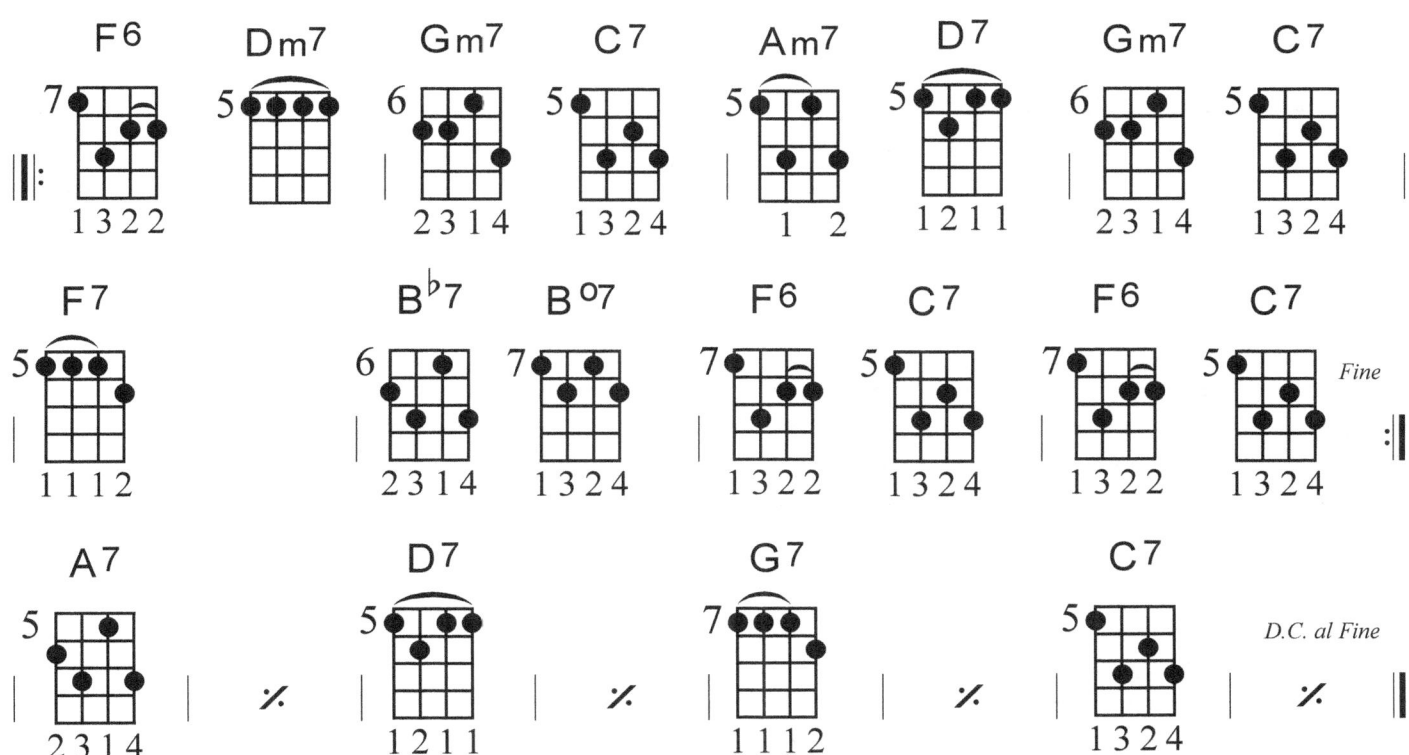

CHAPTER SEVEN – GRADED UKULELE PIECES

Now, it's time to put your ukulele skills into action with the graded pieces. Each piece in this section was carefully selected based on difficulty, hand and fretboard movement, tempo, and overall length.

I recommend you work through the pieces in order, focusing on perfecting each before moving on. Imagine you are preparing to perform the music for an exam or recital. Here are a few more tips to consider:

- Memorize the music.
- Work out all fingerings.
- Use a metronome.
- Play only as fast as your slowest section.

A typical scenario is being able to play most of the piece but struggling with a few specific bars. When this happens, isolate those bars and turn them into focused exercises. When you can play those bars with nearly 100% accuracy, then you are ready.

I always find it easier if you have a clear mental picture of how the tune sounds, so listen to the audio tracks on my website for a reference. While suggested tempos are provided, play at the speed that works for you and keep track of your progress.

Once you feel you have the piece as good as it will get, start a repertoire list. The repertoire list is a collection of pieces that you practice regularly and can perform with ease.

I should note that the fingerings indicated in the pieces worked for me, but you will likely come up with alternatives. Also, the right-hand fingering is optional for several reasons.

- Some players prefer a pick. Playing with a pick means you must adapt some pieces by omitting notes played on different strings or using a hybrid style (a combination of pick and finger techniques).
- If you play fingerstyle, alternate the fingers as often as possible. Occasionally, alternating may not be the best approach, but it is still a good general rule to follow.

Graded Ukulele Pieces:

*Audio tracks available online.

https://brentrobitaille.com/product/ultimate-ukulele-technique-warmup-book

Level 1 - Blues in C

In our first graded piece, we will play three variations on a standard 12-bar blues in the key of C. Notice the finger markings in the notation line. Play with a blues shuffle rhythm and practice with a metronome or blues pattern on a drum machine. The suggested tempo is between 104—116 bpm.

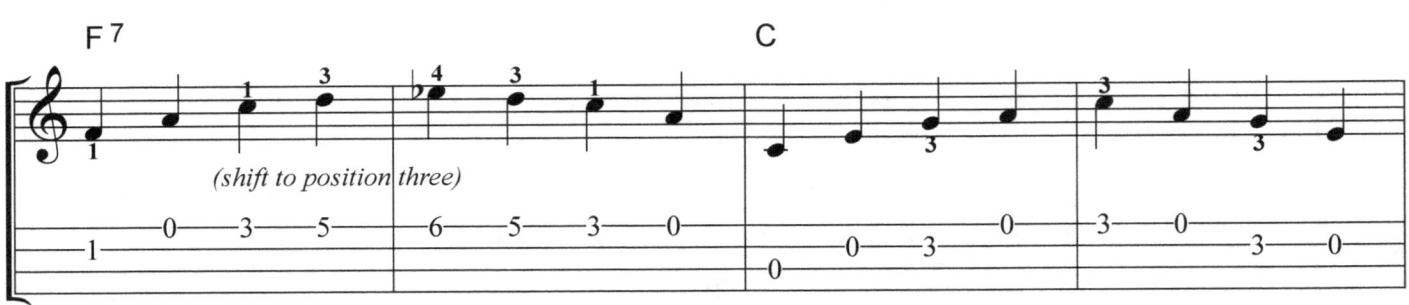

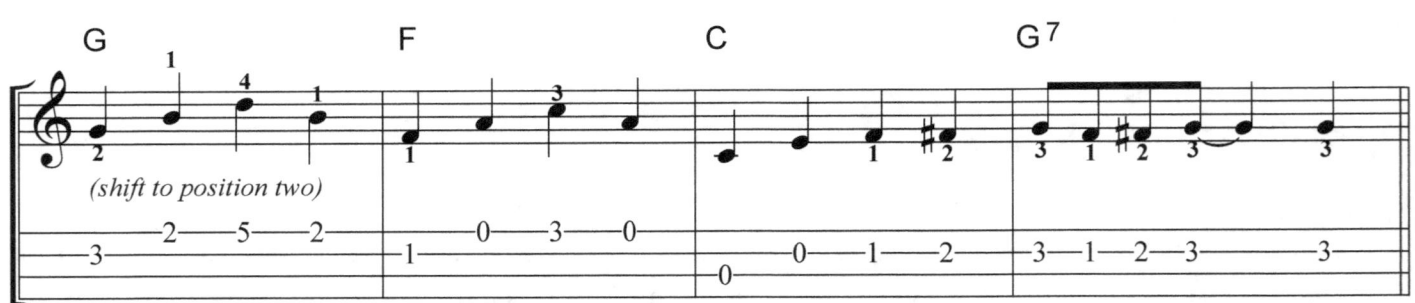

Variation #1 - Use alternate fingering or picking.

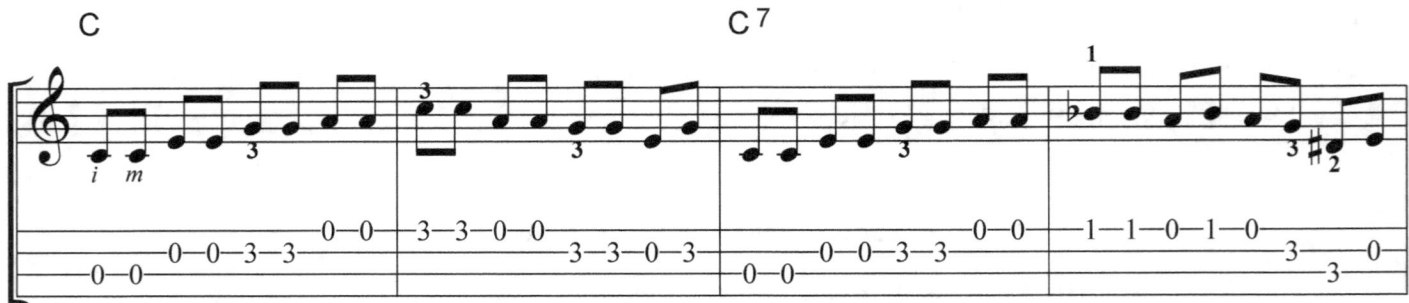

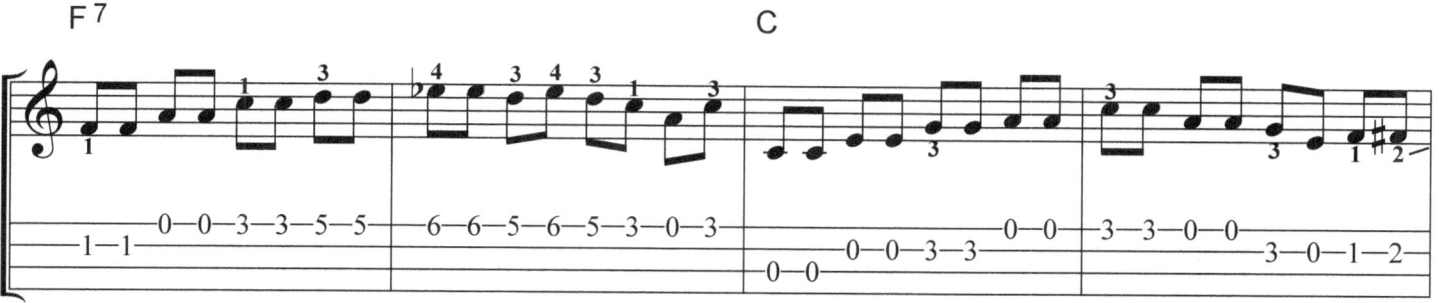

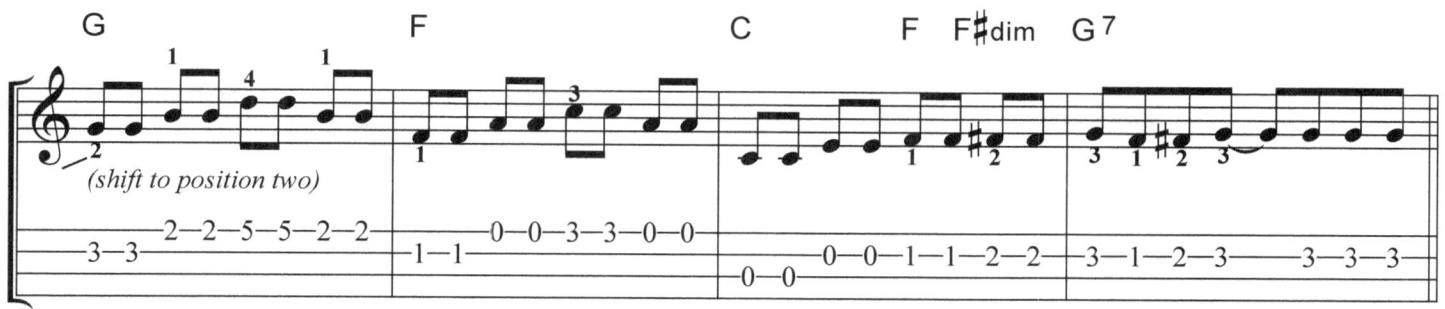

Variation #2 - Rests, Hammer-ons, Triplets and Slides

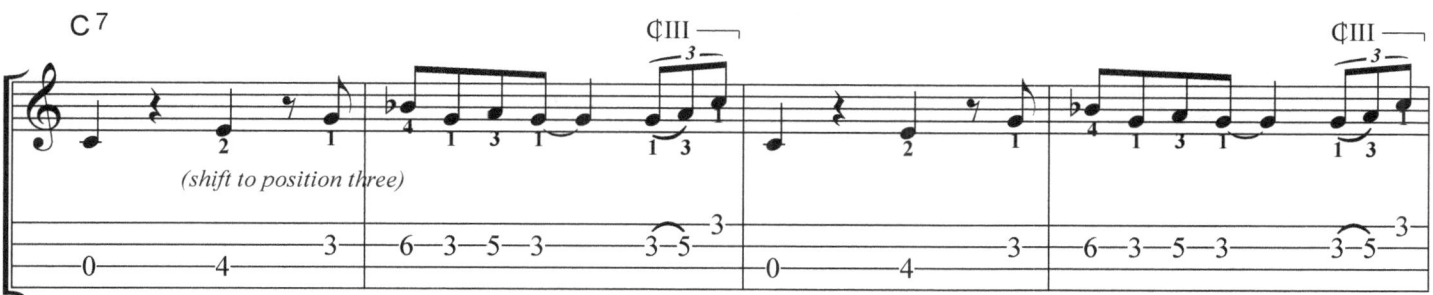

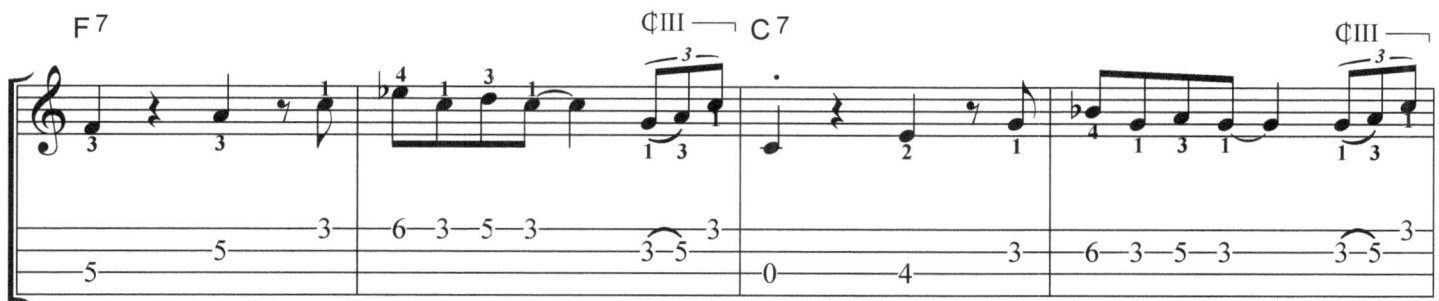

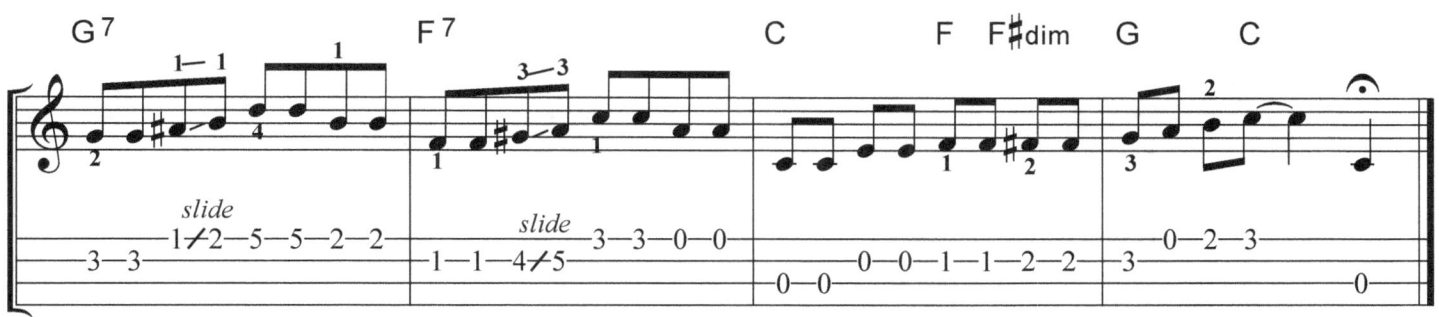

Level 2 - Minuet in G Major

(Transposed to F Major)

Christian Petzold
Previously attributed to J.S. Bach

  Our level two piece pulls from the classical repertoire and is an excellent study to develop hand position changes. For example, notice the change to position five in measures 3, 11, 19 and 22. Also, there are a few places where you will need to extend the 1st or 4th finger, such as in measures 17 and 21.

  We also introduce dynamics and phrase marks to add more scope and variety to Minuet in G (transposed to F to accommodate ukulele). Chords are included, so find a duet partner and play at a moderate tempo between 100—116 bpm.

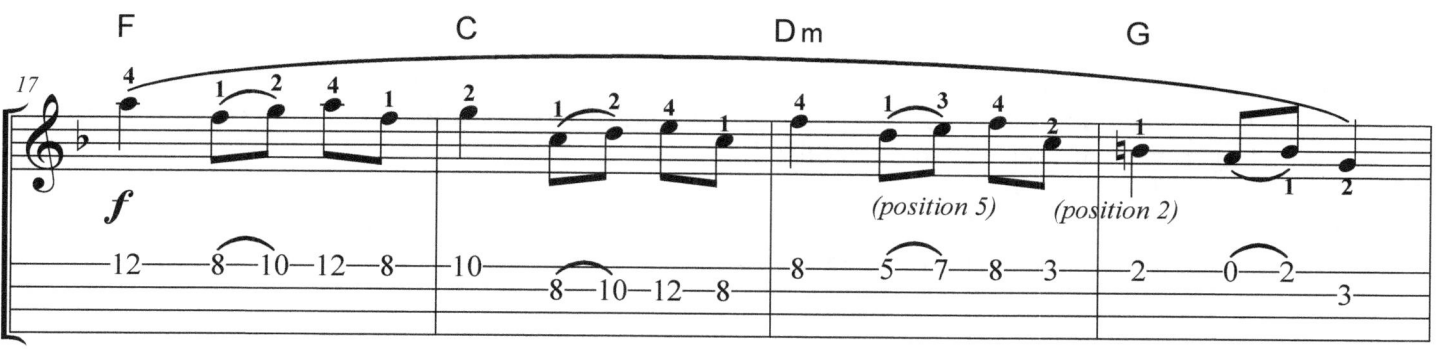

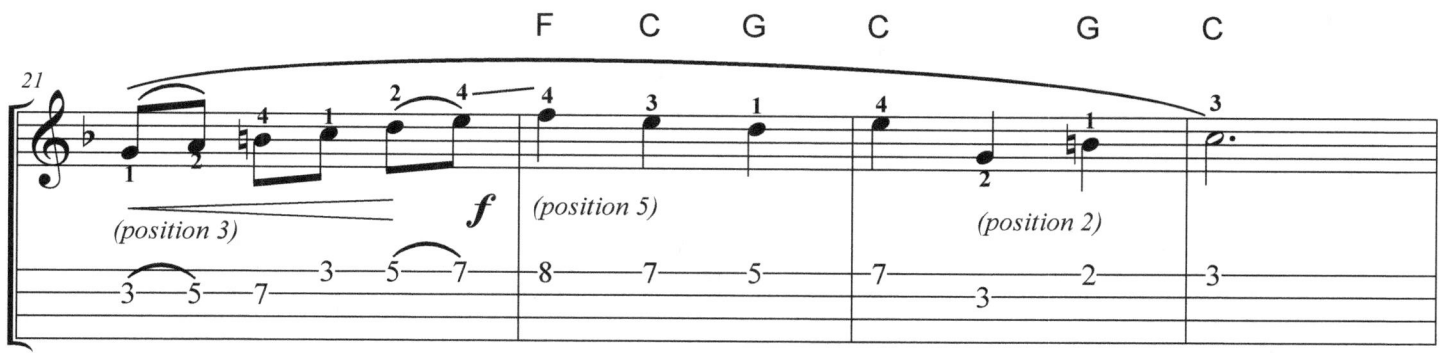

Level 3 - Fire On The Mountain

Bluegrass

The level three pieces may seem reasonably playable, but keep in mind bluegrass tunes often move at an alarming tempo. The sky is the limit for speed on both tunes, but start slow, follow a fingering and use an alternate fingering or picking with the right hand.

Pay particular attention to the extended fingerings in measure 9 and experiment with the 2nd and 3rd fingers to feel what works best in measure 11. The hammer-ons and pull-offs should help move the fingers along, but not set in stone. Work up to 160 bpm and start increasing the tempo from there.

Level 3 - Whiskey Before Breakfast

Our second bluegrass piece is arranged for fingerstyle ukulele playing. The right-hand finger markings are indicated below the notes, and the left-hand fingerings are above the notation line. Like all faster pieces, start very slowly and work through the fingerings, focusing on one hand at a time. Study the hand position changes from measures 11 to 13 and play at 160 bpm and up.

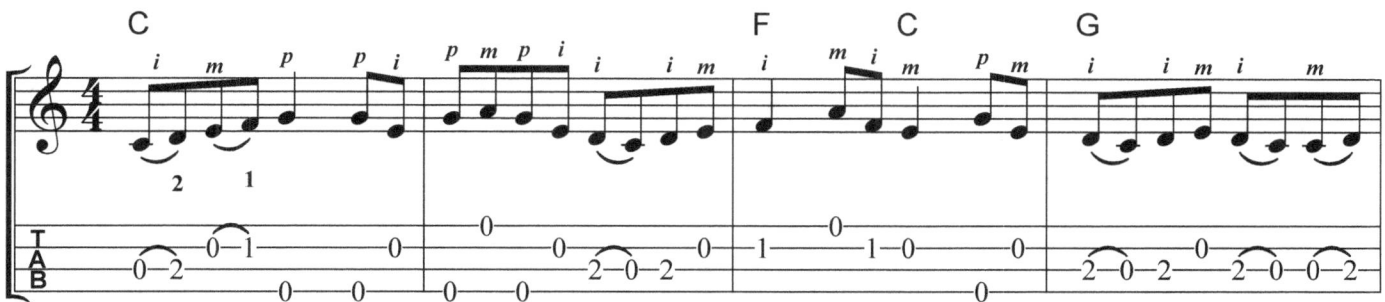

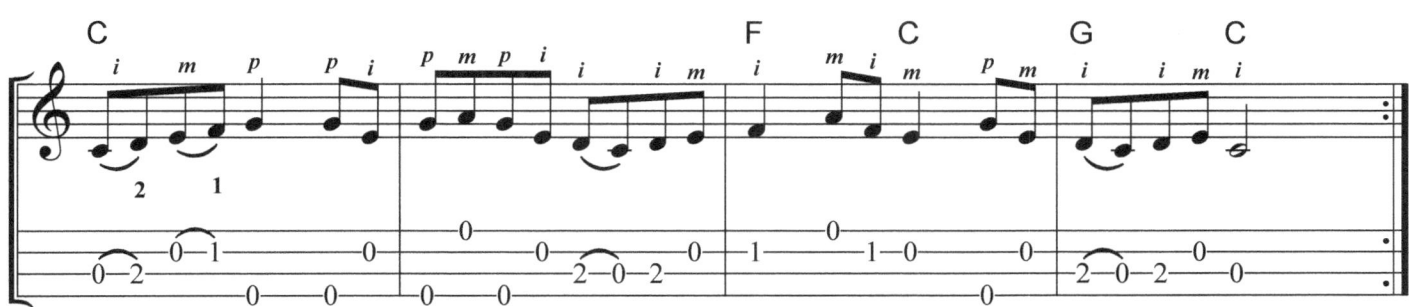

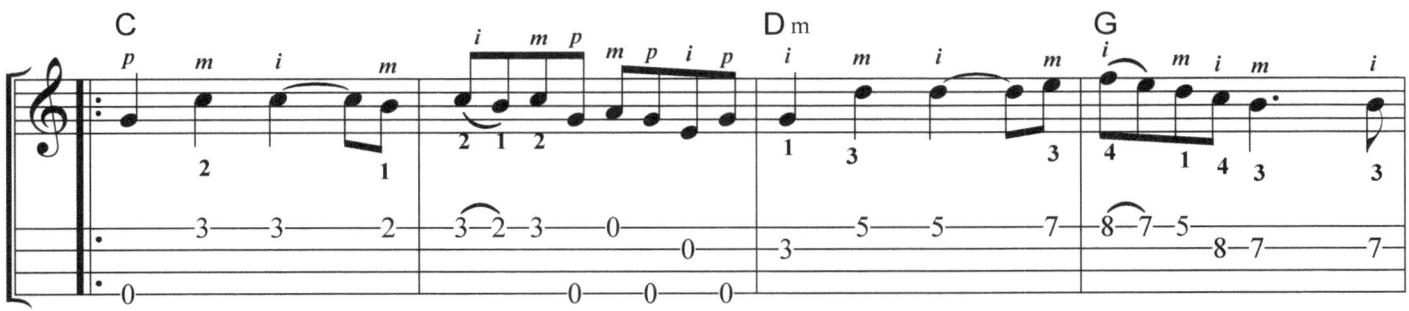

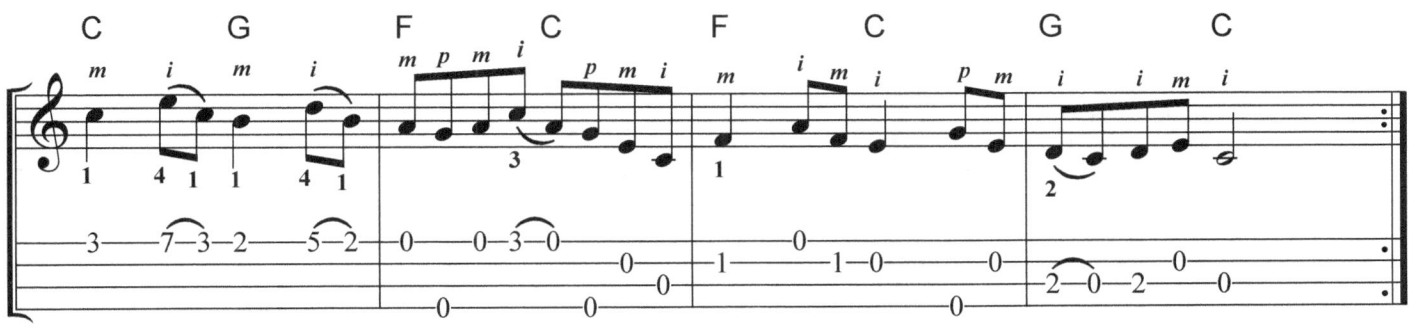

Level 4 - Für Elise

Wo0 59

Ludwig van Beethoven
(1770 - 1827)

Our level four piece is one of the most famous pieces ever written and is instantly recognizable by the first few notes. Beethoven's Fur Elise is played "very gracefully" with a flowing rhythm and phrasing. Identify and practice the more challenging hand position changes, barre chords and finger extensions separately.

Level 5 - Kesh Jig

Irish

The level five piece kicks it up with this well-known Irish tune, "Kesh Jig." Slowly work through the many hammer-ons and pull-offs with intricate and extended fingerings requiring rapid movements and hand position changes.

Ornamenting a note is essential to the Celtic style (measures 6,14,16, 21, 25 and 29), though often left up to the performer to improvise. Jigs are in 6/8 time and typically played quite fast, around 110-135 BPM. As in many advanced pieces of music, identify trouble spots, master the fingering and play with a metronome until memorized.

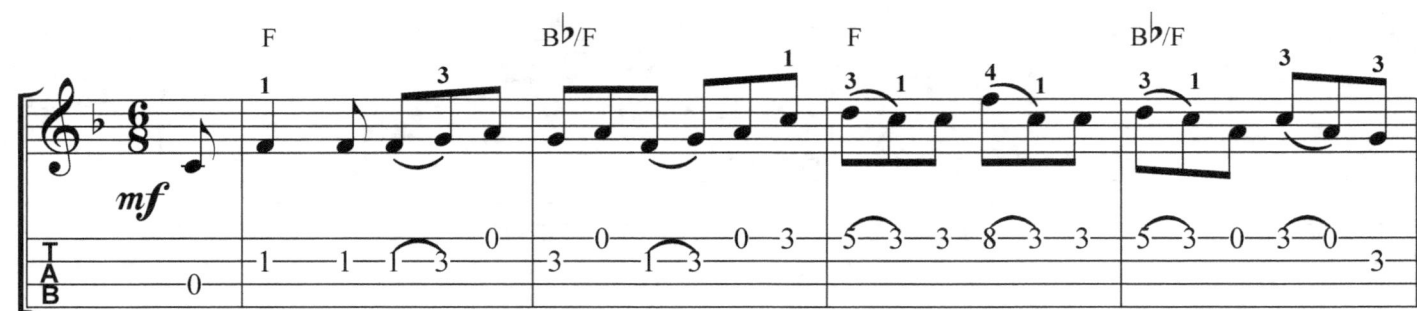

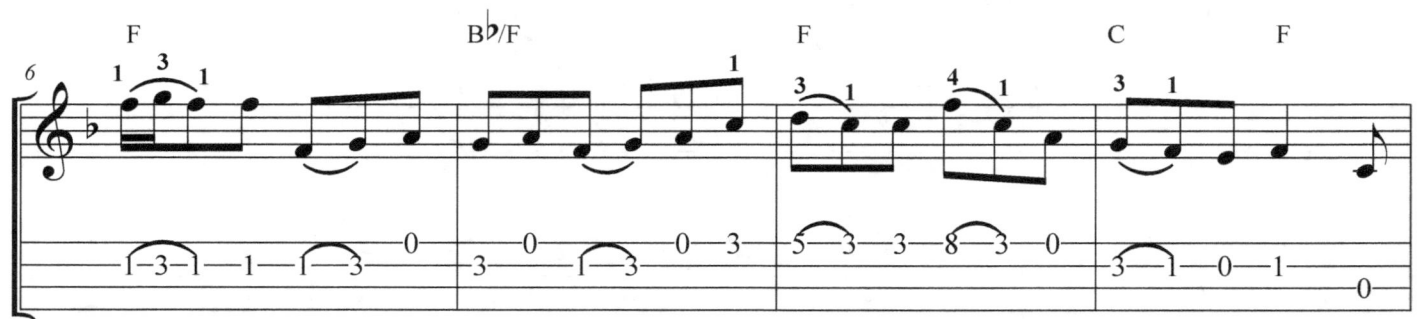

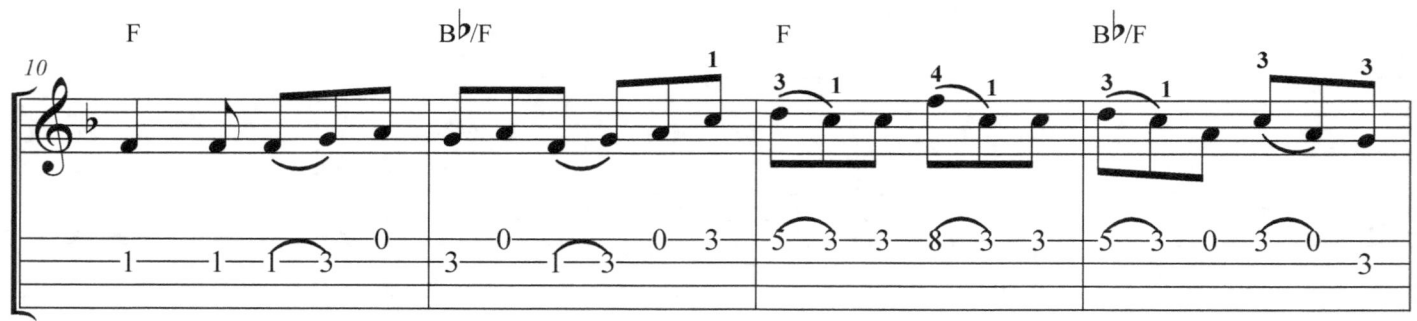

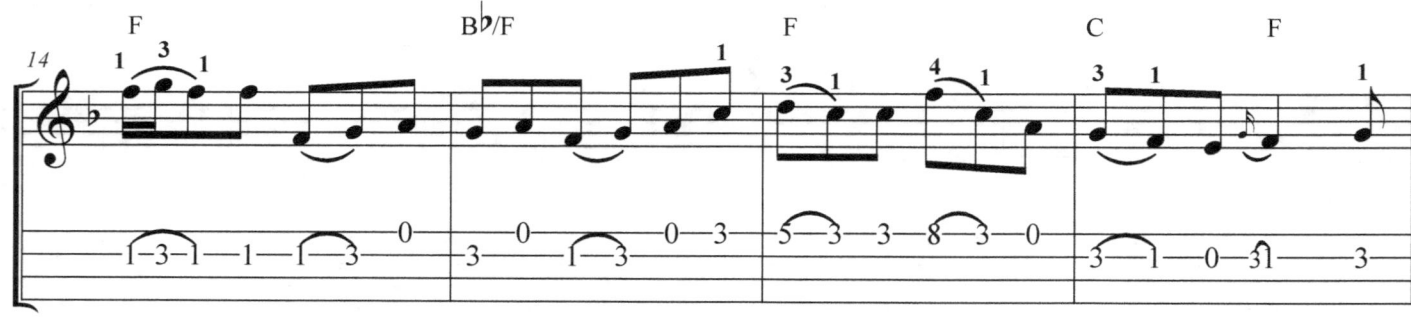

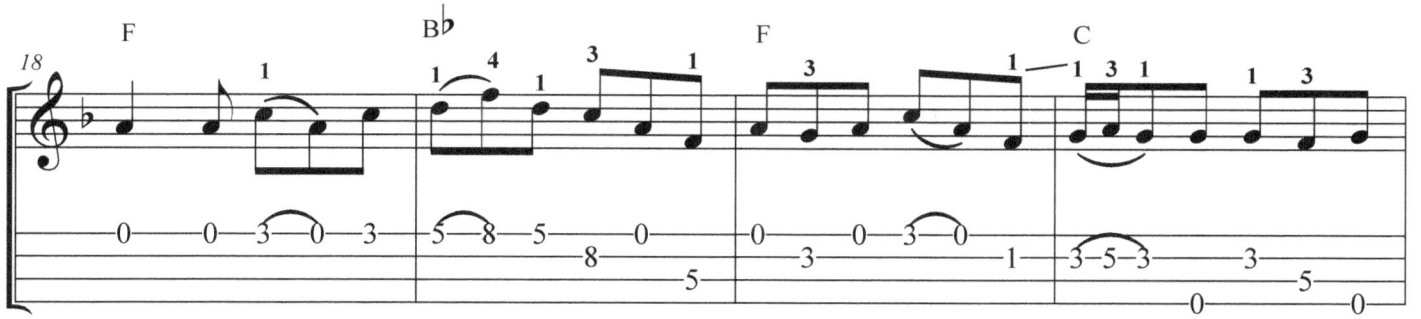

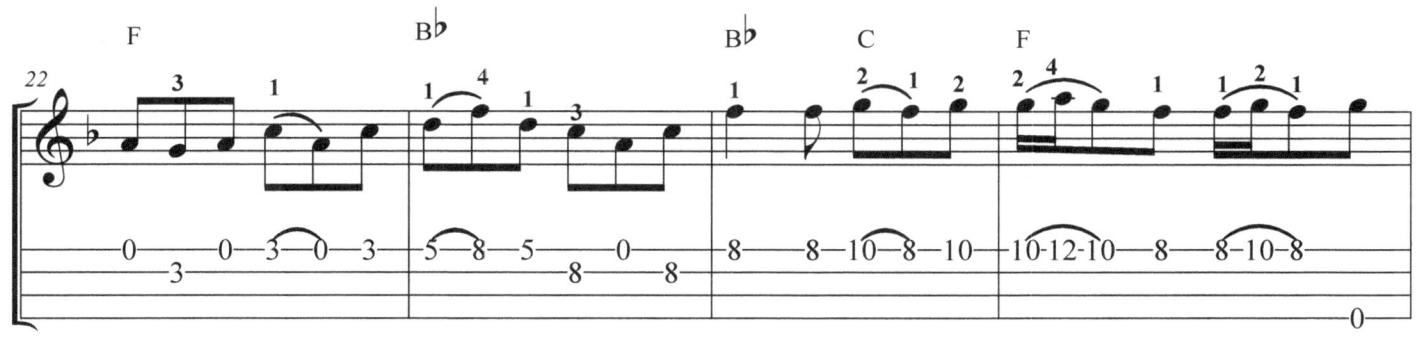

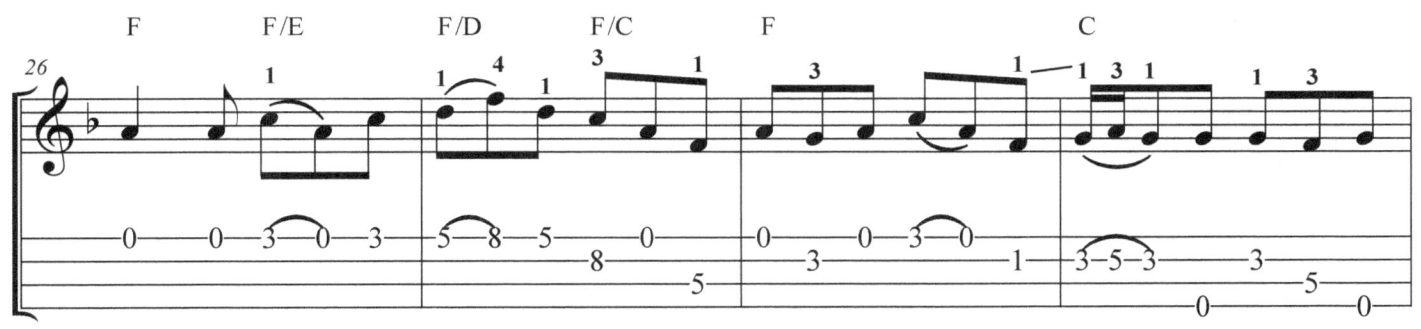

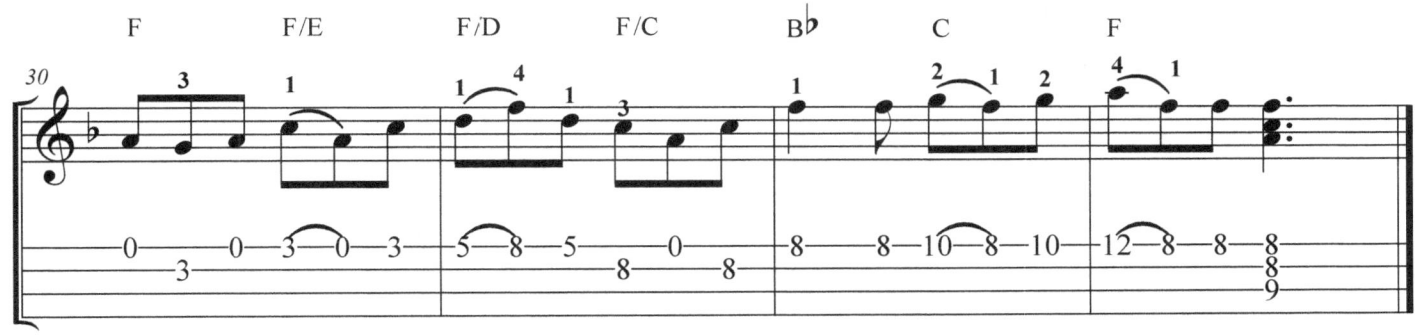

Level 6 - Blues for Chuck

Let's change up the style in our level six piece with an early rock and roll riff in the style of Chuck Berry. Riffs and solos in this style often use double stops with a barre (playing two notes together), hammer-ons, pull-offs, and slides. A suggested BPM would be between 108-120 with a shuffle rhythm and aggressive attack on the strings.

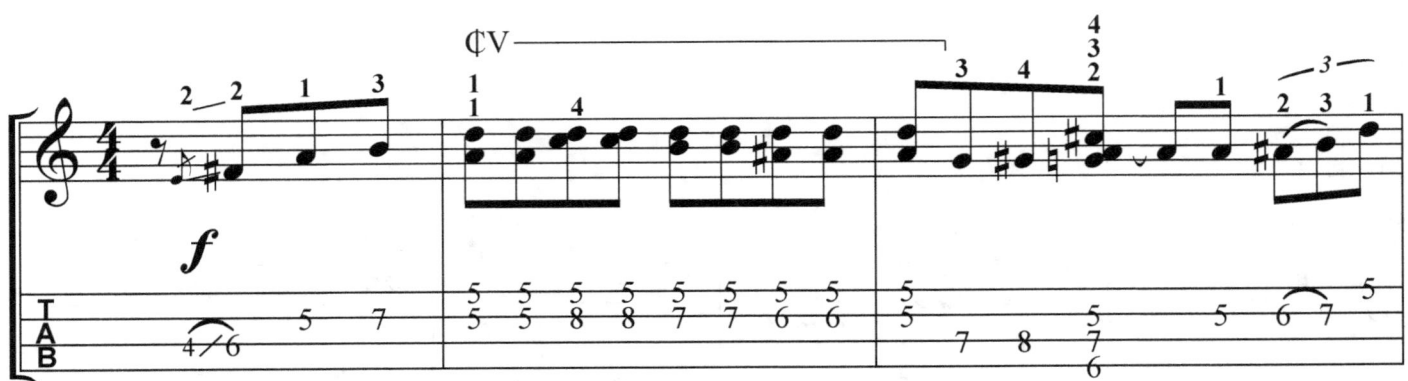

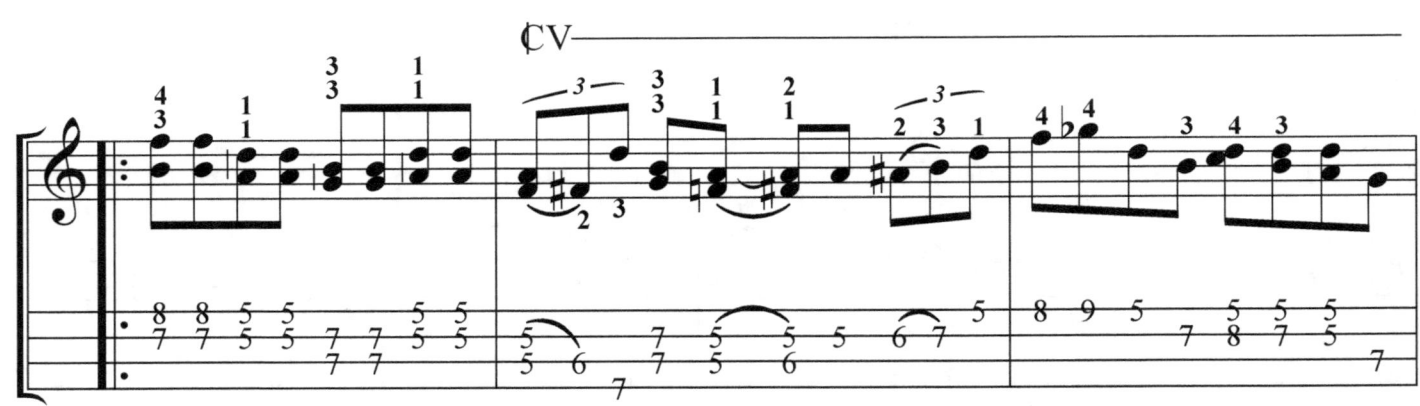

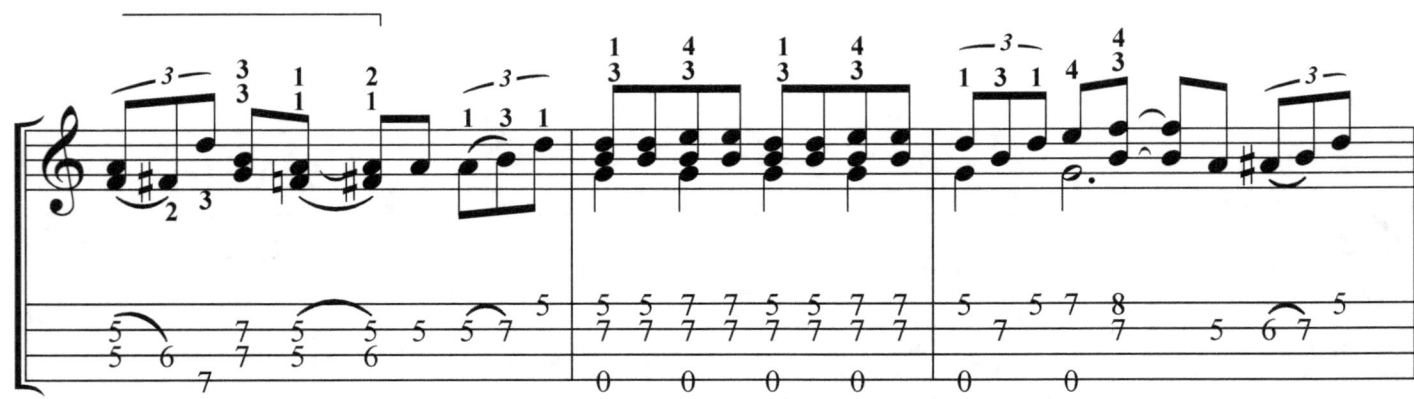

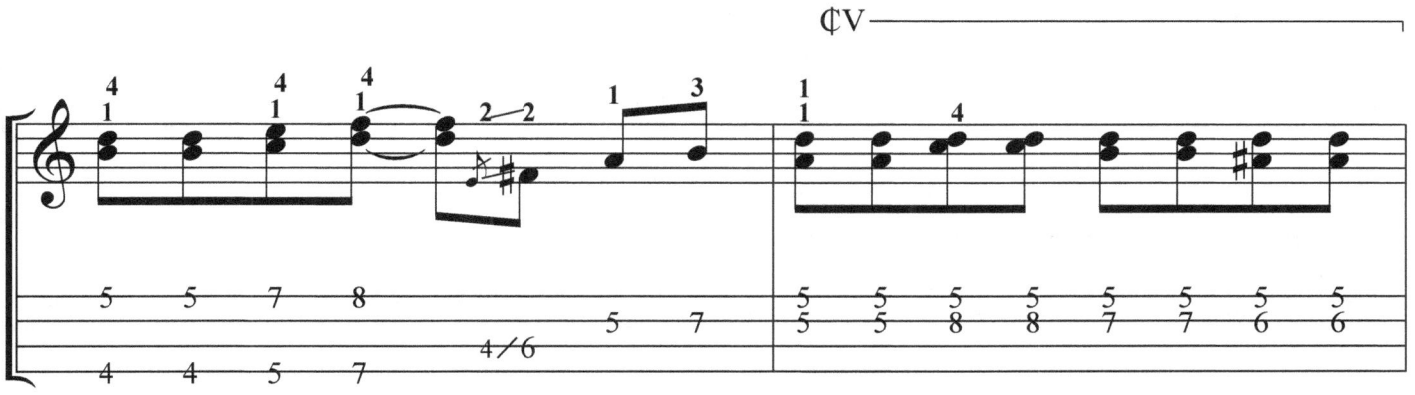

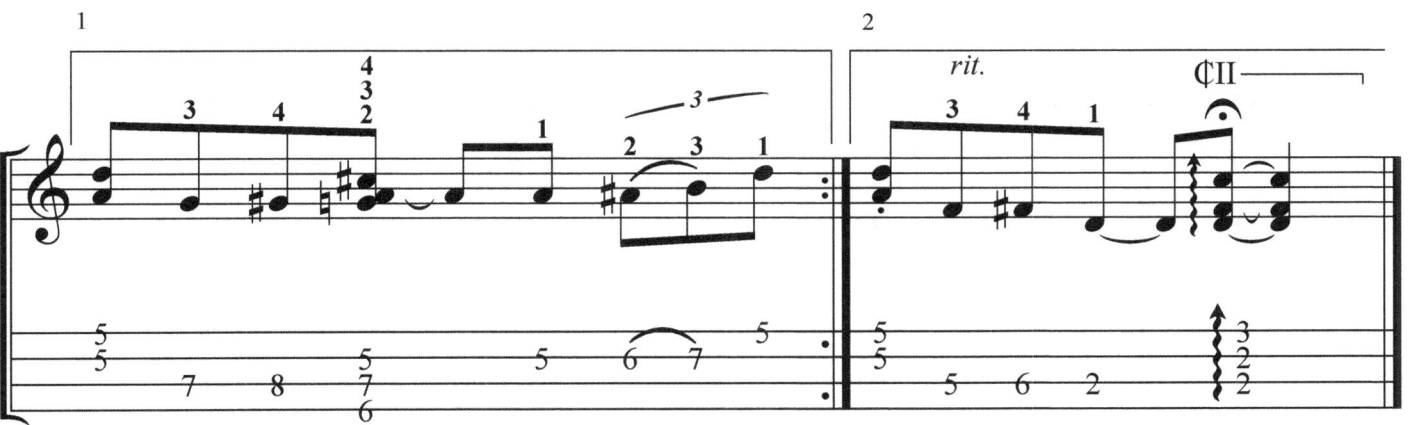

Level 7 - Cello Suite - Prélude No. 1

J.S. Bach

Grading ukulele pieces is not exactly a science, so take the complexity of the graded pieces with a grain of salt. The level seven piece is Bach's Cello Suite No. 1 in G major, BWV 1007. We transpose to the key of C to make it playable and accommodate the range on the ukulele. This arrangement will be very challenging for most players and take many months of practice to perfect. The best advice is to listen to a recording on cello and become very familiar with the tune and phrasing. Recognizing the melody will considerably speed up learning when you begin playing the piece. Please take all the techniques you have developed so far and apply them accordingly.

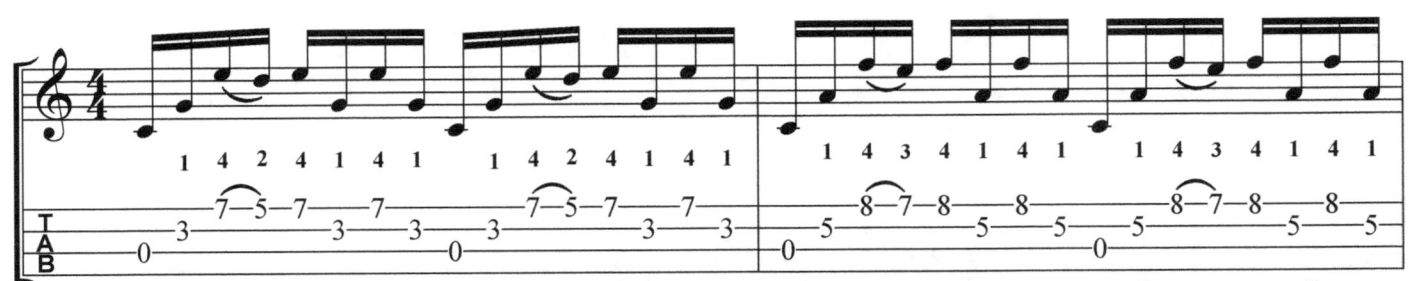

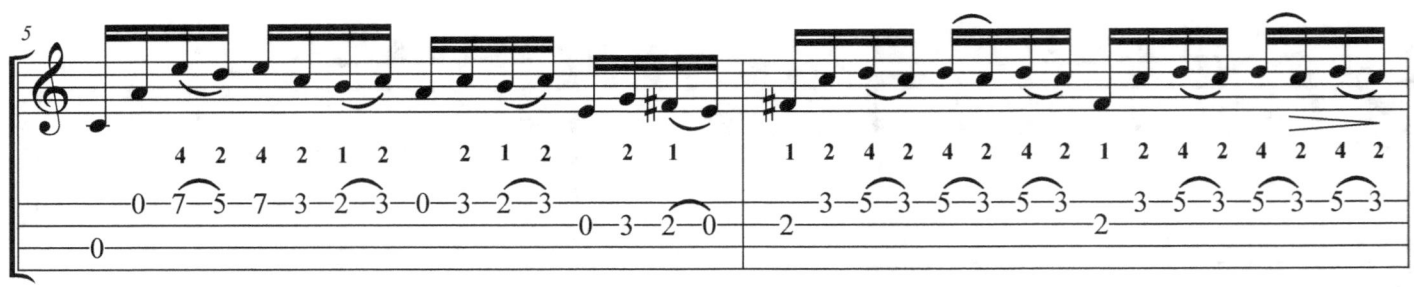

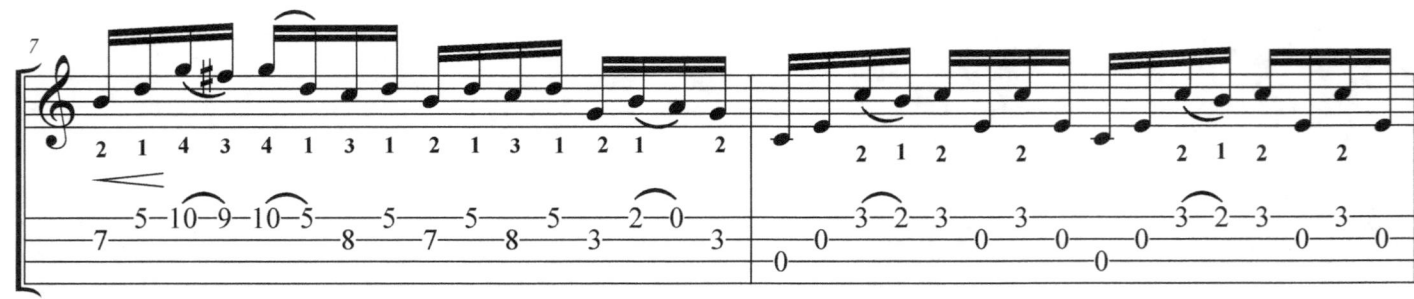

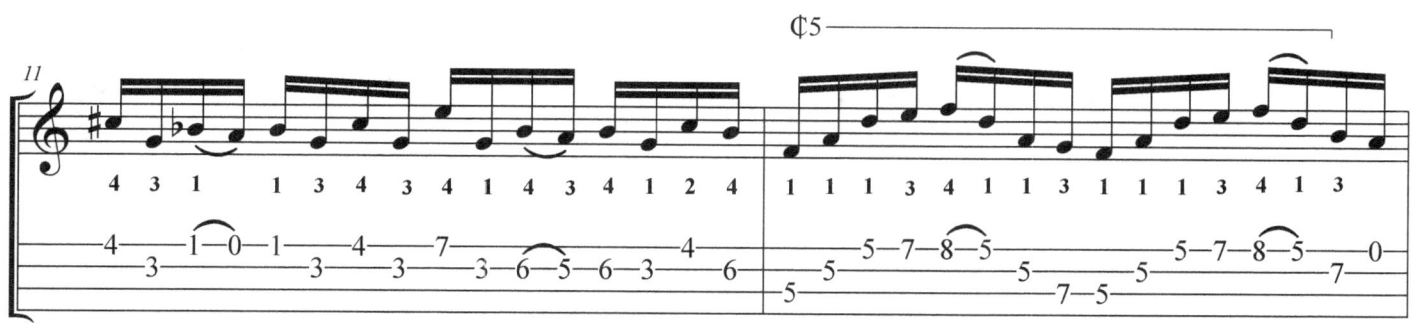

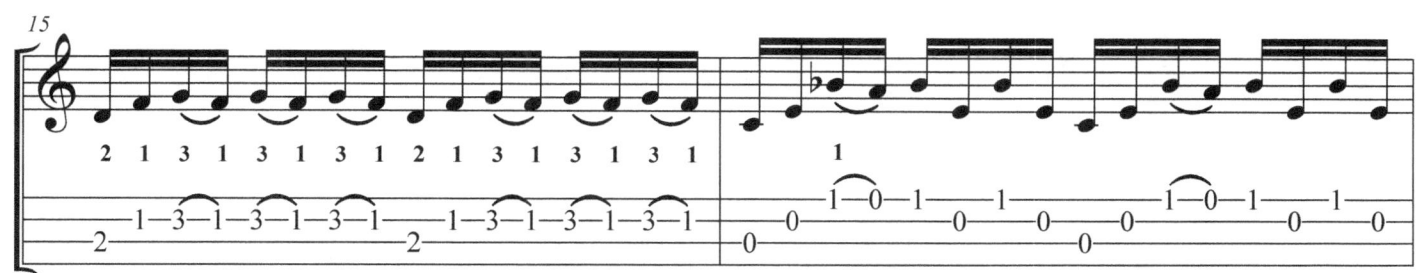

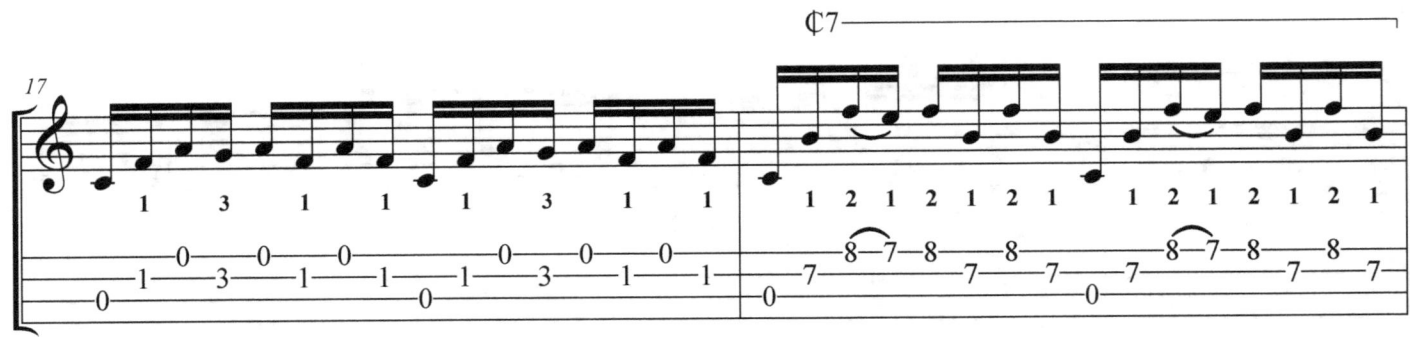

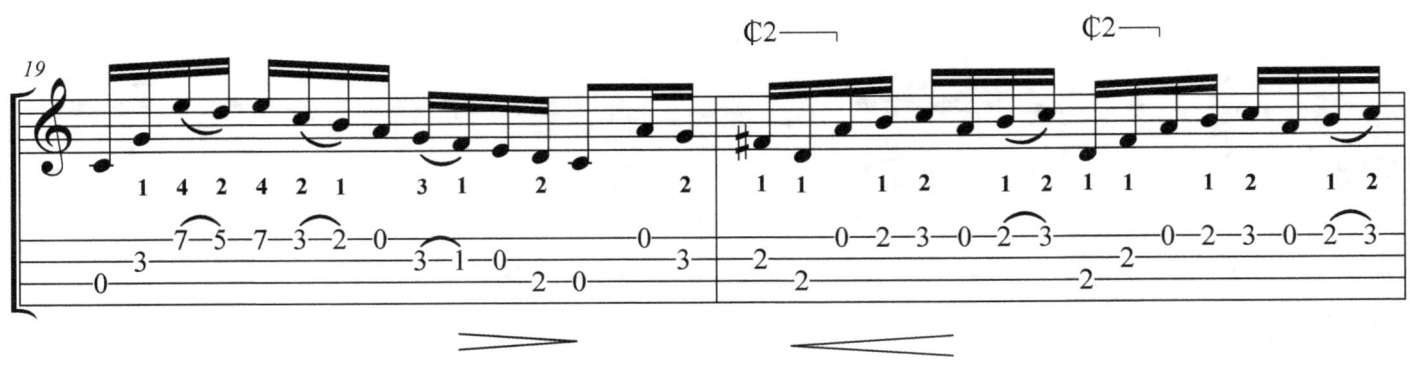

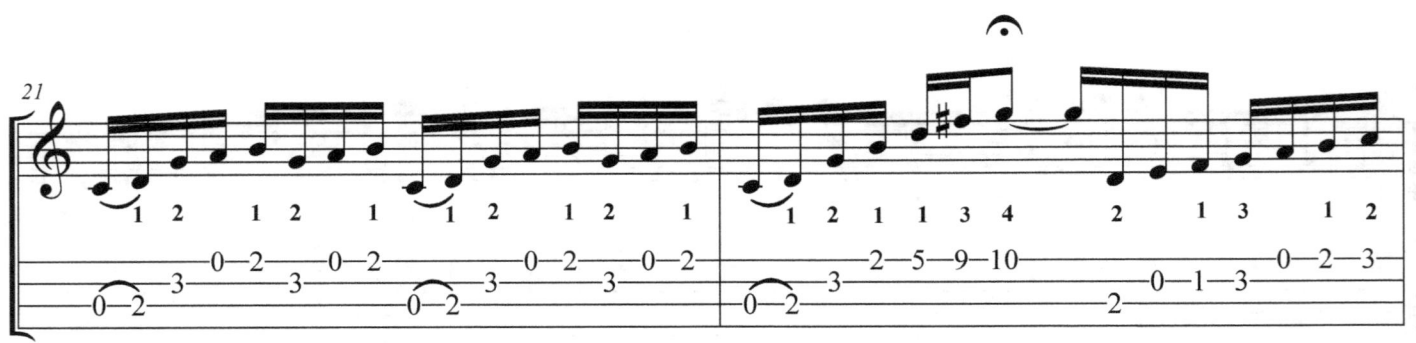

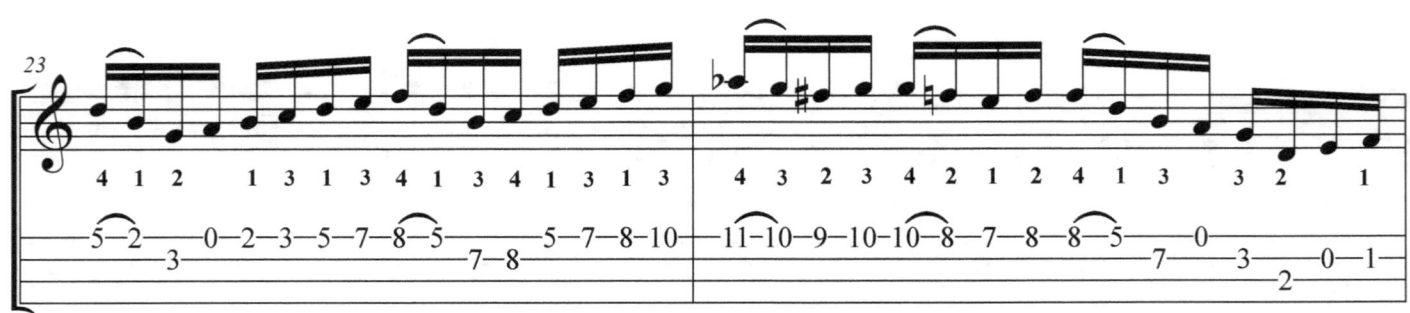

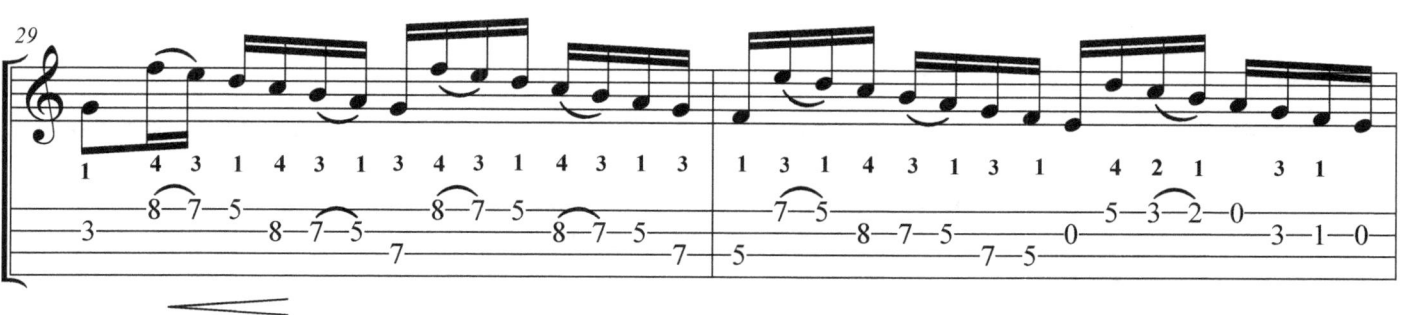

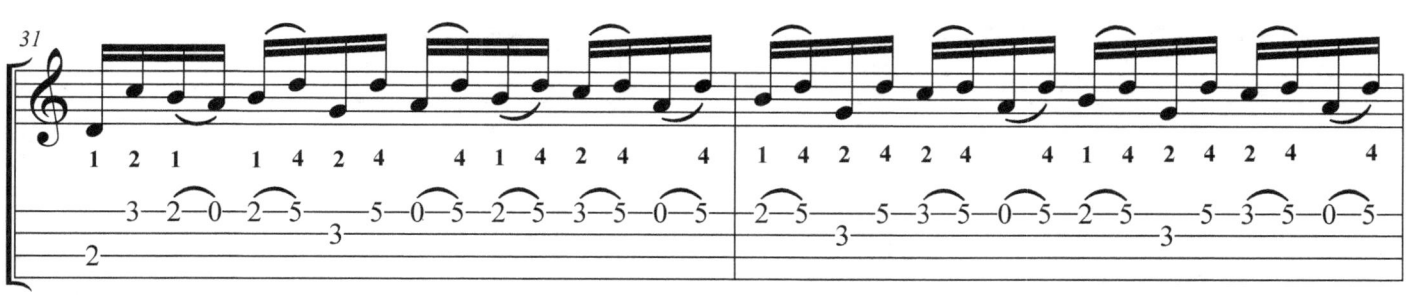

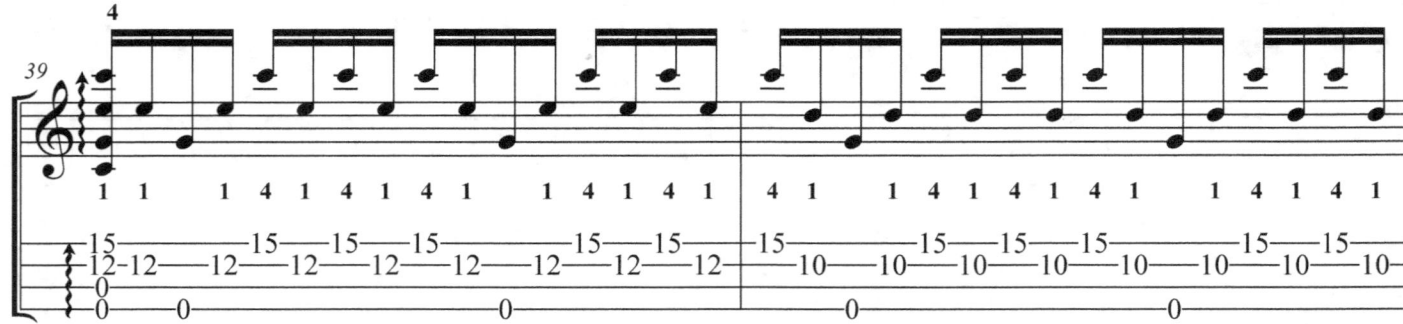

Level 8 and Beyond - Flight of the Bumblebee

Nikolai Rimsky-Korsakov (1899)

   Flight of the Bumblebee is an iconic showpiece that has long challenged the world's finest musicians. Don't feel like you have to master this one; use it as an ultimate exercise. Study this piece one note, measure and phrase at a time until you can play the whole piece extremely slowly. If you listen to the audio online, the first recording is very slow and intended for learning purposes, with a tempo of around 25 beats per minute (bpm). The subsequent four recordings gradually increase in speed: recording 2 = 40 bpm, recording 3 = 56 bpm, recording 4 = 112 bpm, and recording 5 = 156 bpm. The faster recordings were digitally sped up to give you an idea of how the tune is meant to sound at faster tempos. Also, the fingering has been added above the tab line for convenience.

   If learning the entire piece is too much, consider breaking it down into small sections and turning them into technique exercises. For example, take the first two measures and work on hand position changes and accurate tone production. The possibilities are pretty endless!

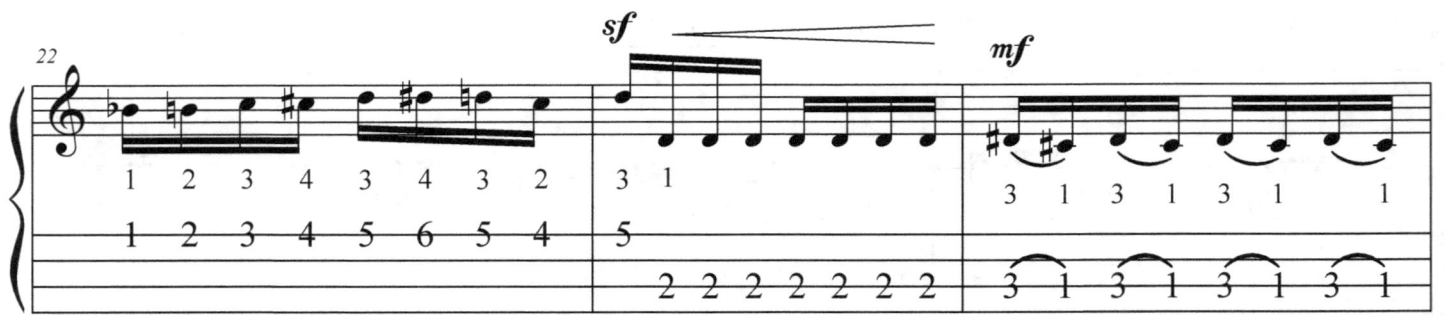

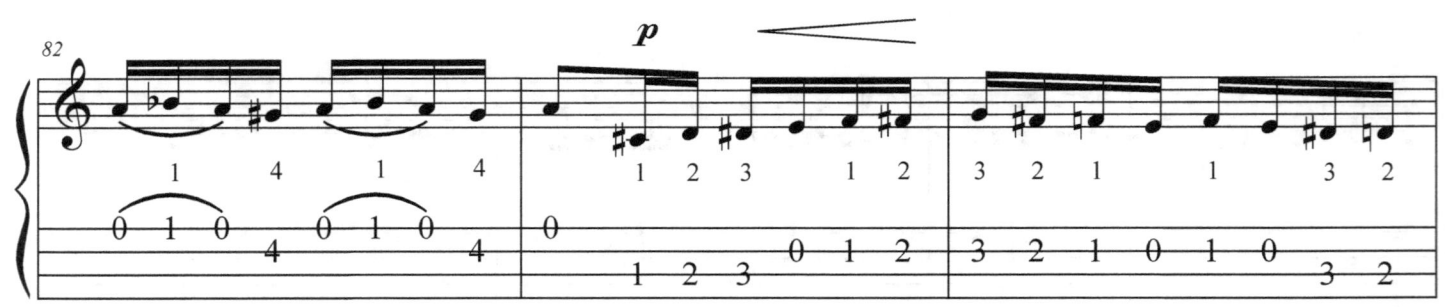

* Binded books create problems when turning pages, so if you want to print all the graded pieces
(digital PDF), then contact me at my website and use the code: **UUTB25**

CHAPTER EIGHT – UKULELE RESOURCES

Our last section of the book is a compilation of many helpful ukulele charts to expand your fretboard, scale, chord, and arpeggio knowledge. We will start with moveable scales below. The square indicates the root of the scale, and the numbers are fingering suggestions. These scale patterns are commonly used for improvisation, composition, and to improve finger positioning.

MAJOR   1 2 3 4 5 6 7

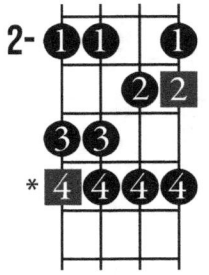 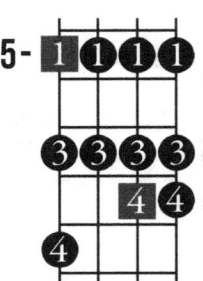 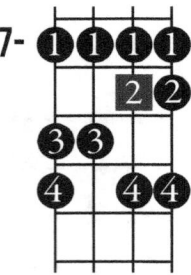 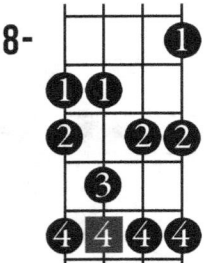 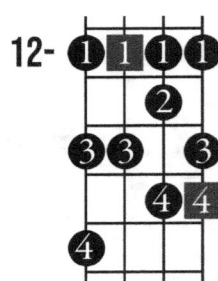

MINOR   1 2 ♭3 4 5 ♭6 ♭7

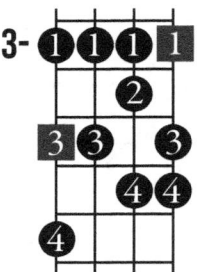 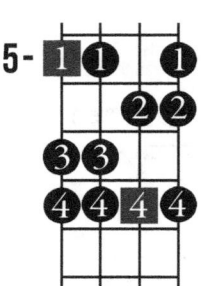 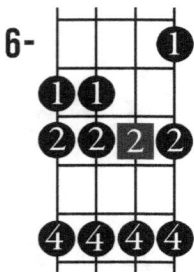 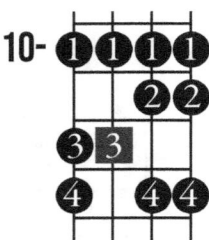 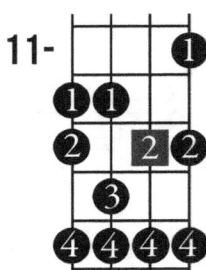

MIXOLYDIAN MODE   1 2 3 4 5 6 ♭7

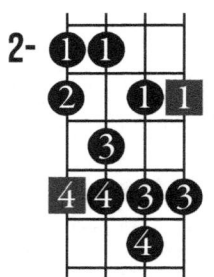 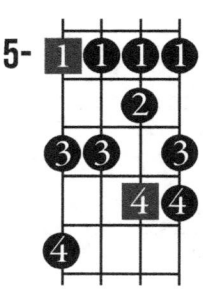 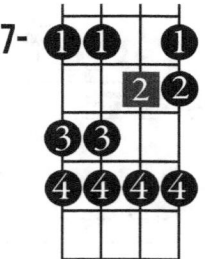 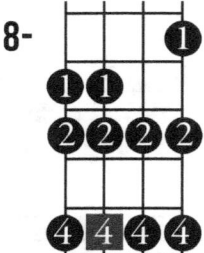 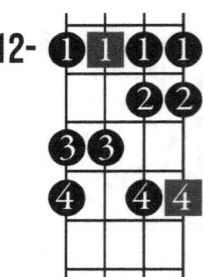

DIMINISHED*   1 2 ♭3 4 ♭5 ♭6 6 7   ## WHOLE TONE*   1 2 3 ♯4 ♯5 ♯6

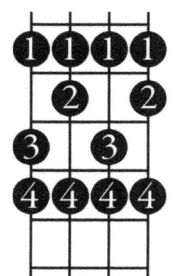

Any note can be the root in diminished and whole tone scales.

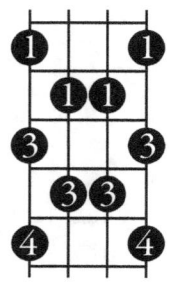

*
■=ROOT

BLUES & PENTATONIC UKULELE SCALES

BLUES MINOR   1 ♭3 4 ♭5 ♮5 ♭7

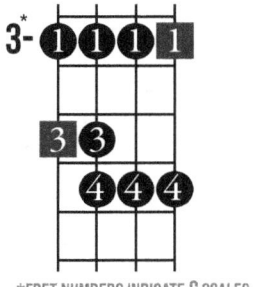 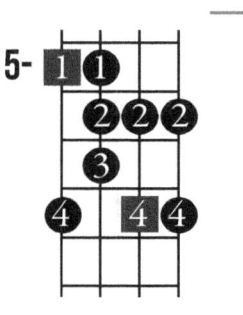 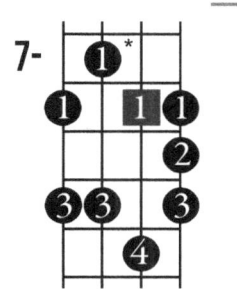 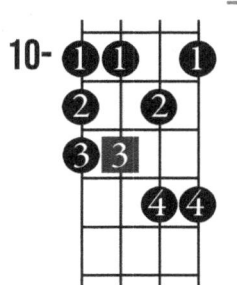 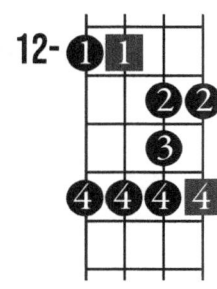

*FRET NUMBERS INDICATE C SCALES.

*ALTERNATE CROSS FINGERING. EXPERIMENT WITH DIFFERENT FINGERINGS ON ALL SCALES.

BLUES MAJOR   1 2 ♭3 ♮3 5 6

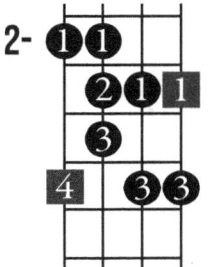 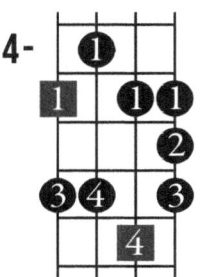 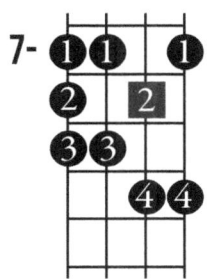 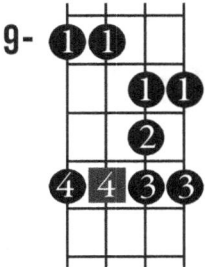 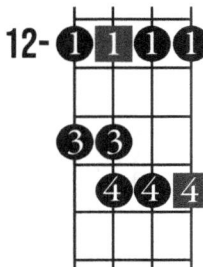

PENTATONIC MINOR   1 ♭3 4 5 ♭7

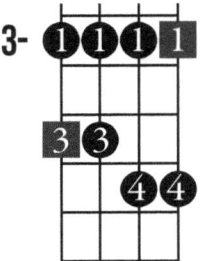 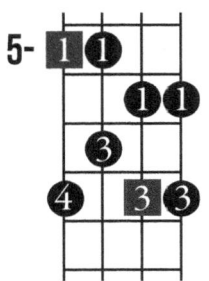 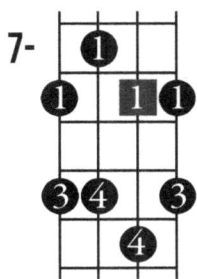 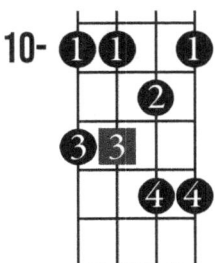 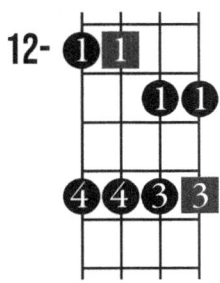

PENTATONIC MAJOR   1 2 3 5 6

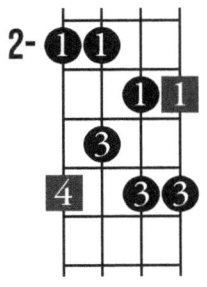 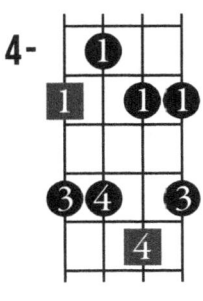 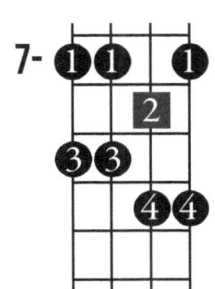 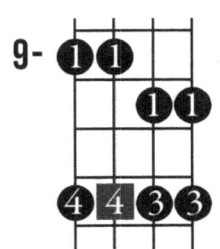 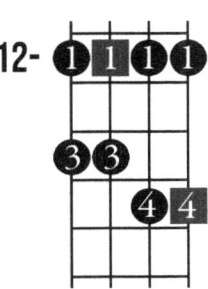

Chords and Arpeggios - A

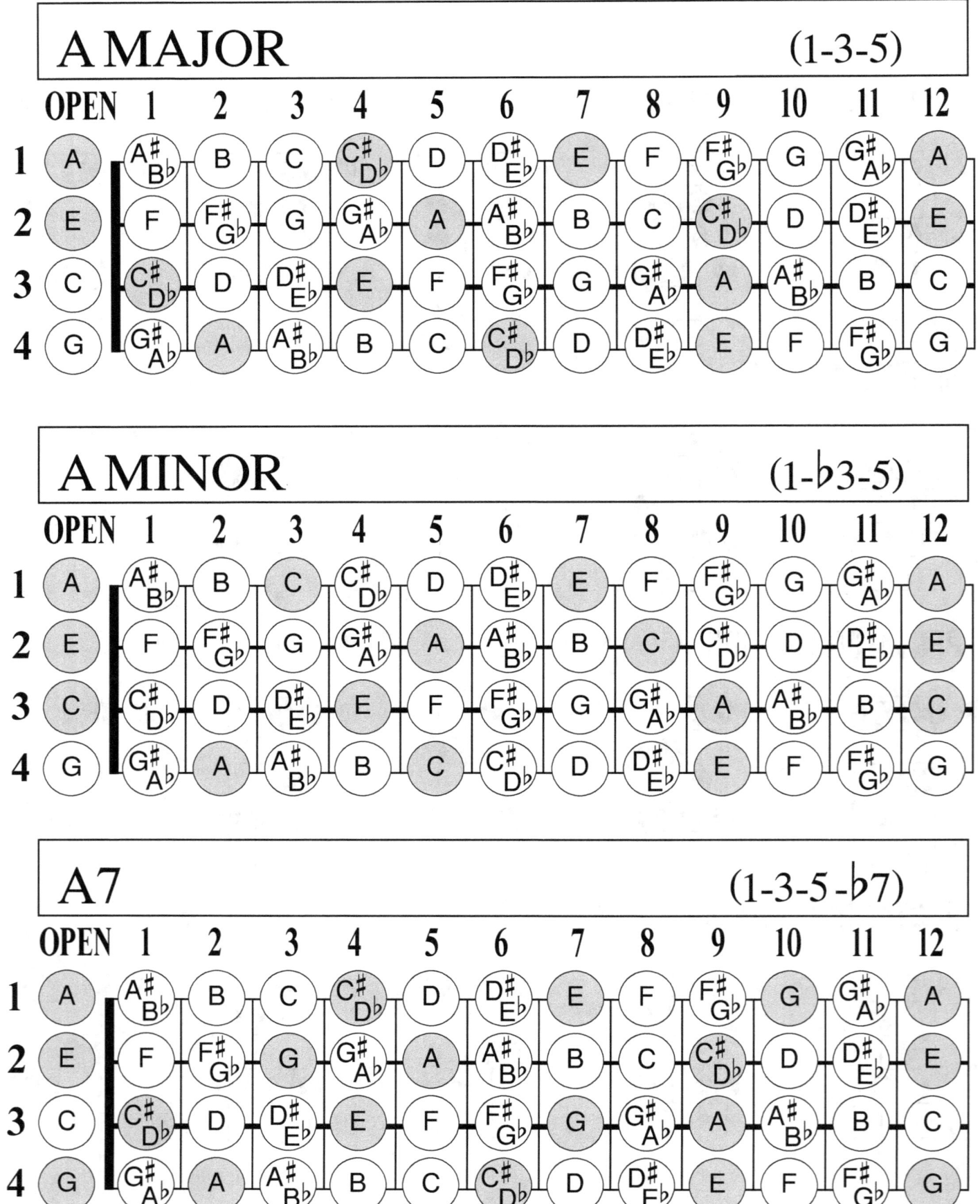

Chords and Arpeggios - B♭

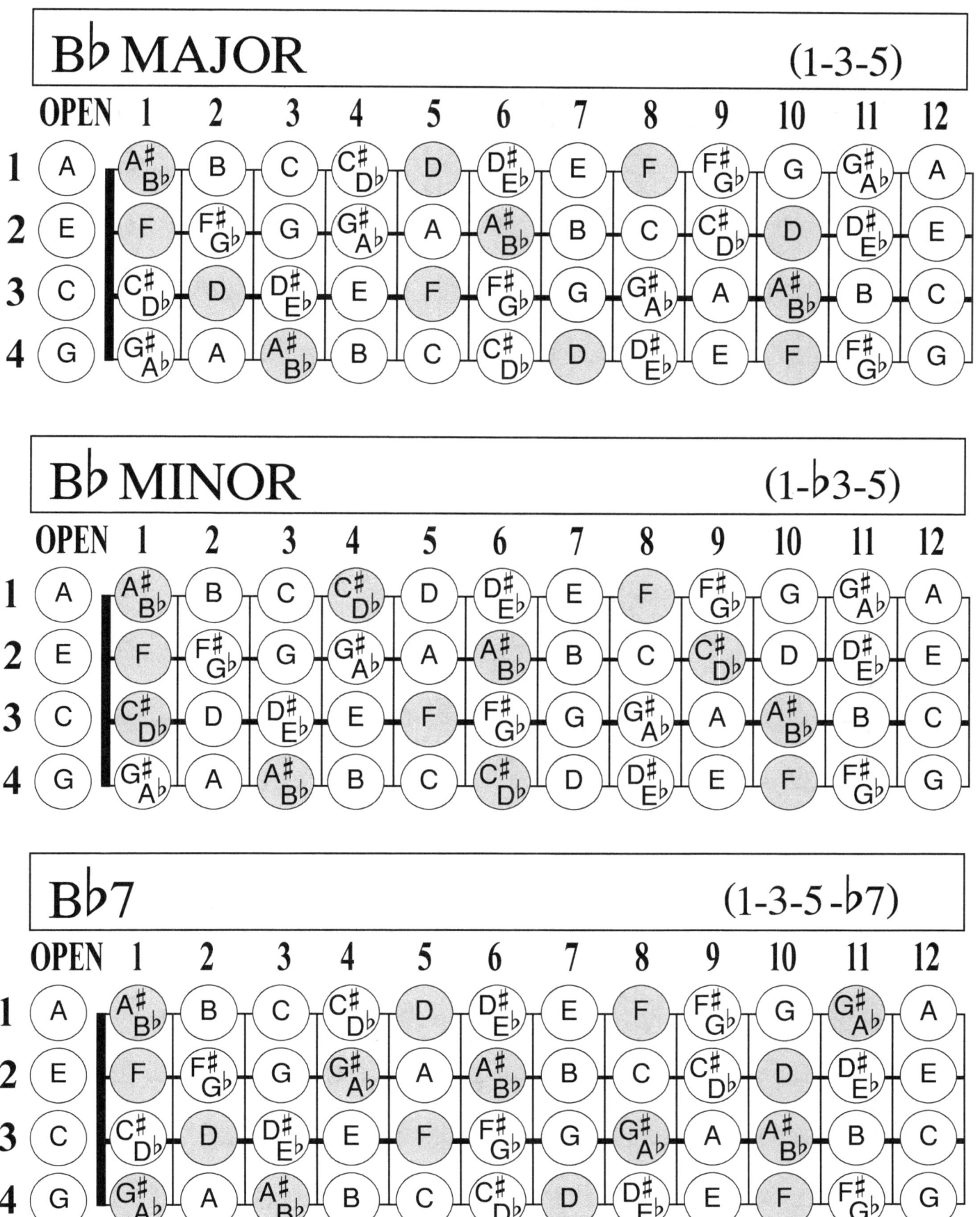

Chords and Arpeggios - B

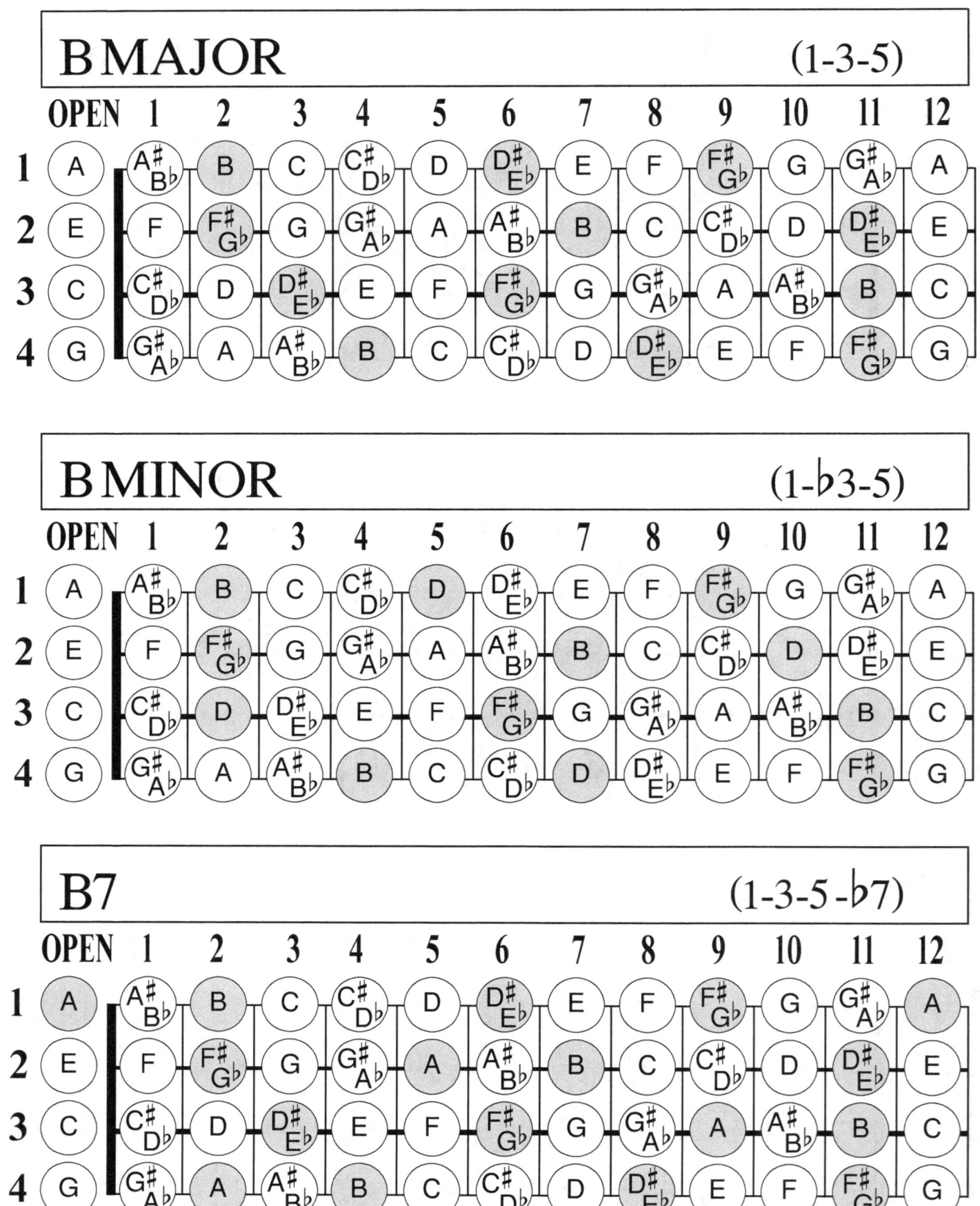

Chords and Arpeggios - C

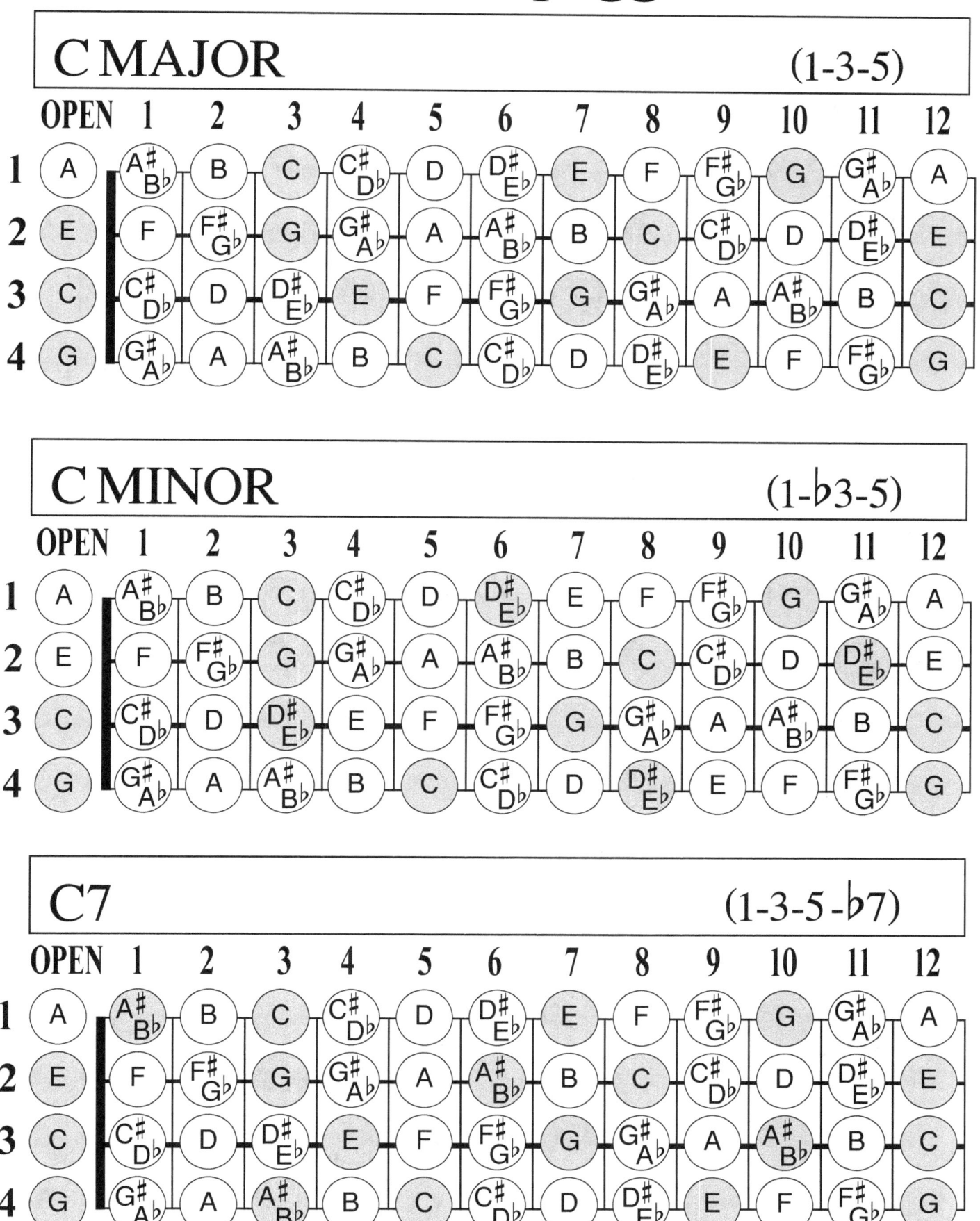

Chords and Arpeggios - C♯ D♭

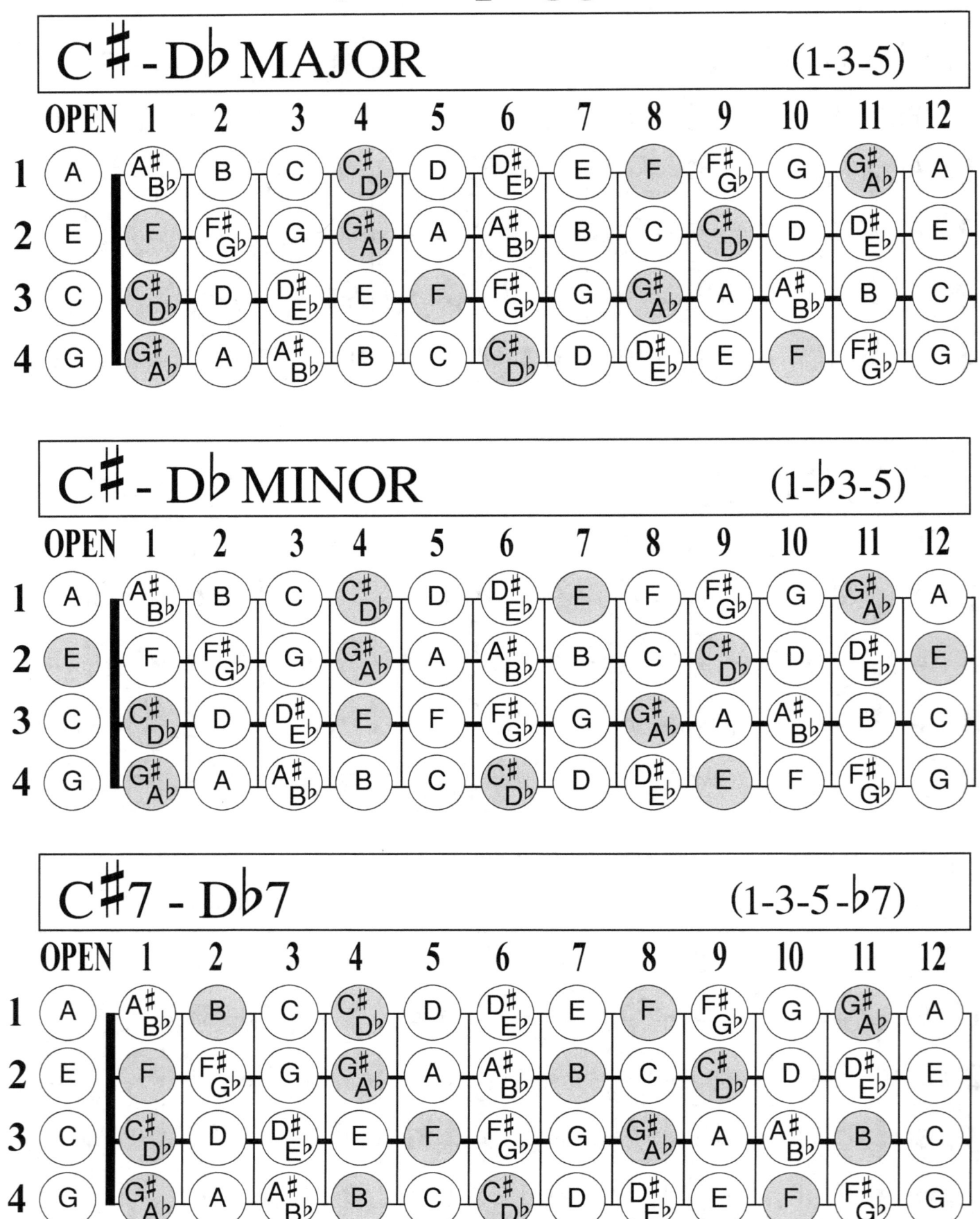

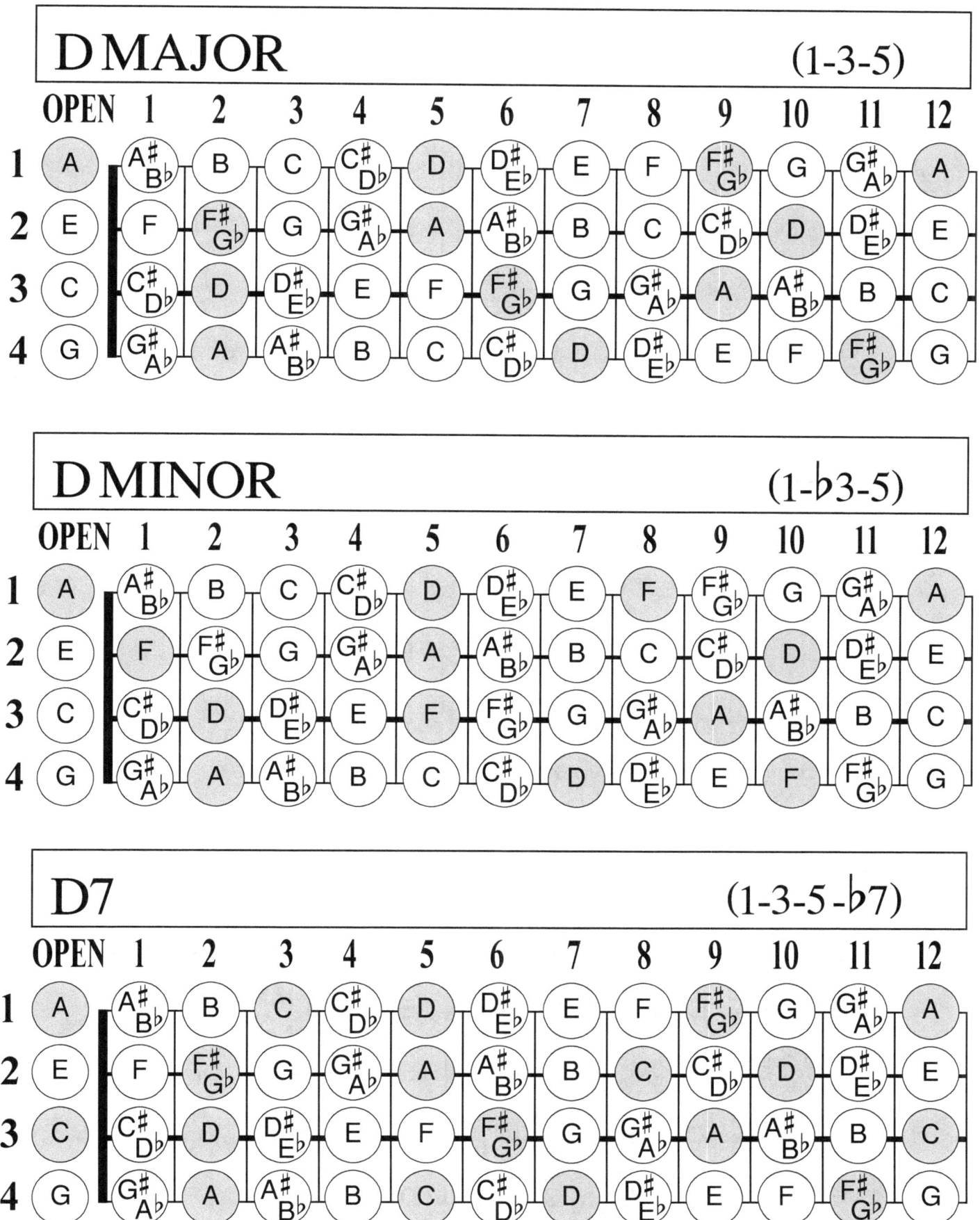

Chords and Arpeggios - D

Chords and Arpeggios - D♯ E♭

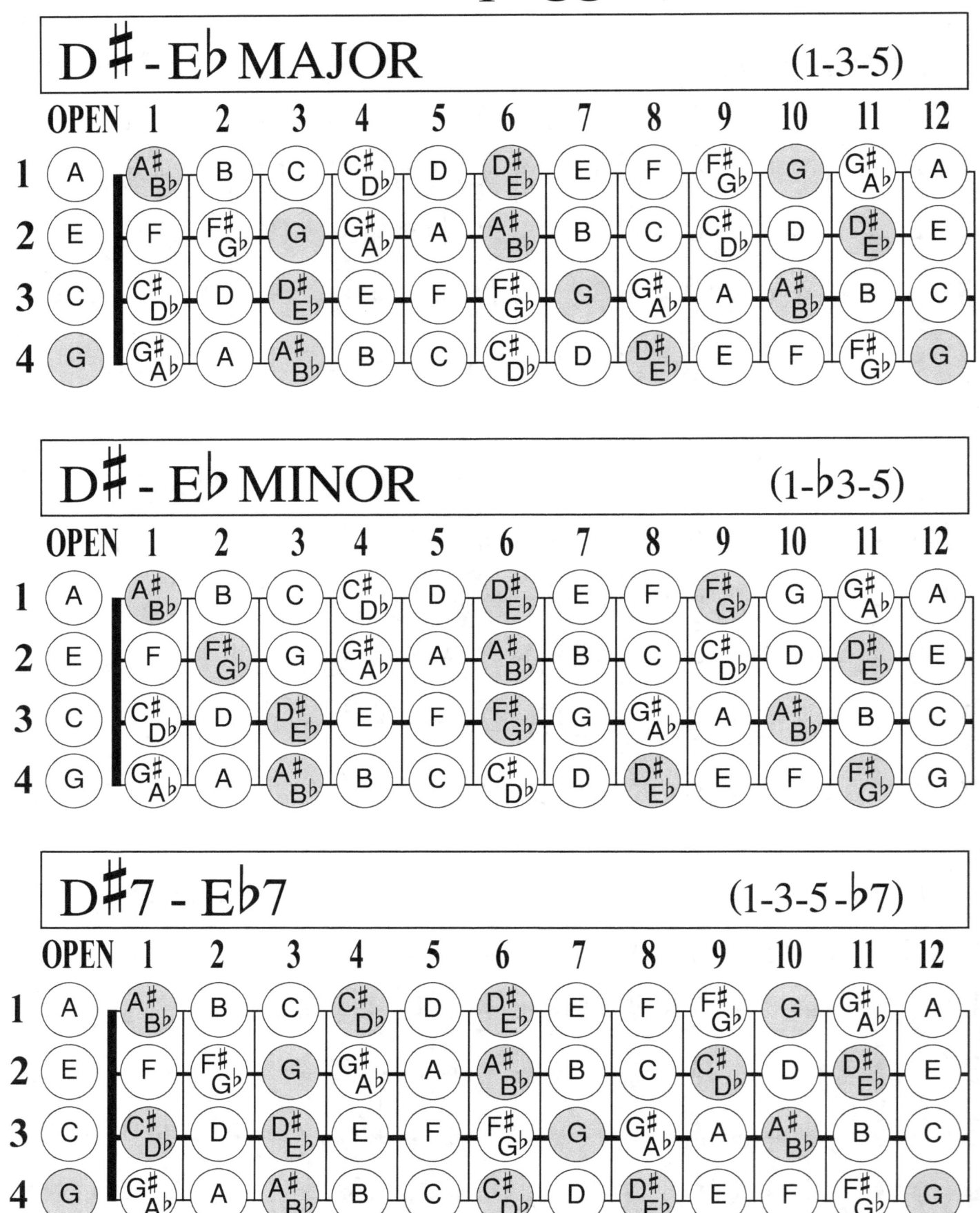

Chords and Arpeggios - E

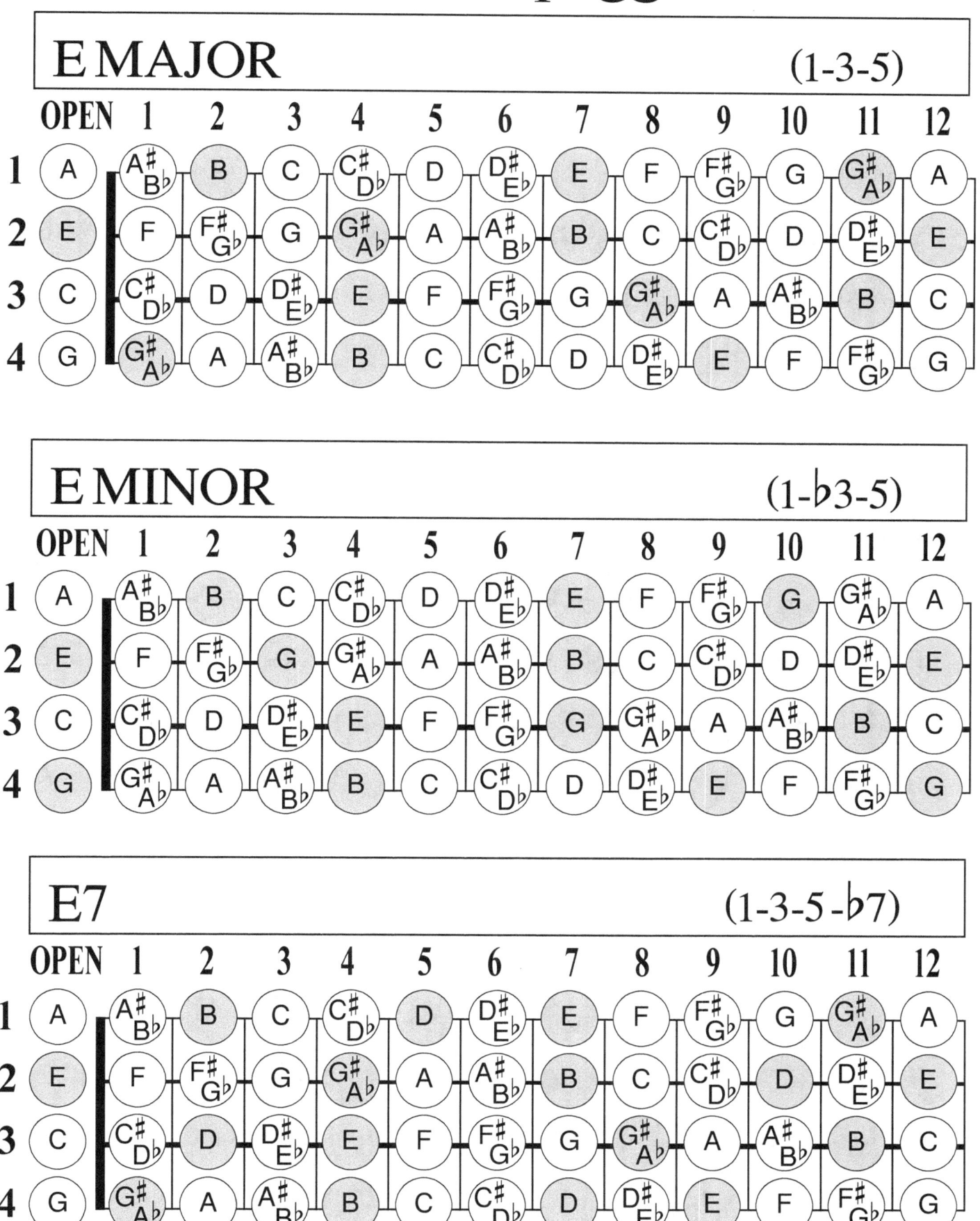

Chords and Arpeggios - F

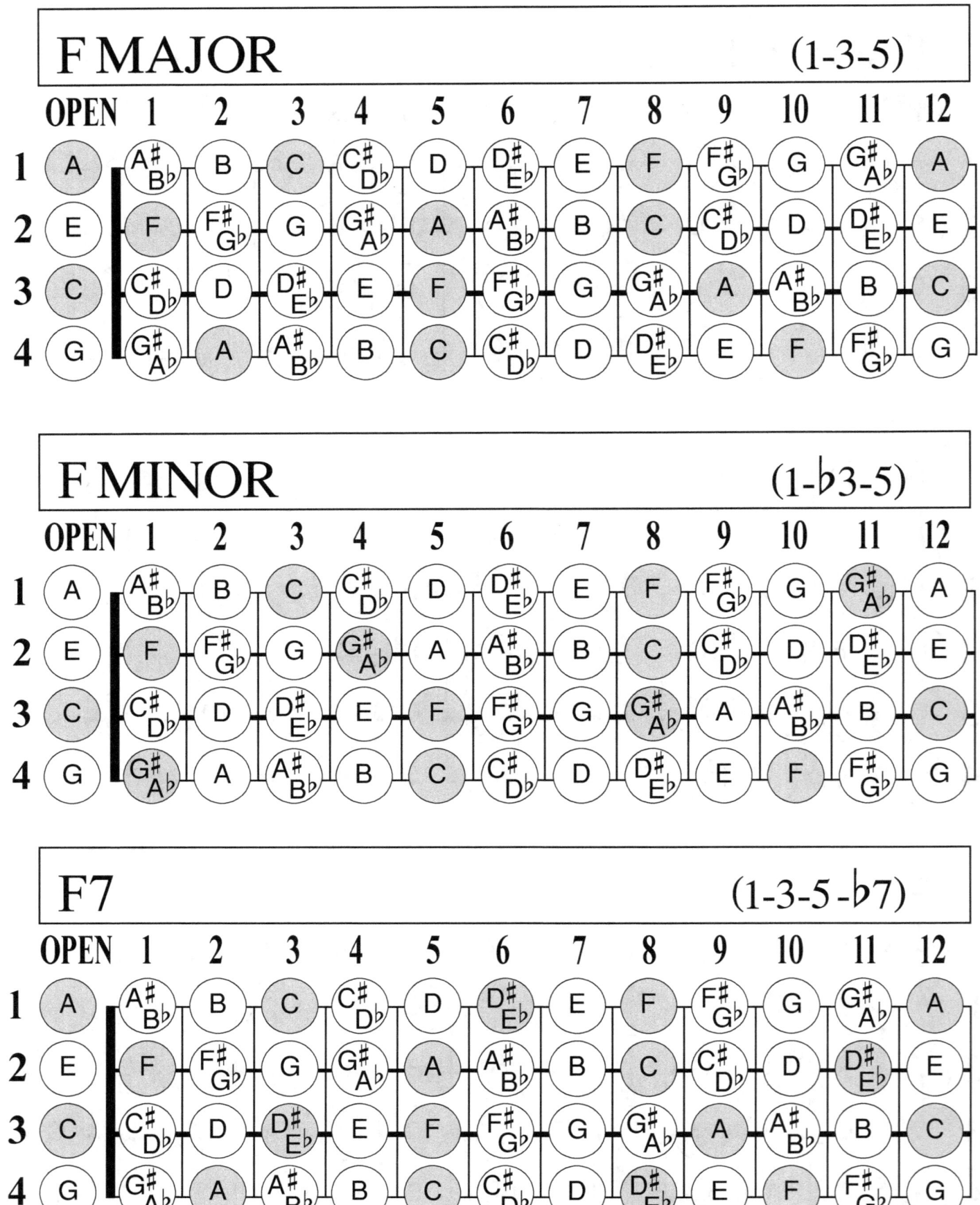

F♯ - G♭ MAJOR (1-3-5)

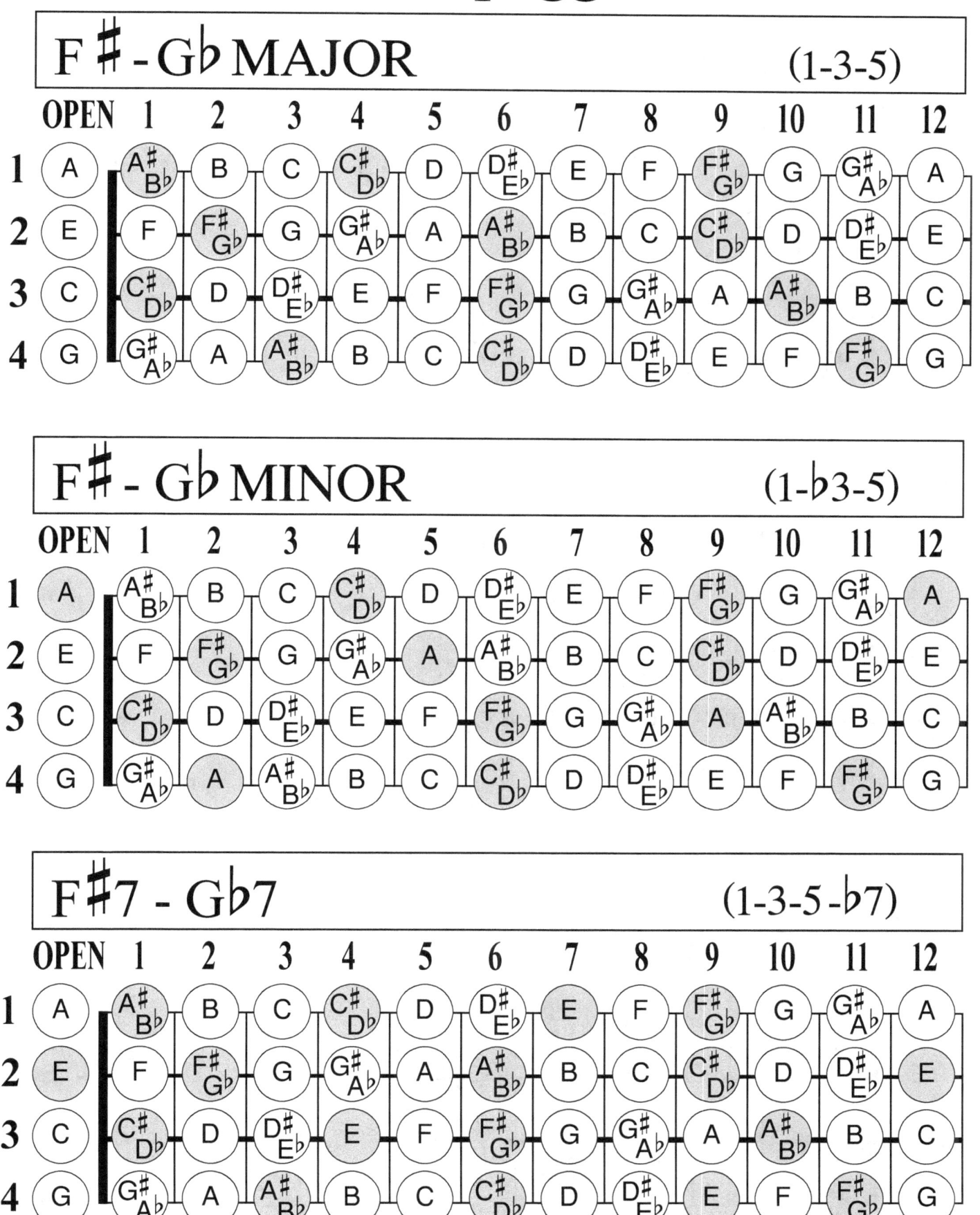

Chords and Arpeggios - G

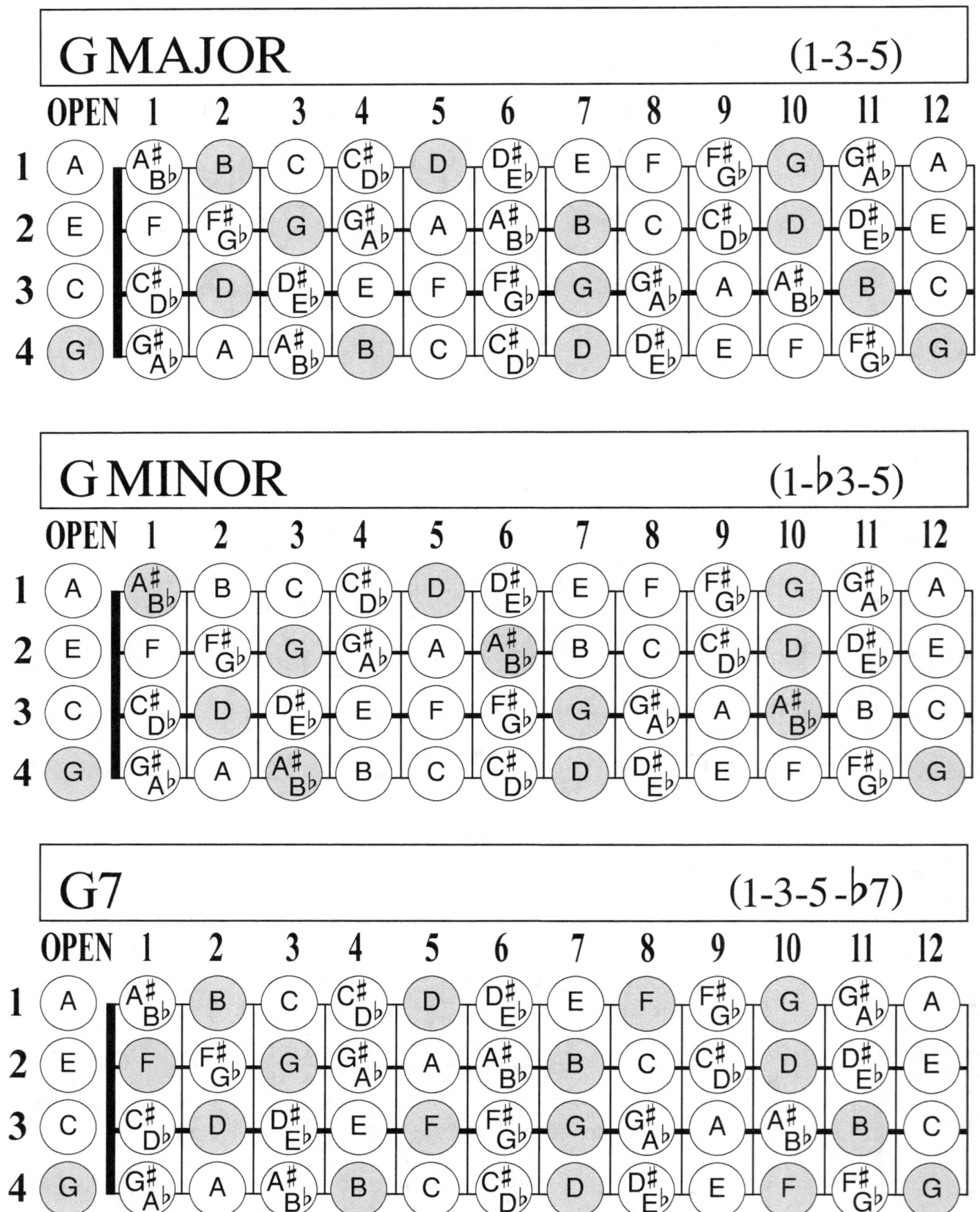

Chords and Arpeggios - G♯ A♭

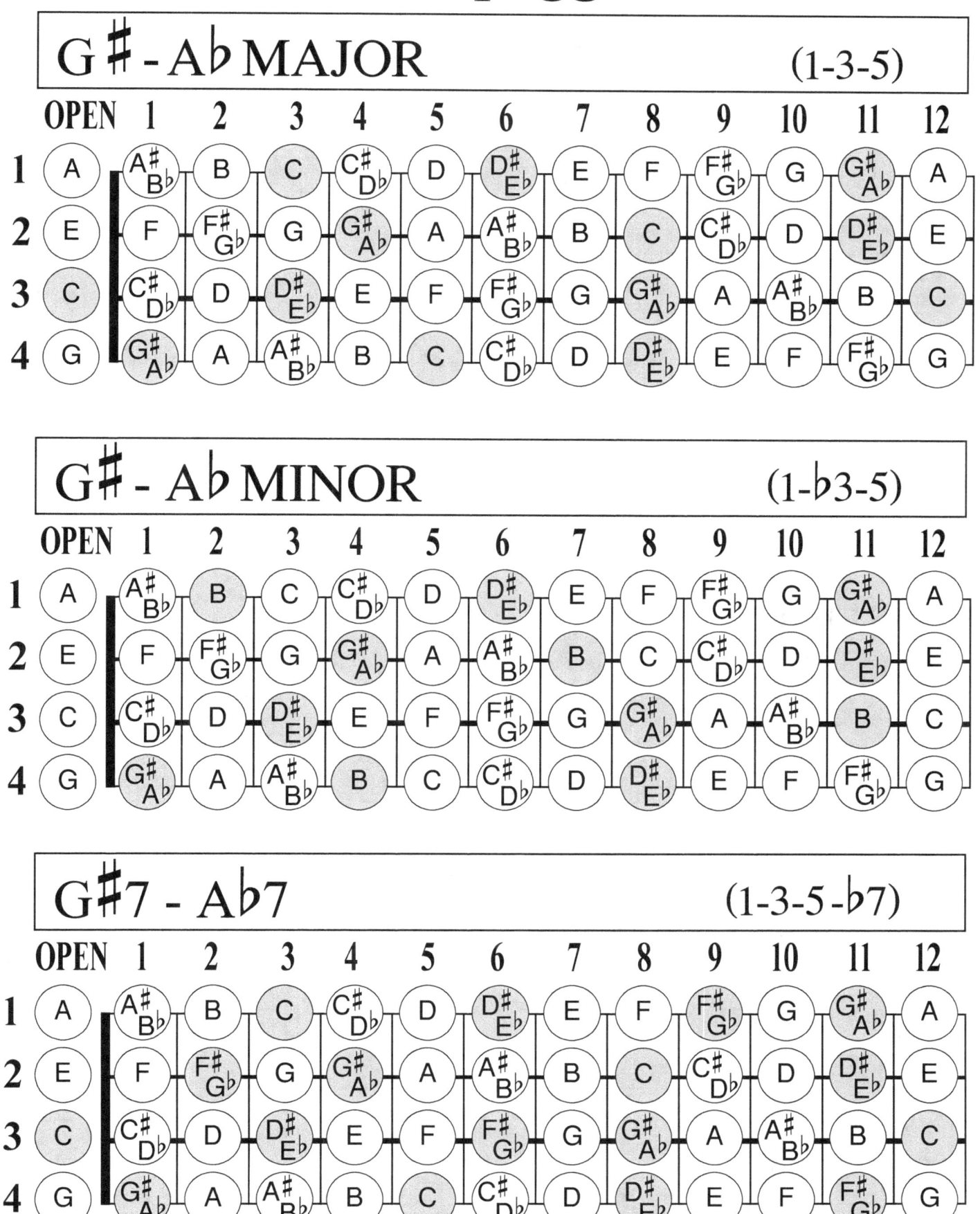

MAJOR CHORDS

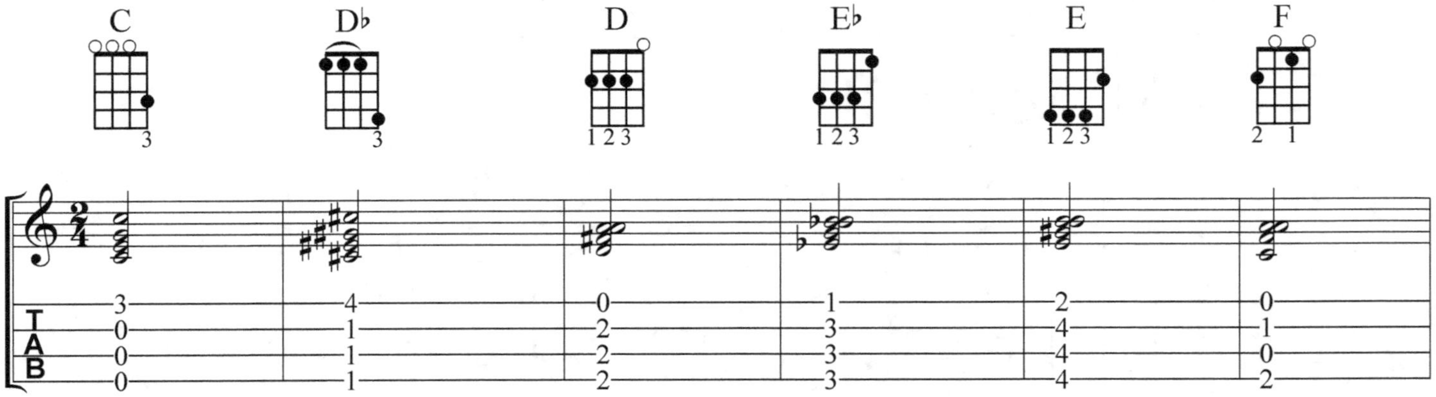

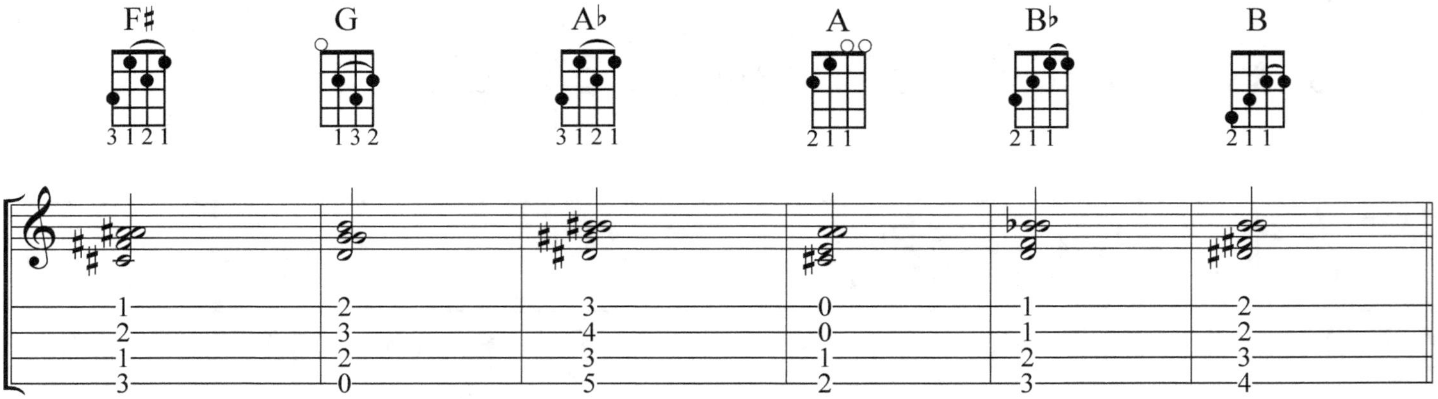

MINOR CHORDS

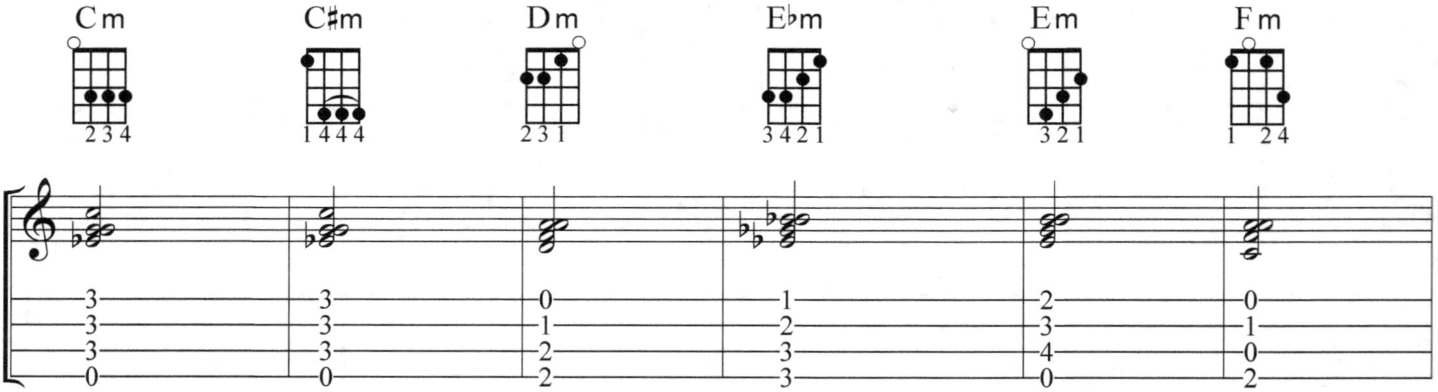

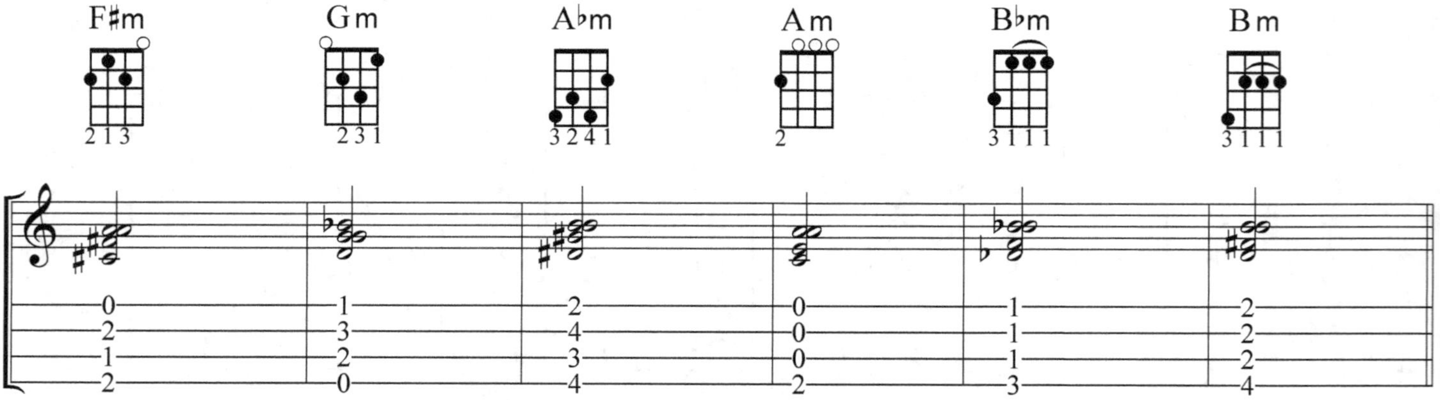

DOMINANT 7th CHORDS

DIMINISHED 7th CHORDS

MAJOR 6th CHORDS

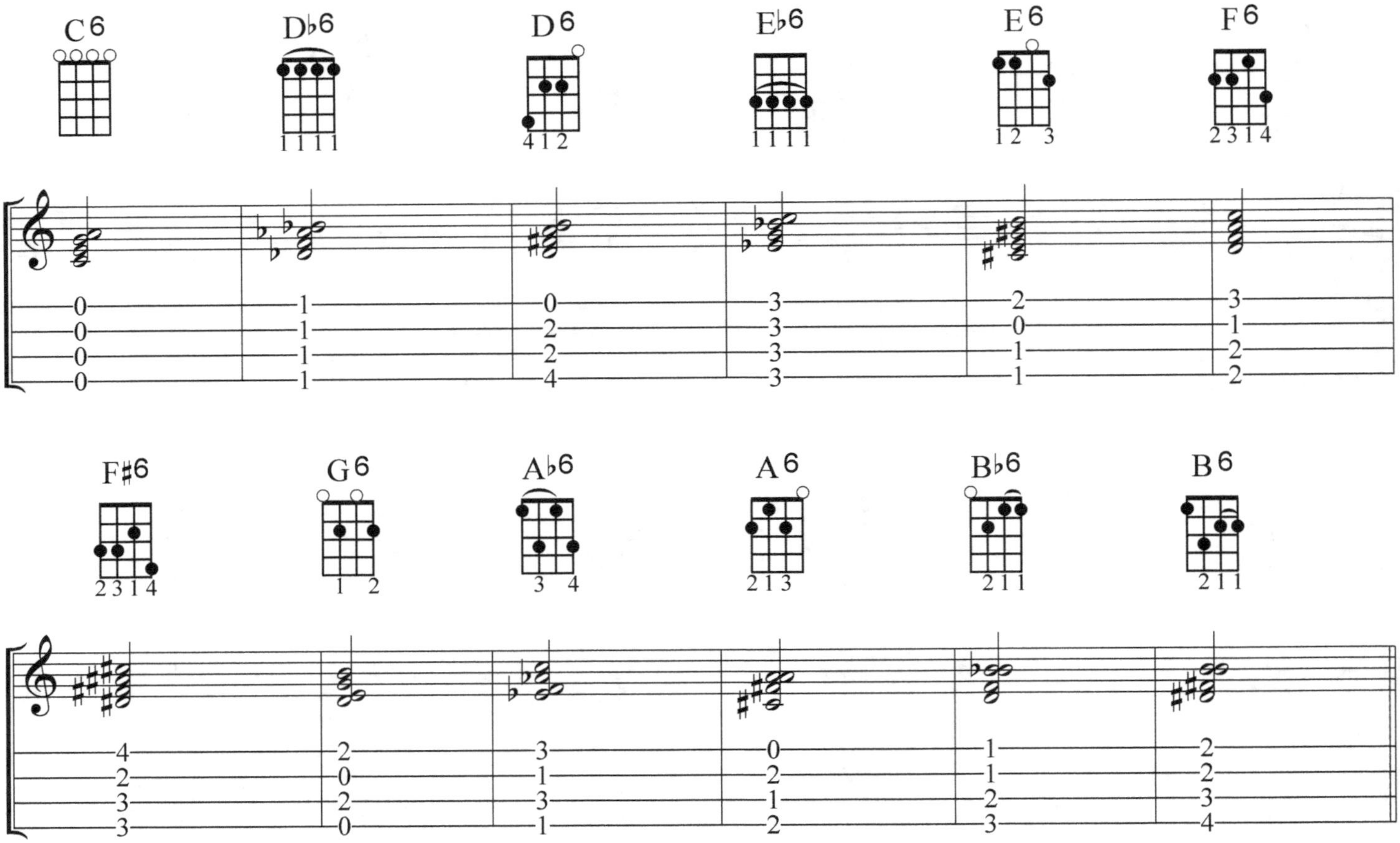
C6
D♭6
D6
E♭6
E6
F6
F♯6
G6
A♭6
A6
B♭6
B6

MAJOR 7th CHORDS

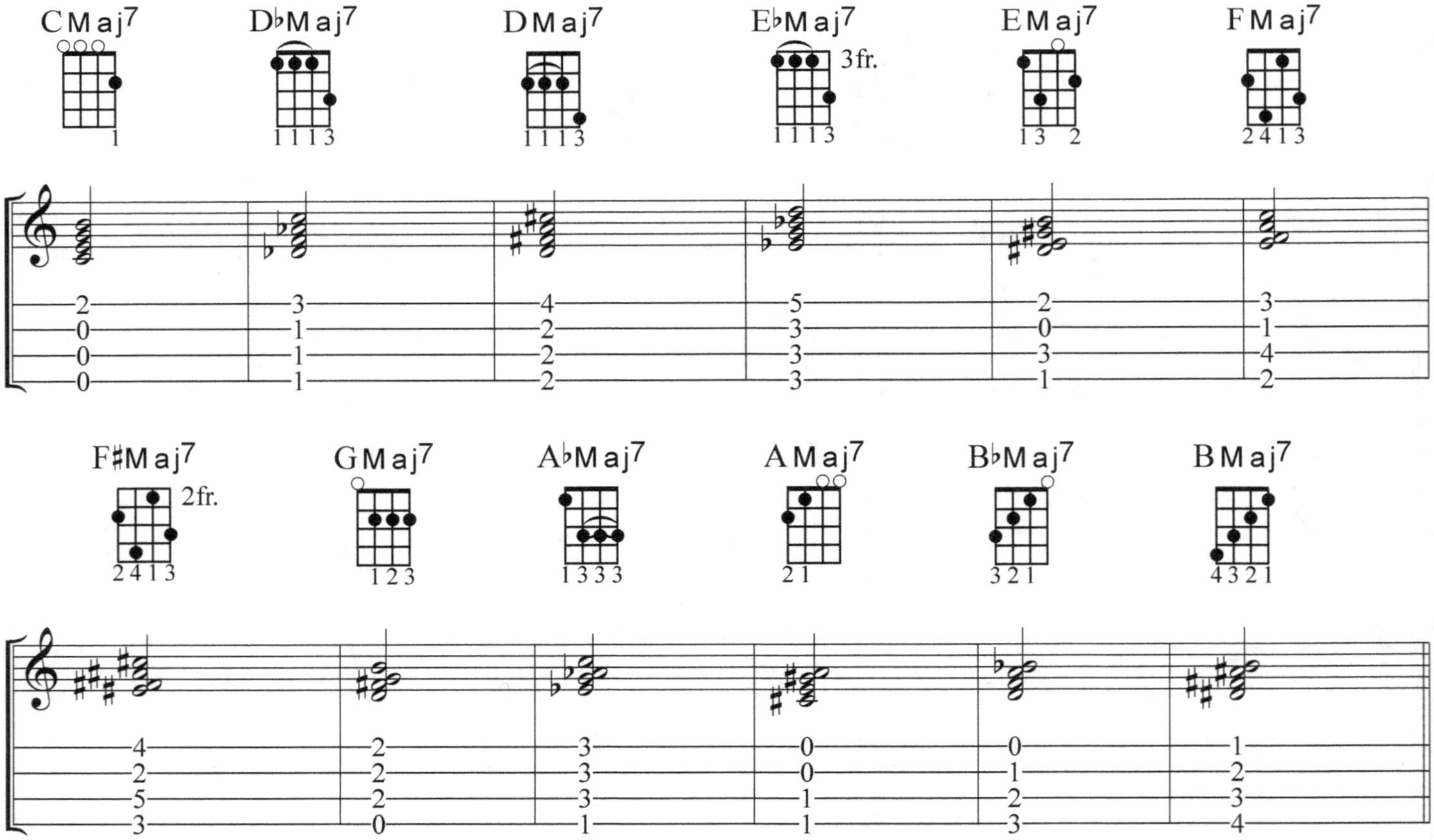
CMaj7
D♭Maj7
DMaj7
E♭Maj7
3fr.
EMaj7
FMaj7
F♯Maj7
2fr.
GMaj7
A♭Maj7
AMaj7
B♭Maj7
BMaj7

MINOR 7th CHORDS

AUGMENTED CHORDS

SUS4 CHORDS

SUS2 CHORDS

Ukulele Notation Guide

Downstroke
Pick down towards ground.

Upstroke
Pick up towards sky.

Accent
Strike the string harder to produce a louder sound.

Strong Accent (Martelato)
Pluck the string forcibly to produce a strong accent.

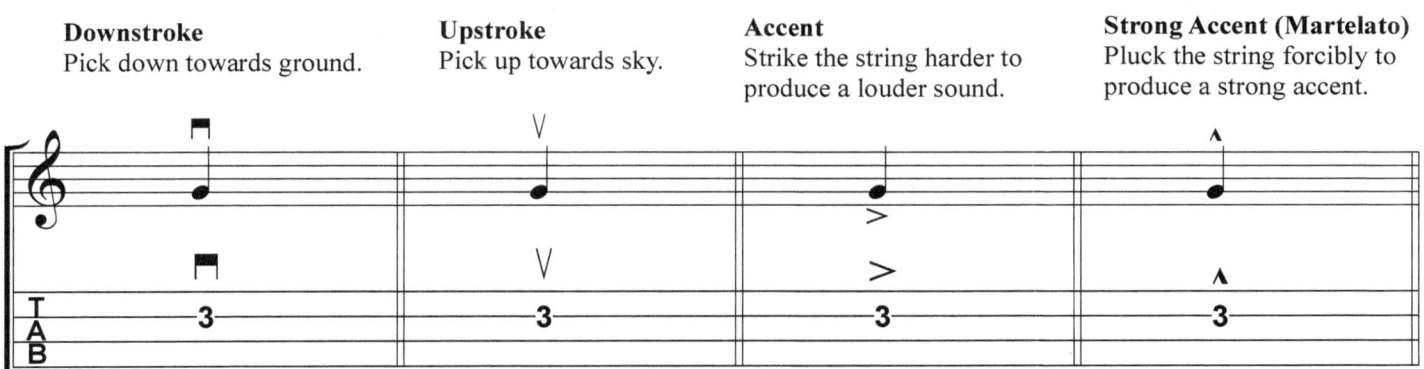

Staccato
Shorten note lengzth.

Accent with Staccato
Strike the string harder and let ring shorter. (Marcatto)

Tenuto
Slight accent. Hold note for full value.

Accent with Tenuto
Strike string harder and let ring for full value of note.

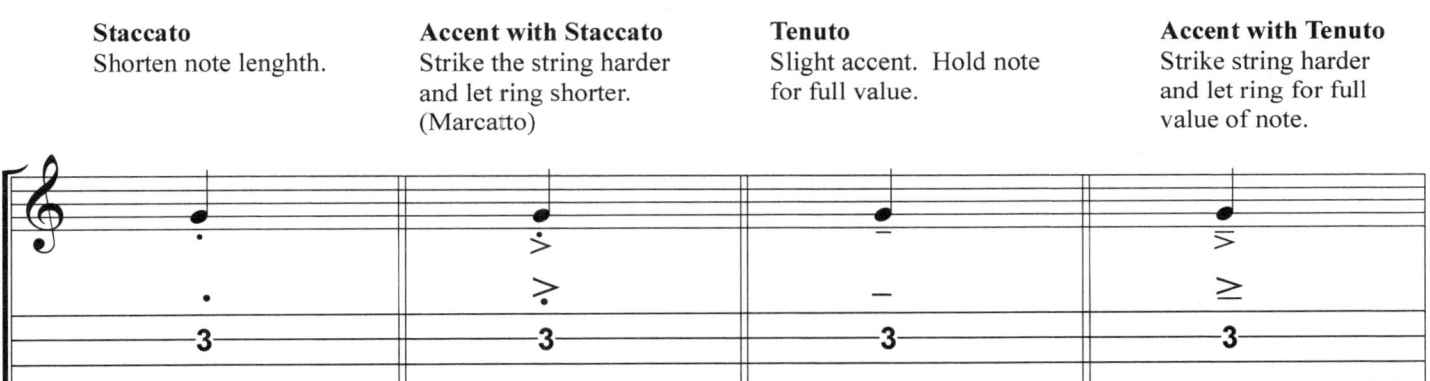

Hammer On
Play first note then hammer down finger without playing higher second note.

Pull Off
Play first note then grip on string and pull off to second lower note without playing.

Shift Slide
Slide finger/slide up or down to the next note on the same string. Pluck both notes.

Legato Slide
Slide finger/slide up or down to the next note on the same string. Play only the first note.

Palm Muting (P.M.)
Place palm on strings near
bridge to muffle the sound.

Left Hand Mute
Place left hand finger(s)
on strings to mute sound.
A percussive sound (x)

Grace Note
The smaller grace note
is rhythmically combined
with large note. Play
quickly before larger note.

Ghost Note (Parenthesis)
An optional note or
bracketed note played
quickly before main note.

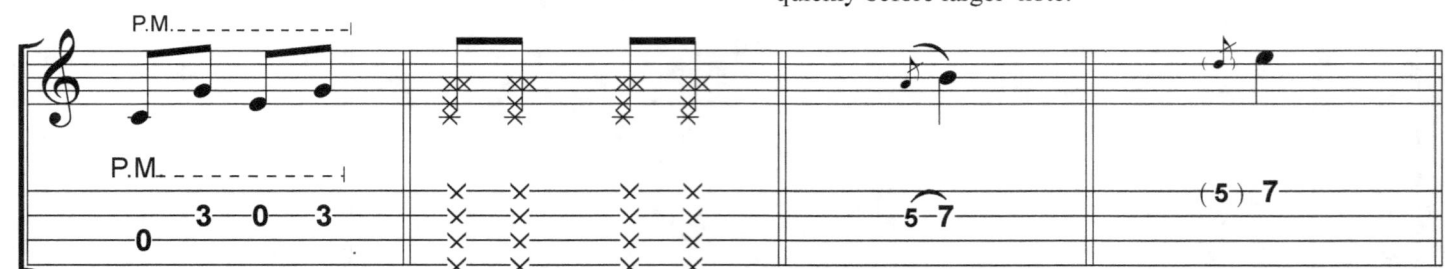

Vibrato
Bend string up and
down. Can be slow
or fast.

Wide Vibrato
Bend string up and down
but with wider arc. Can
be slow or fast.

Slight Bend
Slightly Bend the note
up a 1/4 tone.

1/2 Tone Bend
Bend the note up a half
tone or to sound 1 fret
higher.

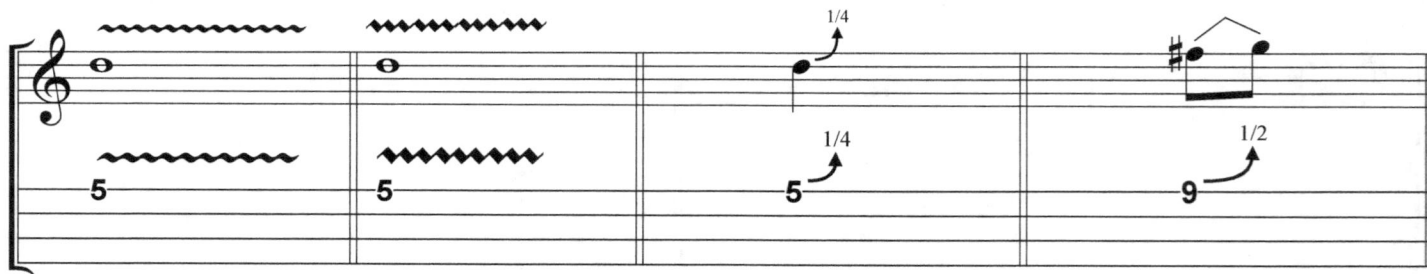

Whole Step Bend
Bend the note up a full
whole tone or to sound
2 frets higher.

Bend and Release
Bend the note up and
release back down to
the original note.

Pre-Bend
Bend the note up then
play note.

Pre-Bend
Bend the note up then
play note.

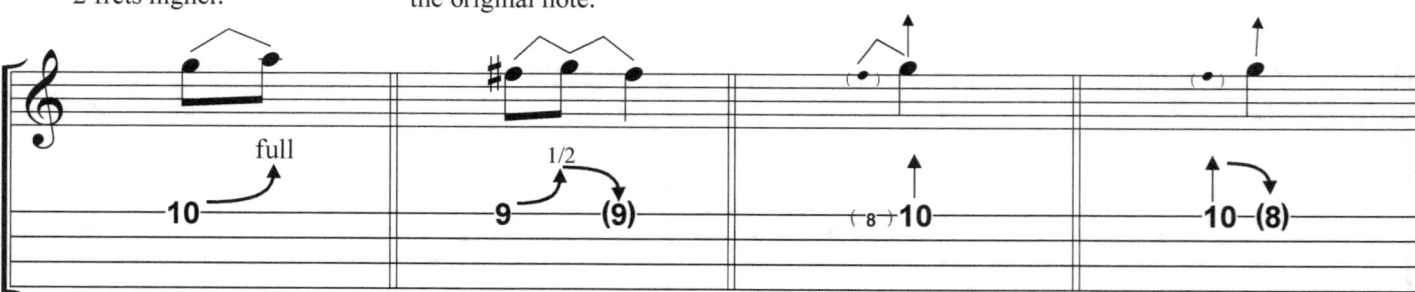

Hold Bend
Hold bend up until the
end of the dashed line.

Multiple Bends
Several bends combined
together.

Bend Neck
Grab headstock while
holding body firm and
bend neck.

Behind Nut Bend
Bend the string behind
the nut at the headstock.

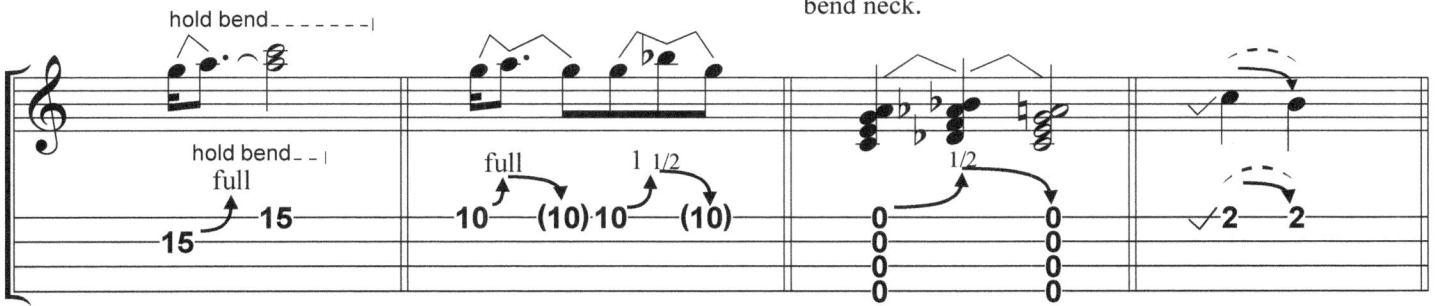

Rake
A percussive clicking sound
before playing a note. Mute the
strings (x) with the left hand.
Often a muted arpeggio.

Arpeggiate
Strum the chord in the
direction of the arrow.

Trill
Quickly alternate between
two notes using hammer ons
and pull offs.

Tapping (+)
Tap fret with finger
or pick.

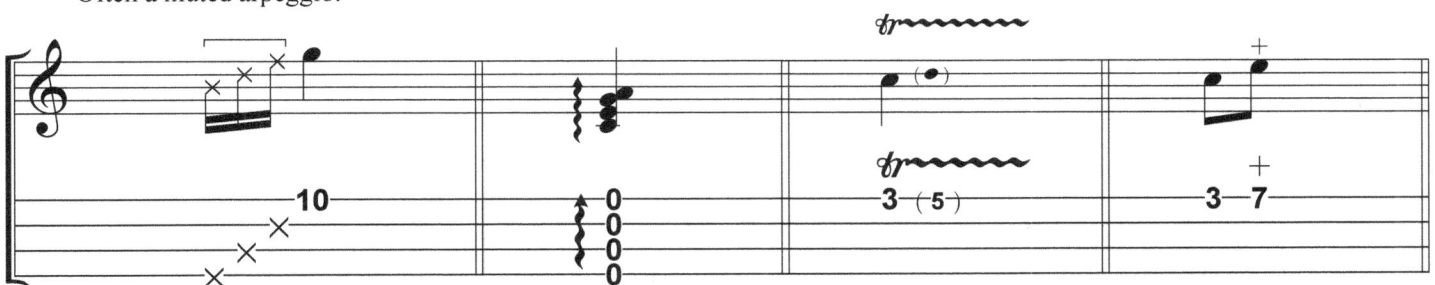

Natural Harmonic
Lightly place finger over
fret indicated and pluck.

Artificial Harmonic
Hold done note indicated
and lightly pluck pick finger
higher up string with thumb.

Pick Slide (P.S.)
Place pick edge on
string and scrape down
or up string.

Tremelo Picking
Rapidly pick down and up
on string.

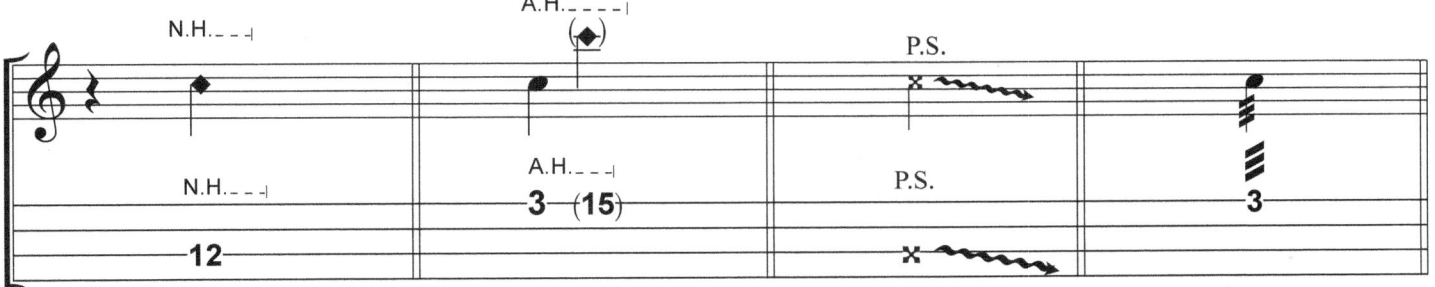

Ukulele Note Chart

1st String - A

2nd String - E

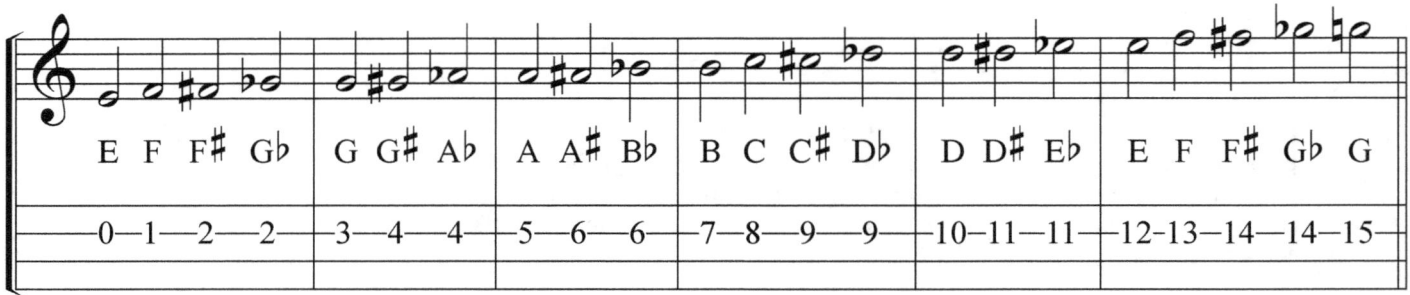

3rd String - C

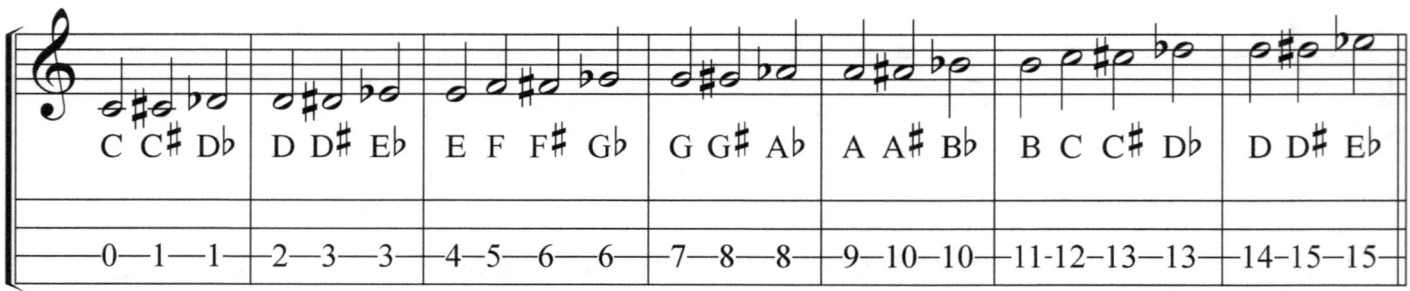

4th String - G

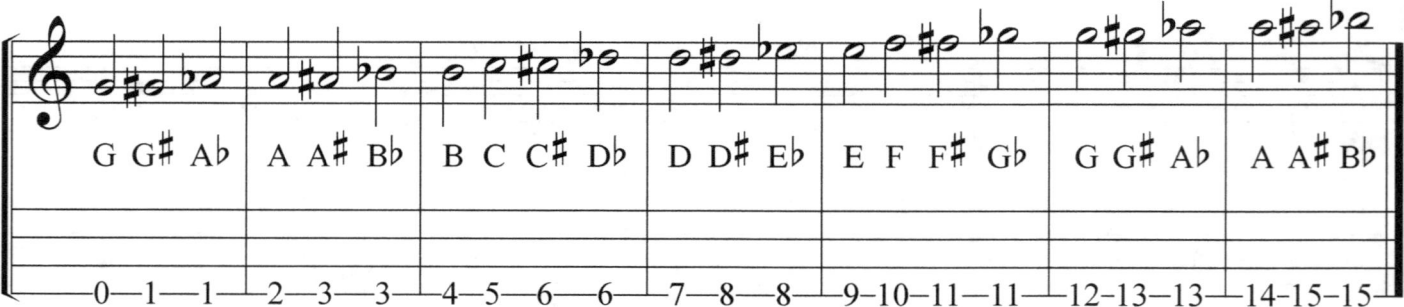

UKULELE FINGERBOARD

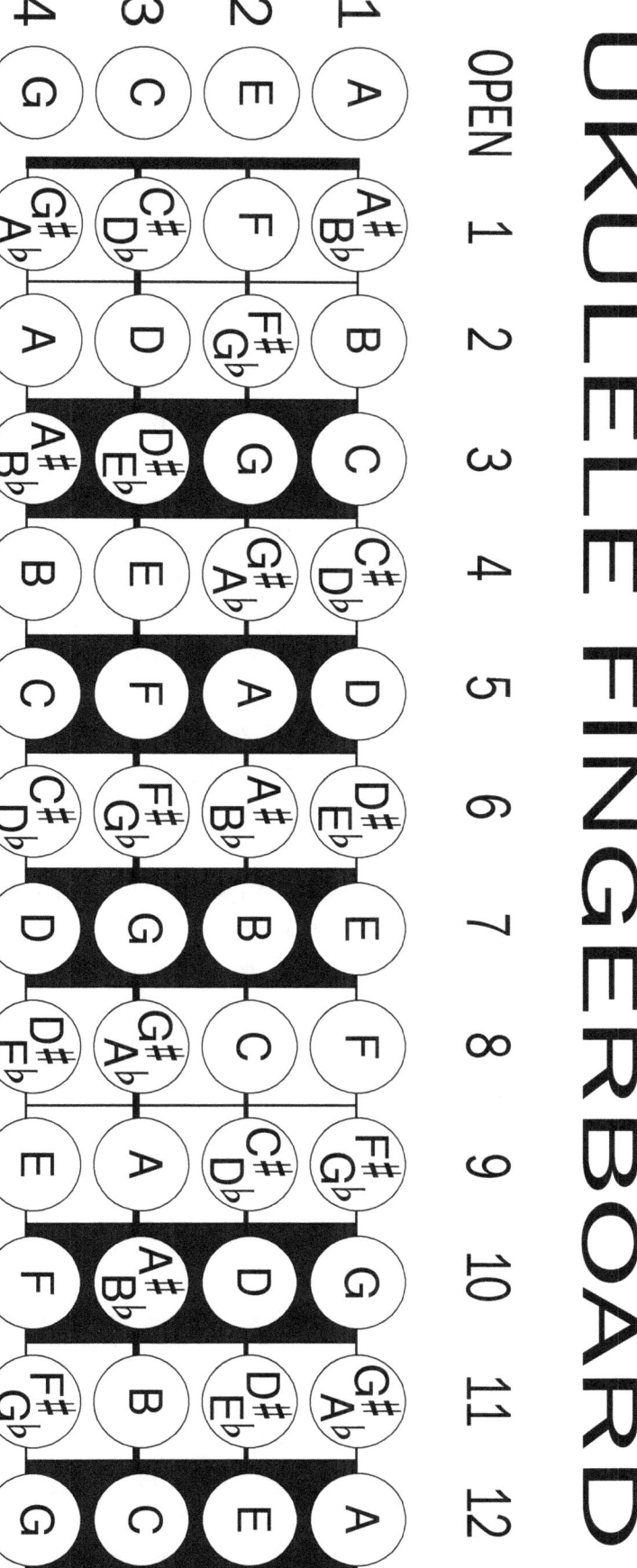

Weekly Practice Schedule

TIME	PRACTICE	MON	TUES	WED	THUR	FRI	SAT	SUN	Rate 0-10
Weekly									
Extra									

TIME	PRACTICE	MON	TUES	WED	THUR	FRI	SAT	SUN	Rate 0-10
Weekly									
Extra									

Mastering Fingerstyle Ukulele
Unlock Your Ukulele Fingerpicking Potential!

"Mastering Fingerstyle Ukulele" is the ultimate guide for ukulele enthusiasts, from beginners to advanced players. Whether you're just starting or looking to elevate your skills, this comprehensive book provides everything you need to become a fingerstyle virtuoso.

What's Inside:

Six Essential Fingerstyle Techniques: Learn the foundational skills that will unlock your full ukulele potential.

Modern Percussive Techniques: Add a fresh, rhythmic sound to your playing with modern techniques that will take your music to the next level.

Advanced Arrangements: Challenge yourself with intricate fingerpicking patterns and arrangements, perfect for showcasing your growing expertise.

Genre-Specific Patterns: Master fingerstyle patterns for blues, country, rock, Latin, and more – adding versatility to your repertoire.

Chord Libraries & Progressions: Build your chord vocabulary with detailed libraries and practice essential progressions.

Fretboard Maps & Note Charts: Gain a deeper understanding of your ukulele with easy-to-follow fretboard maps.

Practice Tips & Warm-ups: Stay sharp with a variety of exercises, including 144 chord riffs for accompaniment.

Plus!

Online Audio & Video Tracks: Access interactive online materials to guide your learning experience every step of the way. Simply scroll down this page to start!

Whether you're strumming for fun or aiming for a professional level, "Mastering Fingerstyle Ukulele" is your all-in-one resource to grow your skills and play with confidence. Start your journey today!

Ukulele Ensemble Arrangements

We have a growing collection of sheet music arrangements with tablature, notations and chords for ukulele ensembles and duets.

Havana
Falling Slowly
Pipeline
Speak Softly Love
Somewhere My Love
Green Onions
Derniere Danse
Free Fallin
Derniere Danse
Si Bheag Si Mhor
Maisie's Waltz
Only Time
After the Goldrush
Carol of the Bells
Just the Way You Are
Tico Tico
Rock Around the Clock
Habanera
Unchained Melody
I Have a Dream
Despacito

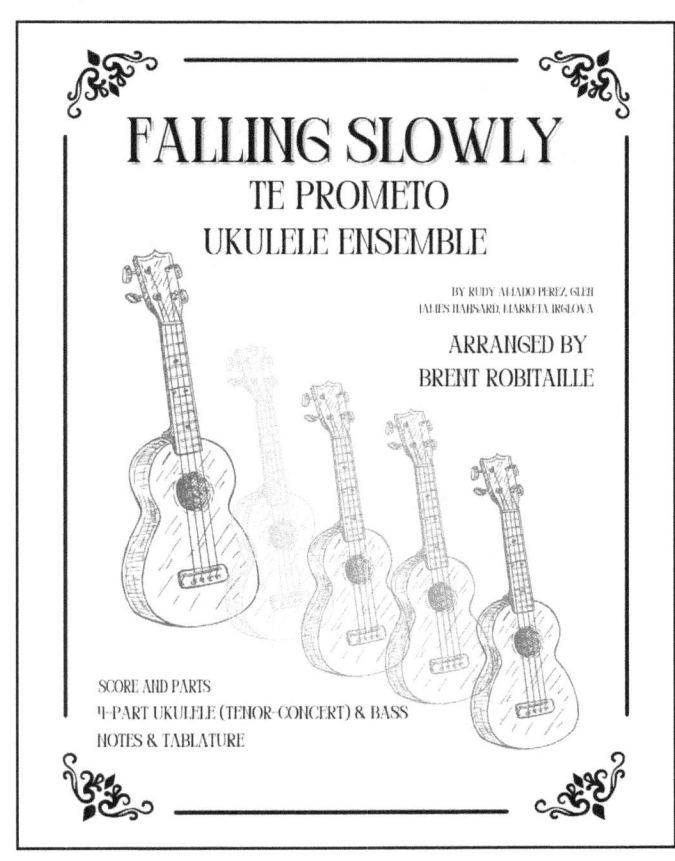

FALLING SLOWLY
TE PROMETO
UKULELE ENSEMBLE

BY RUDY AHADO PEREZ, GLEN
JAMES HANSARD, MARKETA IRGLOVA

ARRANGED BY
BRENT ROBITAILLE

SCORE AND PARTS
4-PART UKULELE (TENOR-CONCERT) & BASS
NOTES & TABLATURE

**brent
robitaille
.com**

Other Book Titles From Kalymi Music

GUITAR

The Blues Guitar Looper Pedal Book
The Pop Rock Guitar Looper Pedal Book
DADGAD Guitar Celtic Flatpicking
Open D Guitar Celtic Flatpicking
Open G Tuning Celtic Guitar Flatpicking
Slide Guitar Collection
Improve Your Guitar Chord Playing
Guitar Blank Tablature & Reference
Beginner Guitar Chord Book
The Open D Guitar Christmas Songbook
101 Blues Riffs and Solos in Open D Guitar Tuning
Classical Guitar Book in Open D Tuning
Resonator Guitar Celtic Book
101 Blues Riffs and Solos in Open G Guitar Tuning

UKULELE

Celtic World Collection - Ukulele
Ukulele Blank Tablature Workbook & Reference
The Ukulele Christmas Songbook
Mastering Fingerstyle Ukulele
Ultimate Ukulele Technique & Warm-Up Book

FIDDLE/VIOLIN

Fiddle Tab Celtic Collection
Fiddle Tab Traditional Collection
Fiddle Tab Holiday Collection
Easy Classical Violin Tabs

MANDOLIN/ MANDOLA

Celtic World Collection - Mandolin
Mandolin Blank Tablature Workbook & Reference
Mandolin Blues Book
The Celtic Mandola Book (Treble and Alto Clef)

CIGAR BOX GUITAR

Cigar Box Guitar Jazz& Blues Unlimited – 3-String
Cigar Box Guitar Jazz& Blues Unlimited – 4-String
Cigar Box Guitar – The Ultimate Collection - 2, 3 and 4-String
Cigar Box Guitar – The Ultimate Collection Volume Two
101 Riffs and Solos for Four String Cigar Box Guitar
101 Riffs and Solos for Cigar Box Guitar
Cigar Box Guitar Blues Overload
The Complete Cigar Box Guitar Chord Book
The Complete Cigar Box Guitar Chord Book 3-String
The Complete Cigar Box Guitar Chord Book 4-String
Celtic Collection 3 and 4-String
Cigar Box Guitar Technique Book
Cigar Box Guitar Classical Collection
Cigar Box Guitar Holiday Collection
4-String Blank Tablature Workbook & Reference for Cigar Box Guitar
3-String Blank Tablature Workbook & Reference for Cigar Box Guitar

Online Store: brentrobitaille.com

A Growing Collection of **Music Posters Available!**

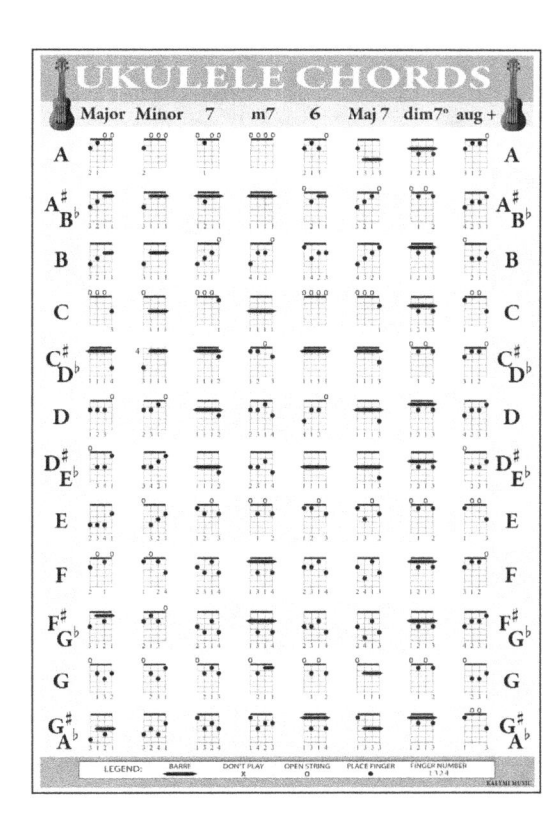

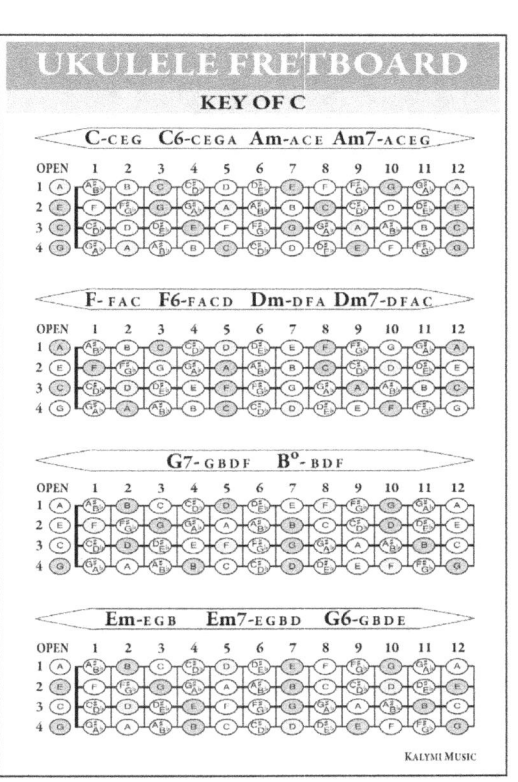

**brent
robitaille
.com**